Food Information, Communication and Education

Also available from Bloomsbury:

Food, Power, and Agency, edited by Jürgen Martschukat and Bryant Simon
Italian Food Activism in Urban Sardinia, Carole Counihan
Proteins, Pathologies and Politics, edited by David Gentilcore and Matthew Smith

Food Information, Communication and Education

Eating Knowledge

Edited by
Simona De Iulio and Susan Kovacs

BLOOMSBURY ACADEMIC
LONDON • NEW YORK • OXFORD • NEW DELHI • SYDNEY

BLOOMSBURY ACADEMIC
Bloomsbury Publishing Plc
50 Bedford Square, London, WC1B 3DP, UK
1385 Broadway, New York, NY 10018, USA
29 Earlsfort Terrace, Dublin 2, Ireland

BLOOMSBURY, BLOOMSBURY ACADEMIC and the Diana logo are
trademarks of Bloomsbury Publishing Plc

First published in Great Britain 2022
Paperback edition first published 2023

Cover design by Rebecca Heselton
Cover photograph © Alexander Schimmeck/unsplash

A catalogue record for this book is available from the British Library.

Library of Congress Control Number: 2022932159

ISBN: HB: 978-1-3501-6250-1
PB: 978-1-3502-9613-8
ePDF: 978-1-3501-6251-8
eBook: 978-1-3501-6252-5

Typeset by Newgen KnowledgeWorks Pvt. Ltd., Chennai, India

To find out more about our authors and books visit www.bloomsbury.com
and sign up for our newsletters.

Contents

Illustrations

Figure

Tables

Contributors

François Allard-Huver is Associate Professor of Strategic and Digital Communication at Lorraine University, Nancy, and researcher at the Center for Mediation Research (CREM). His research focuses on environmental and scientific controversies – especially regarding pesticides and GMOs – fake news and health and food communication issues. He is currently directing three research projects on environmental controversies (Cap-Controverses), transparency in the public sphere (DISTIC) and food supplements (Manger-Droit).

Marie Berthoud holds a PhD in Information and Communication Sciences; her research focuses on public communication related to food and health. She studies the circulation and appropriation of normative discourse produced by public health authorities. Her most recent article is 'Prescribed Roles, Roles Played: When Children Thwart Their Role as "Good Consumers" in School Canteens' (*Revue des sciences sociales* 2020).

Philippe Cardon is Associate Professor of Sociology at the University of Lille. His research focuses on changes in eating habits in contemporary societies, with regard to three specific areas: household food, public nutritional policies and citizen food movements. He has recently published *Sociologie de l'alimentation* (2019) with co-authors Thomas Depecker and Marie Plessz.

Viviane Clavier is Associate Professor of Information and Communication Sciences. She is a member of the Communications Research Group (Gresec) at the University of Grenoble-Alpes. Her research interests include knowledge organization and information practices in the professional context of health and nutrition. Her most recent book is *Food and Health: Actor Strategies in Information and Communication* (2018).

Simona De Iulio is Full Professor of Information and Communication Sciences and a member of the Interdisciplinary Research Group in Information and Communication (GERiiCO) of the University of Lille. Her research focuses on advertising, culture and society. Her recent work investigates food communication strategies in educational environments. Her most recent publications on this topic are: 'Food Marketers at School: The Challenge of Trustworthiness in France (1900–2013)' (2019); *Cantine et friandises. L'école et l'alimentation des enfants* (2021), co-edited with Philippe Cardon.

Laurence Depezay is a doctoral candidate in Information and Communication Sciences at the University of Lille, the Interdisciplinary Research Group in Information and Communication GERiiCO and researcher in the private sector (EJS-Aymara). Her research focuses on scientific communication and nutrition and on the popularization and mediation of scientific food knowledge.

Laura Guérin is a sociologist and post-doctoral fellow at the CERIES Sociology Research laboratory of the University of Lille. Her research focuses on the study of the medicalization of human problems. Her work probes different areas of research that intersect: health, ageing, disability, the construction of public problems, bodily constraint, care and the dilemmas of professional practice in the field of care. She teaches at Paris I Sorbonne University.

Thomas Heller is Associate Professor of Information and Communication sciences at the University of Lille. His research focuses on the link between communication and managerial governmentality in organizations from a critical perspective. He also explores the analysis of filmic representations of organizations and work. His recent publications include: 'Scientific Knowledge as a Key Issue for Food Service Business Activity' (*Les Enjeux de l'information et de la communication*, 2020) co-authored with E. Sevin.

Susan Kovacs is Full Professor of Information and Communication Sciences at the ENSSIB National School of Library and Information Sciences and a member of the ELICO Information-Communication Sciences research laboratory (Lyon). Her research interests include scientific knowledge circulation, food information practices, food literacy programmes and media and information literacy. She recently co-edited a special issue of the journal *Les Enjeux de l'information et de la communication* on 'Food Information, Communication and Education' (2020) with Simona De Iulio.

Justine Le Floc'h holds a PhD in French literature and the history of ideas. Her research focuses on the history of emotions, moral literature and the Early Modern period. She studies representations of anger in seventeenth-century French treatises on medicine, theology, philosophy, morals and civility. She has published several articles about metaphors of anger in theological and medical discourse.

María Dolores Martín-Lagos López is Lecturer at the University of Granada (Spain) in the Department of Sociology. Her research focuses on consumption, education and family involvement. She has published on gender studies in the household and on social inequalities based on the Coleman Report. She co-authored, with Philippe Cardon, 'Un cambio en los hábitos alimentarios desde la base: comedores escolares y asociaciones de madres y padres en Granada', in Cecilia Díaz-Méndez and Isabel Garcia-Espejo, *El malestar con la alimentación* (2021).

Elisabetta Moro is Full Professor of Cultural Anthropology at the University of Naples Suor Orsola Benincasa. She is Co-director of the Virtual Museum of the Mediterranean Diet and of MedEatResearch (Center of Social Research on the Mediterranean Diet). Moro is Director of the Mediterranean section of 'Granaries of Memory' at the University of Gastronomic Sciences and Slow Food in Pollenzo (Cuneo), and a member of the Scientific Committee of FICO Foundation for Food Education and Environmental Sustainability in Bologna. Her research interests span several areas and fields: food studies, cultural heritage of the Mediterranean diet, ancient and contemporary mythology, anthropology of symbols. She is the author of *Sirene: La seduzione dall'antichità ad oggi* (2019) and co-editor with Marino Niola of *The Secrets of the Mediterranean Diet: Eat Well and Stay Well* (2020).

Didier Nourrisson is Emeritus Professor of History at the University Claude Bernard Lyon 1. His research focuses on the history of food and drink and the history of food practices. He has authored the following: *Cigarette: histoire d'une allumeuse* (2010); *Crus et cuites: Histoire du buveur* (2013); *Une histoire du vin* (2017).

Christian Orange is Emeritus Professor at the University of Nantes and Professor at the Université Libre de Bruxelles (Belgium). His research focuses on learning and problematization in the natural sciences. His most recent publications include: *Enseigner les sciences: problèmes, débats et savoirs scientifiques en classe* (2012); the article 'Les résultats des recherches en didactique des sciences et des technologies: quelle validité et à quelles conditions?' (*Recherches en didactique des sciences et des technologies*, 2019) with C. de Hosson; the article 'La modélisation des savoirs dans les analyses didactiques des situations d'enseignement et apprentissage' (*Recherches en éducation*, 2017) with F. Ligozat.

Denise Orange-Ravachol is Emeritus Professor at the University of Lille. Her research focuses on functionalist and historical problematizations in biology and geology, and on educational approaches to sustainable development and health. She is the author of *Didactique des SVT, Entre phénomènes et événements* (2012). She co-authored 'Knowledge and Values Youngsters Can Trust: Nutrition and Food Practices in French Life Science Teaching since 1945' (*Food and Foodways*, 2019) with Susan Kovacs, and 'Éducation nutritionnelle et acculturation scientifique: quelles circulations de normes et de savoirs dans les discours adressés aux jeunes?' (2018) with Susan Kovacs and Christian Orange.

Vincent Schlegel is a doctoral candidate in Sociology at the School for Advanced Studies in the Social Sciences (EHESS) and a member of the Interdisciplinary Research Center on Medicine, Science, Health and Society (Cermes3) of the French National Centre for Scientific Research (UMR CNRS 8211 – Unité Inserm 988 – EHESS – Université de Paris). His main research interests include socialization, health education and chronic disease management. His current research involves ethnographic inquiry into therapeutic patient education programmes and focuses on the 'making' of self-controlled diabetic patients.

Elodie Sevin is Associate Professor of Information and Communication Sciences at the University of Lille. Her current research interest is the transformation of management practices in organizations. She also studies local public policy on waste reduction and the zero waste movement. Her most recent publications include 'Norms in the School Canteen: A Case Study of Primary School Canteens in a Large City of Northern France' in Philippe Cardon and Simona De Iulio, *Cantine et friandises* (2021).

Virginie Córdoba-Wolff is a PhD candidate in Sociology at the University of Strasbourg and a member of the Interdisciplinary 'European Dynamics' research laboratory of the French National Centre for Scientific Research (Dynamiques Européennes – UMR 7367/CNRS). Her doctoral dissertation is on food avoidance: she studies personal itineraries of gluten avoidance in France and Germany. Her research focuses on the conflicts generated by changing norms related to food, health and the body. She has published 'Food Sensitivities and Bodily Sedition: From Vulnerability to a Moral Ideal?' (2019). She is co-editor of the *Revue des Sciences Sociales* and co-coordinator of issue No. 61 'Dissidences Alimentaires' (on Food Dissidence; published in 2019).

Acknowledgements

We gratefully acknowledge the institutional and financial support we received from three University of Lille research units, GERiiCO, CIREL and CERIeS. We would also like to thank the University of Lille research commission for a 2019 grant to cover translation costs for several chapters of this book. We extend our sincere thanks and appreciation to Patrice de la Broise, director of the research unit GERiiCO, for providing an encouraging environment for our work and for this editorial project.

We wish to acknowledge all contributing authors for their insights, their commitment and for the time and energy devoted to developing individual chapters. Heartfelt thanks go to our colleagues Philippe Cardon and Denise Orange-Ravachol, members of the 'Food Information, Communication and Education' research programme we initiated in 2012, for their stimulating collaboration and unflagging support over the past ten years. As part of this programme, we organized a two-day international conference in December 2018, 'Eating Knowlege: Interdisciplinary Perspectives on Food Information, Communication and Education'. The conference and the exchange of ideas which grew out of it were the starting point for this book. We would like to thank Peter Scholliers, keynote speaker at the conference, for his generous advice and guidance.

Special thanks to Martin Breughel for valuable suggestions which helped us improve the manuscript and to Carole Counihan for her encouragement and input.

We wish to thank Siofra Dempsey, Mickaël Mariaule, Corinne Wecksteen-Quinio and Anna Marrinan for their help in revising the English versions of certain chapters.

Our thanks go as well to Miriam Cantwell, Lucy Carroll, Lily McMahon and Saranya Manohar for their enthusiasm, thoughtful assistance and editorial support starting from the early phases of this book project.

Introduction

Simona De Iulio and Susan Kovacs

In today's world a wide variety of corporate, public and media-based actors have taken on the responsibility of informing and educating the public about food and eating: food producers, advertisers, celebrity chefs, teachers, food bloggers, food activists, national and local councils and governmental agencies. Such actors, each with their own objectives and communicational strategies, contribute to the public's 'eating knowledge' or, in other words, to what people know about eating and what they do with this knowledge. Given that so many diverse social actors are involved in the process of production, reformulation, diffusion and appropriation of knowledge about food, it is apparent that different kinds of knowledge exist simultaneously: institutional and traditional knowledge, scientific and lay knowledge, consensual and disputed knowledge and so on. In addition, knowledge claims can take many different forms including advice, expertise, nutritional guidelines and models, and can be disseminated within a wide variety of media (internet, cooking workshops, school textbooks, mobile apps, etc.). Mediatized forms of knowledge about food and eating are embedded in specific social contexts and participate in the shaping of these contexts.

The first aim of this book is to explore how eating knowledge has been disseminated and continuously configured over time and in specific social spaces and circumstances through the action of various actors and through different media. In accordance with recent approaches to the history of knowledge (Östling et al. 2018; Sarasin and Kilcher 2011), we consider eating knowledge as a communication process by which theories, norms and beliefs about food and food practices circulate in different spheres. Analysis of the circulation of eating knowledge can help reveal how different media and mediators intervene in this process, how they seek to advance their interests and how they attempt to impose specific views about health and eating. The second fundamental objective of this book is to consider the ways in which eating knowledge has been interpreted and appropriated by different publics. The study of the use and recontextualization of eating knowledge sheds light on the often subtle ways in which aspects of this knowledge are accepted, interpreted, adapted or contested within specific cultural contexts and social realities.

The overriding goal of this book is to analyse, from a diachronic and interdisciplinary perspective, the emergence and current proliferation of actors and discourses, each with various claims to authority and legitimacy, concerned with explaining how and what to eat. The contributions assembled in this book, which focus on case studies in several Western European countries (France, Italy, Belgium and Spain), seek to advance our understanding of the processes of mediatization, circulation and reception of knowledge relating to food. These processes are analysed within specific social environments (including schools, businesses, hospitals) and media contexts; authors are in particular concerned about the ways in which communication artefacts – public communication tools, social media platforms, popular science publications and pedagogical materials – transport, shape and transform knowledge about food.

Information, education, communication: A driving force in contemporary food and nutrition policy

The study of eating knowledge as a communication process raises key questions about how different media and mediators clamour for attention and seek to influence beliefs, values and practices about a range of issues surrounding health, food traditions and culinary practices.

Knowledge circulation strategies have, for example, become central to government agencies' health and nutrition policies and politics. Contemporary European food and nutritional policies have given increasing importance to the creation of pedagogical and awareness-raising messages in order to foster certain eating behaviours. Starting in the mid-twentieth century, governmental and public institutions, at international, national and local levels, began to invest significant time and resources in the development of programmes and tools for promoting food-based dietary guidelines and guidance on how citizens can and should 'eat well'. A so-called 'information, education, communication' approach has become an important component of the World Health Organization's (WHO's) public health policies; this approach also guides the policy creation of other international public institutions such as the Food and Agriculture Organization (FAO) and the United Nations Children's Fund (UNICEF). This approach is defined as follows:

> Information, education and communication initiatives are grounded in the concepts of prevention and primary health care. Largely concerned with individual behaviour change or reinforcement, and/or changes in social or community norms, public health education and communication seek to empower people vis à vis their health actions, and to garner social and political support for those actions. (WHO 2001)

Information campaigns and other messaging initiatives in line with this approach play an increasingly prominent role as part of a range of strategies and roadmaps devised at the European Union (EU) level to promote healthy diets among school children and the wider public. Examples include the 2007 'Strategy for Europe on Nutrition, Overweight and Obesity-Related Health Issues', and the EU 'Action Plan on Childhood Obesity 2014–2020'. In addition, EU member states have aligned themselves with the WHO 'European Food and Nutrition Action Plan 2015–2020' by developing awareness-oriented resources, publications and events at national and local levels.

In order to influence diets and, ultimately, the food system itself, the FAO recommends coherent integration of dietary prescriptions into national food, agriculture, education and health policies and programmes. The FAO also recommends involving a wide range of stakeholders from governments, non-governmental organizations, mass media, the private sector and communities to carry out these so-called information-education-communication initiatives.

Our observation of these current health policy trends and messages led us to question the larger social and historical contexts in which they emerge. Through this book, we seek to promote an understanding of the ways by which information and teaching initiatives reproduce, renew or seek to overshadow or replace other types of mediated knowledge about food and food practice. As the essays in this book show, while recent measures and programmes designed by today's policymakers bring knowledge circulation strategies to the forefront of dietary reform initiatives, nutritional precepts have been published and disseminated over the centuries in many forms and for various reasons. The objective of this book is not to provide a complete historical account of eating knowledge processes and artefacts across time; through reference to significant historical examples and trends, however, individual chapters provide insight into how and why nutritional policies have increasingly sought to encroach upon the daily lives of eaters. The generalization of such policies coincides, as of the twentieth century, with the expansion of rationalized health and education infrastructures, the growth of consumer society and the increasing medicalization of eating and health. These policy orientations and socio-economic changes are analysed through exploration of the mediators and mediatized messages which embody, promote or challenge them over time.

Through close consideration of the forms and sources of mediated knowledge about food, this book addresses significant questions about how individuals and groups are imagined by social and political policymakers. Today's public awareness campaigns, for example, aim to disseminate nutritional norms and to incentivize normalized food conducts. Food-based dietary guidelines promoted within current public health and nutrition campaigns tend to take the form of simple, short messages visually illustrated with graphic tools (e.g. nutritional pyramids, food plates, flags). Such guidelines also seek to correlate, to varying degrees, chronic disease, illness and food consumption. Advice is given about topics such as the amount and types of food groups to consume on a daily basis, meal planning techniques, nutrient and disease interactions, strategies to reduce or prevent chronic disease, and dietary advice for particular life stages (FAO 2016; FAO/WHO 2006). Such messages, and their mediatized forms, are predicated on the assumption that audiences are rational subjects who can act willingly on such advice and that food knowledge transfer and appropriation requires above all effective, well-planned and easy to comprehend content.

Public policy messaging in pedagogical resources, information campaigns and other initiatives seek in fact to convey the idea that the primary responsibility for food choices and behaviour lies with individuals themselves. In this respect, two critical phenomena should be pointed out. First, most food policy actions remain focused on consumer-centred, education-based self-help approaches to promote healthy eating, rather than addressing the contextual phenomena shaping people's choices. Thus, recent eating knowledge disseminated through public messaging paradoxically reflects a move towards strong interventionist health policy while positioning individuals as the ultimate monitors of their own health and nutrition. Second, while the primary objective of today's public policies in food education is to improve health, the process of learning to 'eat well' is inextricably linked to a political ambition, that of producing certain types of subjects and citizens.

This book seeks to question and deconstruct the promotion of today's desirable subjects as they are defined and typified through mediated and often normative knowledge about food: the health-conscious worker, the rational young eater, the self-reliant diabetic patient, the enterprising gluten-free eater and so on. Our book concurs with current critical research in food studies undertaken by scholars such as Charlotte Biltekoff and Jo Pike. These authors show how the government of food behaviour is linked to processes of social normalization and involves attempts to inculcate norms and values that are considered relevant to the stability of the social order. From this perspective, we consider that the production and dissemination of eating knowledge through health policy initiatives raise issues and concerns of a political nature; the study of public food knowledge information strategies shows the extent to which health and education policy surrounding food derives from 'a moral project: the kind of people we are, what we aspire to be and the role that food plays in this process' (Pike and Kelly 2014: 19).

New critical perspectives in food knowledge circulation

As the above considerations suggest, knowledge circulation about eating raises important questions not only for policymakers and information professionals but also for scholars of food studies, media studies and more broadly for those involved in humanities and social sciences scholarship: What kind of knowledge about food and nutrition is disseminated in society? For what purpose? Through which media channels? By which social actors? What authority and legitimacy do these actors have? How has such knowledge been interpreted and used by different audiences?

Although actions of knowledge dissemination are considered as fundamental in food policy and food politics, and despite the crucial importance of the issues raised, critical study of the strategies and logics underlying food knowledge circulation and mediatization has not yet been widely developed. Among the few studies devoted to the communicational dimension of food is a collection of essays edited by Janet M. Cramer, Carlnita Green and Lynn M. Waters (2011) entitled *Food as Communication, Communication as Food*. The aim of the book is to explore and understand the increasing prevalence of food-focused consumption, media and culture. Contributors provide different examples of how food operates as a system of communication, and how communication theory and practices can be understood by considering food in this way. Another volume of scholarly essays edited by Rick Flowers and Elaine Swan (2015), *Food Pedagogies,* argues that food has become the target of intensified pedagogical activity across a range of domains, including schools, supermarkets, domestic spaces, advertising and TV media. The authors assess the moral dimension and politics of teaching and learning about food inside and beyond the classroom. These two exceptions aside, much of the work of communication and education scholars and professionals has focused on how to improve the effectiveness of awareness-raising campaigns or in-school initiatives with little consideration of the social, ethical or political implications of these practices and the discourses they promote and convey.

The present book, in addressing these questions, highlights the relationships between eating knowledge, society, politics and culture. In this sense, our book shares perspectives with aspects of Science and Technology Studies (STS) (Felt et al. 2017; Latour 1987). Like STS, the chapters in this book recognize that food, as a technical, social and symbolic process, functions through the interweaving of people, things, information objects, knowledge and values. Further, as in STS scholarship, the book adheres to the principle of the social construction of knowledge and seeks to understand scientific and technological innovation as it emerges through the interactions of networks of actors. Following an STS approach, the book questions the role of technologies, specifically information and communication technologies, in the circulation of knowledge over time and in social spaces; authors consider how different media contribute to the shaping of what people know and think about food and food practices.

However, while STS research and actor network theory are often primarily concerned with exploring the connections between different stakeholders and their underlying power positions, this book is more interested in how knowledge about food and food practices has been popularized, adapted, recontextualized or 'trivialized' in Jeanneret's sense of the term (2008). In addition, the aim of the book is not to study scientific and technological knowledge production in academic or laboratory settings. In recent years, a growing body of work has been devoted to the construction of scientific expertise in the area of nutrition and in the domain of food science and technology (Gentilcore Smith 2019; Neswald, Smith and Thoms 2017; Penders 2010). The originality of this book resides rather in the attention given to the dynamic cultural processes of transforming, rewriting, mediating and reusing concepts and beliefs derived from both academic and non-academic sources. Moreover, contrary to diffusionist and linear models of knowledge transfer and sharing, we assume that when media and mediators communicate theories, beliefs and experiences about food and eating, they inevitably transform them. Such processes of knowledge circulation in the field of food and eating remain largely unexplored. Our ambition is to bring to the fore new critical perspectives through exploration of how knowledge sources derived from expert and lay domains are disseminated, revived and shared across society; how they are used to support advice, precepts and behavioural guidelines; how they are interpreted by different actors.

Structure of the book

Contributing authors employ a variety of methodological approaches to examine two primary issues related to eating knowledge. Part 1 of the book explores how different media and mediators, through their dissemination of knowledge about food, have sought to impose an increasingly normalized vision of food practice. Part 2 focuses on the reception and use of eating knowledge messages and initiatives by the general public and by specific actors including patients, students and parents. The chapters in the second part of the book also explore the extent to which the appropriation of eating knowledge has led to the emergence of renewed food information and communication practices and alternative food pedagogies.

Part 1: Construction and circulation of eating knowledge: Mediators and mediations

Part 1 of the book addresses how different forms of eating knowledge have circulated within and across public arenas through the actions of both human actors and knowledge artefacts. Authors explore, on the one hand, the status, authority and objectives of the various actors who, over time, have taken on the role of food knowledge mediators. On the other hand, contributing authors analyse the role and characteristics of visual, oral, printed and electronic media in the circulation of food knowledge within different social spaces.

In Chapter 1, anthropologist Elisabetta Moro shows how the uses as well as the meanings and values associated with food have their roots in the ancient past. She argues that contemporary food-based dietary guidelines tend to ignore the wealth of cultural knowledge developed over centuries. The case she examines, that of olive oil, is exemplary in this respect. As literary, historical and religious texts attest, different kinds of practical and symbolic knowledge have been associated with olive oil over the centuries in the Mediterranean regions, since ancient Greek civilization. Olive oil has long been considered a 'precious' substance, used in cooking, cosmetics, pharmaceuticals, soaps as well as in religious ritual to bless and to anoint the sick. Today, olive oil is often considered only from a nutritional point of view, so that this rich and ancient store of knowledge and symbols is in danger of disappearing. Nutritional 'yellow or red traffic light' warnings which appear on bottles of olive oil discourage its consumption, thus 'demonizing' a food once considered sacred. Reconstructing the key issues and controversies surrounding traffic light recommendations and olive oil, Elisabetta Moro provides an overview of the political and economic wrangling behind the terminology and principles of nutritional labelling for consumers. Moro shows how contemporary food knowledge mediators including dieticians and governmental experts play a key role in determining how nutritional knowledge is transposed into cautionary messages for consumers. Paradoxically, the dietetic and communicational ostracism of olive oil has confirmed and reinforced its historic and symbolic value in certain contexts. Elisabetta Moro explores the tensions between proponents of the

Mediterranean diet, who call upon cultural heritage to defend their views, and critics of olive oil who appear determined to banish this substance from the table of today's '*Homo Dieteticus*'.

While Elisabetta Moro offers a broad historical perspective on the evolution of ancestral knowledge about food, as such knowledge is transported through ritual, practice and myth, Justine Le Floc'h focuses in Chapter 2 on a specific form of popularized dietetic knowledge, the seventeenth-century printed *regimina sanitatis* (health regimens or living regimens). Le Floc'h identifies the rhetorical strategies developed by the authors of these treatises to influence intended readers. Authors present their writings as contributions to the emerging domain of disease prevention. In so doing, their intent is to promote the legitimacy of the medical field as the professional sector uniquely qualified to produce reliable knowledge about the body, health and self-government. According to the *regimina sanitatis*, physicians – rather than apothecaries – are to be seen as the sole repositories of valid knowledge about food choices. Written in accessible vernacular style, this narrative form is composed of medical *doxa* and examples from Antiquity and various historical sources. As such, this medical book genre constitutes one of the first examples of published medical casuistry accessible to a wide readership through the printed medium. Le Floc'h's analysis of rhetorical strategies and figures reveals the importance given to instructive and pleasant discourse and to the use of persuasive language for disseminating valuable eating knowledge in this period.

The remaining chapters of Part 1 are devoted to knowledge created and mediatized in post-war and contemporary Europe with reference to specific publics: school children, the elderly, salaried workers and consumers seeking reliable information in times of food crisis. In Chapter 3, historian Didier Nourrisson addresses the problem of food and nutrition education in the changing landscape of the French school setting in the mid-twentieth century. In addition to traditional pedagogical tools used by teachers (textbooks, posters and murals, award cards for good students), twentieth-century schools developed an innovative method for mass teaching through visual language: the pedagogical film strip. Such 'silent' films allowed teachers to personalize their explanatory discourse while projecting successive images to their class. Didier Nourrisson analyses a corpus of a hundred film strips on the theme of food produced between 1930 and 1970 by ten different editors in France. His analysis shows that the vision of the history and geography of food, of natural science, of civic education (table manners) and of home economics (including the art of cooking) is significantly modified by this medium. He also investigates the ways in which these film strips display the role of consumer brands within the school environment, during the period of post-war prosperity which sees the rise of consumer society in France.

In Chapter 4, sociologist Laura Guérin examines different fields of knowledge that have shaped the fight against malnutrition in old age since the beginning of the twentieth century. As Guérin explains, current public health policy describes undernutrition as one of the major medical issues affecting older populations. At the beginning of the twentieth century, however, the issue of nutrition among the elderly was framed in an entirely different light. Based on a sociological study of food practices in residential care for the elderly (EHPAD) in France, Guérin analyses the ways in which knowledge circulation has led to an emphasis on maintaining and guaranteeing a sufficient level of food consumption as a central criterion of good professional practice in elder care facilities. Guérin's study of the medical literature, including medical theses and archives of Parisian public hospitals from the end of the nineteenth century to the beginning of the twenty-first century, shows how unhealthy food habits in the elderly have become a medical issue designated by the term 'undernutrition'. Guérin's analysis illustrates the scientific construction of a social reality: in less than a century, what was considered to be a private issue gradually aroused public interest to become an issue worthy of public action. This chapter contributes to a more general reflection on the 'government' of so-called old-age dependent populations.

In Chapter 5, communication scholars Thomas Heller and Elodie Sevin address two preoccupations that characterize issues raised by 'food at work': the concern for workers' well-being and the need for sustained productivity. As the authors show, today's context of late capitalism is marked on the one hand by the rise of junk food, the risk of obesity, and increasing sources of competition and stress in the workplace and on the other hand by new practices of food-based well-being. In this context, new professional actors have emerged (such as coaches, local or bio-food delivery personnel, taste educators), who seek to inform and to sensitize employees about specific food philosophies and behaviours (vegan practices, nutrient timing, etc.). Yet as the authors explain, concerns about 'food at work' characteristic of our post-modern age were expressed by scholars and industrial actors alike by the second half of the nineteenth century. 'Food at work' in the nineteenth century was addressed in scientific and professional literature as part of the development of industrial capitalism and was linked to questions such as work rhythm and the need to create cafeterias in firms. Heller and Sevin highlight the similarities between the issues and types of knowledge about 'food at work' which are debated today and those which were current 150 years ago. While these questions differ in meaning for each period, the authors argue that historical analysis of industrial work and industrial thinking allows for better understanding of contemporary discourses and practices as a heritage from the past.

In Chapter 6, the final chapter in Part 1, François Allard-Huver examines the ways in which knowledge about food risks is disseminated in the public sphere in the context of controversy and sanitary crisis. Recent sanitary crises and food scandals (such as the 2013 horsemeat scandal) have increasingly led consumers to demand information about the food they eat. At the same time, however, consumers tend to mistrust information provided by retailers, producers or food safety authorities. Consumers as well as consumer associations criticize the confusion and the lack of coherent data provided by government and industrial actors. Similarly, scientific experts struggle to provide trustworthy dietary and nutritional guidance to eaters; expert studies are increasingly challenged by actors defending their own businesses and commercial interests. In order to explore these phenomena as they are exacerbated by the mediatization of sanitary controversies, François Allard-Huver first analyses the processes of media coverage of food scandals over the last decade, beginning with the 2011 *E. coli* outbreak. His discussion considers the role of experts and food safety institutions in their attempts to control food narratives. Second, he shows how the emergence of new actors and mediators, exploiting the potential of digital media and alternative modes of online publication, has led to a reorganization of the information-communication apparatus of food knowledge.

Part 2: Uses and appropriations of 'eating knowledge' in everyday practices

Part 2 of the book addresses the ways in which an increasingly diverse array of messages about food and eating are perceived, interpreted and used in everyday life.

In the first chapter of Part 2 (Chapter 7), sociologist Vincent Schlegel considers the history of dietary prescriptions for diabetes mellitus patients through the twentieth century as well as the ways in which these prescriptions are interpreted and put to use by specialists and by patients themselves. As Schlegel demonstrates, the history of dietary prescriptions for diabetic patients is related to concurrent evolutions of medical practices and of patients' involvement in their own care. Schlegel examines the gradual transformations in dietary prescriptions from dietary restrictions imposed on diabetic patients by medical professionals to self-restraint through patient training. As the author shows, while the pre-insulin era (1900–21) is characterized by strict disciplinary methods ensuring that patients follow starvation diets, the discovery of insulin was a turning point: insulin deeply reshaped the experience of those who suffered from diabetes. By the early 1990s, European diabetologists started developing new training practices. The growing interrelations between patients and doctors, structural changes in the medical field as well as therapeutic innovations led to a recognition of the patient's role as 'auxiliary' to the medical profession. In return, dietary prescriptions became more flexible and reached the point where treatment was adjusted to patients' eating habits rather than the reverse. The development of educational programmes has reduced imposed dietary 'constraints' in order to encourage patients' self-control by offering them knowledge, know-how and life skills. Through this historical overview as well as ethnographic analysis of patient training initiatives in different contexts, Schlegel shows that the fostering of patient empowerment has also led to increased responsibilization of individuals. Schlegel concludes that the socio-economic profile of diabetes patients remains an important determining factor influencing the nature of appropriation of medical advice and recommendations.

In Chapter 8, information-communication science scholar Viviane Clavier explores the resources used by dieticians during professional practice and consultations with patients. As Clavier explains, in France the profession of dietetics was recognized in the 1950s, much later than in the United States. High expectations are currently placed upon dieticians, who are considered to be one of the primary vectors of government initiated and supported nutrition education and prevention programmes (especially with regard to type 2 diabetes, obesity and cardiovascular diseases). In the context of the wide-ranging care and networking missions now entrusted to these professionals, Clavier describes and analyses the ways in which dieticians seek information for themselves and how they inform their patients. Her study presents results of an online survey distributed to members of the French Association of Dieticians and Nutritionists (AFDN) from the Auvergne-Rhône-Alpes region. The analysis reveals wide disparities: some professionals never or rarely seek information, while others have very specialized information practices. Clavier's study provides important insight into the types of sources favoured by dieticians in their information-seeking practices. Yet as Clavier shows, while expert knowledge in nutrition has become highly specialized, the expertise of dieticians is often called into question. Dieticians are more frequently asked about issues relating to food and society rather than about nutritional information. Consequently, these professionals are considered for the most part as information mediators rather than as nutrition consultants. Clavier examines the ways in which these professionals take on their role as information mediators, developing personalized information artefacts during consultation sessions through a process of exchange with patients; these practices suggest that dieticians seek out new ways to formulate knowledge in order to avoid prescriptive or normalized communication.

While medical professionals including dieticians and diabetes specialists thus often engage in reformulating 'eating knowledge' for their patients, individuals and the interest groups to which they belong have also become increasingly involved, in part due to the expansion of the internet, in seeking out, creating and disseminating new forms of food knowledge. These knowledge circulation practices participate in establishing underexplored medical issues as legitimate social concerns. In Chapter 9, sociologist Virginie Córdoba-Wolff shows how the increasing visibility of substance-free diets (gluten-free, milk-free, sugar-free, etc.) and of food sensitivities and intolerances has been made possible by the action of various social actors. These actors, including health professionals, journalists and non-professionals, present themselves as competent on the subject of food sensitivities and special diets by virtue of their own experiences. Córdoba-Wolff's analysis of French and German blogs promoting gluten-free diets as well as results of survey interviews that she conducted with individuals who avoid gluten show that these new knowledge mediators use a variety of sources (scientific and popular literature, personal experience narratives) and a wide range of fields of discourse (gastronomy, commercial discourses, health and nutrition guidance, etc.). By offering both cooking recipes and scientific news, these actors have become new prescribers of norms and values, as they seek to capture the attention of their audience and to influence contemporary representations and practices in relation to food, health and the environment.

Just as new nutritional concerns such as gluten intolerance can be legitimized and materialized by the efforts of scientific, media-based and informal mediators, other issues in eating knowledge have been shaped by such contrasting mediating forces as advertisers and school publishers. The popularization of the vitamin is a case in point, studied in Chapter 10 by Simona De Iulio, Laurence Depezay, Susan Kovacs, Christian Orange and Denise Orange-Ravachol. The authors of this chapter focus on the ways in which school resources and commercial advertising – both considered as forms of recontextualized and rewritten scientific discourse – contribute to increasing public awareness of nutritional discoveries in the second half of the twentieth century. The chapter highlights the contrast in approaches to mediatizing the vitamin: while magazine advertisements in women's publications of the post-war period portray and promote the idea of health-as-capital to be developed through vitamin-rich products, school biology textbooks of the mid-twentieth century present a harsh clinical view of the vitamin-deprived body to drive home a lesson in nutritional prevention aimed at school children. As the authors show, these opposing visions of the vitamin, euphoric and preventive, are specific to the communicational contexts from which they arise, and reveal a marked tension between innovative marketing discourses and traditional food pedagogies in the elaboration of cultural imaginaries of food and eating.

The school setting has in fact long been a privileged place for inculcating food behaviours and norms. In Chapter 11, as Marie Berthoud shows, the role of schools in food education has intensified in France since the end of the 1990s. In order to tackle the problem of sanitary risks associated with food, schools have taken on an increasingly central and explicit role in sensitizing children to so-called proper eating behaviour. In France, public authorities disseminate information through national health campaigns, and these national messages are in turn 'translated' into prescriptions, protocols and instructional missions on local and institutional levels. Berthoud explores the transformations of healthy eating messages by public authorities and school actors. Her semiotic and pragmatic analysis of national programme statements (2010–15) and of pedagogical documents coupled with observations and interviews conducted with school actors show that such transformed messages seek to instil normative models in children so that they learn to manage their own conduct and the conduct of others. This complex communicational process is explored in order, first, to show how school food has become a public policy issue. Second, the author reflects upon attempts to empower children to make their own food choices during lunchtime meals at school; Berthoud shows however that such dietary prescriptions embodied in documents, activities and daily routines are often diverted from their primary objectives by the school canteen staff as well as by school children themselves.

In recent years, official instructions governing food pedagogy at school have undergone considerable change, especially with the importance given to so-called 'educational approaches' (the French *éducations à*) including health education. In Chapter 12, education scholars Christian Orange and Denise Orange-Ravachol study the consequences of this evolution for students' learning and their access to scientifically reasoned knowledge. Their objective is to identify conditions for the development of critical thinking and the ability to make educated choices. Their discussion shows the importance, for students, of breaking with common sense reasoning patterns (such as simple causality, storytelling and the focus on the attributes of food) in order to acquire 'disruptive' ways of thinking (relationships between objects, input–output reasoning and systems functioning). The authors analyse several examples of classroom situations, student interviews and school textbooks to illustrate the challenges inherent in developing new reasoning patterns in biology teaching.

Food education is however not reserved to the classroom and can be taken up by new actors including parents who are dissatisfied with approaches to food and eating embodied in the modern impersonal and industrialized school canteen. In Chapter 13, sociologists Philippe Cardon and María Dolores Martín-Lagos López illustrate how in Spain, today's dietary directives have become a political tool for social groups who consider that public schools do not adequately fulfil their role of protecting children by offering them a healthy diet. Their chapter reports on the results of an ethnographic study of five parent-run canteens recently created in the Andalusian city of Granada, Spain. Such associative canteens, set up and managed by parents starting in 2013, offer an alternative mode of nutrition and education (via meals and lunchtime activities) for children in primary education. These associations seek to educate children about nutritional and civic principles; the direct experience of a community-based ethos is meant to foster responsible and ethical eating through social practices around food. Beyond the strictly health and environmental aspects, food and meals are seen as complex learning objects used to promote citizen involvement, autonomy and responsibility. These principles derive in part from the Grenada nursery school canteens founded after the Spanish transition to democracy in 1975. The authors show that these new associative canteens, representative of bottom-up nutrition reform through education carried out by citizen groups, have been created by a relatively homogeneous group of upper-middle class parents. Despite similarities in their socio-economic background which unite these new food and nutrition mediators, their motivations and commitments vary widely, thus hindering the development of a uniform societal ambition for this food reform and educational movement.

Conclusion

The chapters in this book show that the dissemination and reception of food knowledge are in fact part of a complex process of continued rewriting, transposing and reuse of dogma, tradition, research, advice and expertise. The study of the dynamics of food knowledge circulation thus implies a wide-ranging diachronic approach, exemplified here by authors who have pushed the limits of their own disciplinary boundaries, blending, for example, public policy sociology with the evolving epistemology of ageing; rhetorical analysis, medical history and book history; media analysis and information-seeking trajectory ethnographies. The different case studies illustrate the profound paradoxes of eating knowledge mediators and mediations, be they cultural artefact, document, object, social actor or policy. Food knowledge mediators and mediations, in seeking to facilitate access to culturally valued behaviours and insights, reveal and embody lasting tensions between eating norms and eating choices.

Part 1

Construction and circulation of 'eating knowledge': Mediators and mediations

Who is involved in the production, circulation and mediatization of knowledge about food? What role do experts and expertise play in these processes? What kind of knowledge comes into circulation? Through which media and in which environments is such knowledge diffused? The essays in Part 1 of the book seek to answer these questions and to explore the changing material, social and institutional forces at play in the dissemination of advice about nutrition, eating and health.

As historical and socio-anthropological research demonstrates, for many centuries food products and choices have been the subject of heterogeneous sets of beliefs and symbols handed down from generation to generation, through religious precepts, culinary techniques and practical cooking experience. Examination of historical and contemporary sources of knowledge about food shows that public and private actors with diverse interests have been involved in the changing processes and practices that generate, transform and disseminate 'eating knowledge' across time and space and across different cultures.

Since the seventeenth century, the knowledge developed in the medical field of dietetics has sought to shape the ways in which individuals define and govern their own food practices. Mediators of medical food knowledge (physicians, apothecaries, medical writers, educators) while taking up the challenge of popularizing advice and information about eating have advanced their own interests and expertise. This medicalization of knowledge about food has not taken place without rivalry, debate and controversy especially in times of crisis and concern about food risks. Eating knowledge has often been accompanied by feelings of fear, insecurity and mistrust, particularly with regard to the consumption of industrially produced food products.

Based on the authority and expertise of various actors, different types of knowledge about food vie for preeminence in a continuously changing knowledge landscape. While knowledge about food is constantly renewed over time, new knowledge does not inevitably impose itself as authoritative nor does it erase previously held knowledge by taking its place. Phenomena of accumulation, juxtaposition as well as sedimentation of norms, beliefs and opinions occur over time.

As media have evolved, from print to audiovisual culture and the internet, knowledge about food has become increasingly diversified and has taken on new communicational and socio-political properties and objectives within the public sphere. All the contributions gathered here show the central role played by the media dimension of knowledge circulation and appropriation. The cases analysed highlight the variety of media utilized over time: knowledge about food is relayed by medical books, textbooks, film strips, the professional press, cookbooks as well as by blogs, internet forums, websites and social networks. In addition, the written and visual forms and genres used to disseminate this knowledge are also very diverse, ranging from institutional directives to scientific reports, from petitions to 'faqs', from computer graphics to press releases.

And finally, the chapters in Part 1 show the variety of social environments through which knowledge about food circulates: from classroom to workplace, from dieticians' offices to hospitals and hospices. This heterogeneous set of media, documentary forms and environments plays an important role not only in the sharing and appropriation of knowledge about food, but also in its reformulation, transposition and transformation within various social contexts and spaces.

Athena, Jesus Christ and the traffic light: The history and anthropology of knowledge about olive oil

Elisabetta Moro
English translation by Richard Bates

Introduction

The objective of this chapter is to reconstruct the meanings associated with the olive and olive oil from the ancient world to today, from an anthropological and historical perspective. For centuries these plants and the oil produced by pressing their fruits have been regarded as precious, not only nutritionally but also on aesthetic and pharmaceutical levels, since olive oil has traditionally been used to heal and to prepare medicinal lotions. Olive oil is also a substance that can preserve food for very long periods, even in the hot summer months. The combination of these physical properties explains why the use of this oil became so widespread and why it has been traded since Antiquity. Apart from its physical characteristics, olive oil is equally valued for its symbolic associations; the history of olive oil becomes increasingly complex (Geertz 1973) as we move from Minoan to Hellenic civilization, from the Magna Graecia to the Roman Empire, from mediaeval monasticism to the first 'faculties' of medicine – until its final consecration when the Mediterranean diet was introduced as a constructed medical concept in the 1950s. However, while the reputation of olive oil has grown steadily, from the age of Minos to the policies of the World Health Organization (WHO), an educational model known as the 'traffic light diet', conceived – significantly – far from the geographical-cultural area of the Mediterranean, has recently called into question its role in a healthy, balanced diet. This model places olive oil on the same level as other vegetable and animal fats. The intention of this chapter is not to defend olive oil from a nutritional point of view – a job for nutritionists – but to demonstrate that a simplified, if not mistaken, educational model can end up underestimating and obliterating a thousand-year-old cultural heritage. As we will see, this heritage of knowledge, traditions, recipes, preservation techniques and care of the body became widespread in the popular culture of the Mediterranean peoples.

This anthropological analysis is designed to respond, at least in part, to some fundamental questions. The first concerns the validity of a visual symbol such as the food traffic light system for educating the population of the West into adopting a healthy lifestyle. The second invites us to wonder if traffic light labelling, quite apart from its promoters' intentions, does not risk sending out contradictory messages. Indeed, the schematism of current medical-scientific trends tends to relegate the cultural elements of food to a secondary position, favouring the nutritional aspect, which, more often than not, is reduced to mere calorie-counting. But food, as the French anthropologist Claude Lévi-Strauss has taught us, is not only good to eat but also good to think, in that it creates social identity, systems of collective representation, family memory, a language of the heart and material expression of feelings (Granet-Mauss 1975; Lévi-Strauss 1962). One also wonders if the traffic light label on food products does not tend to cancel centuries of history, values, cultural practices, poetics, and customs in the name of a reductionism that stigmatizes and prohibits for educational ends.

To restrict the field of analysis, I have chosen to focus in this chapter on the Mediterranean diet, which is regarded by the international scientific community and the WHO as one of the healthiest lifestyles in the world. In 2010 it was also proclaimed a cultural heritage of humanity by the United Nations Educational, Scientific and Cultural Organization (UNESCO). As it is a complex eating model with many variables, I have chosen to examine just one of the constituent elements in the Mediterranean diet – extra virgin olive oil. This gastronomic ingredient has a cultural history going back thousands of years as one of the three symbolic pillars of the memory and history of the Mediterranean – olive oil, wine and cereals. Despite this, olive oil is currently at the centre of a controversial public health campaign. Through both 'penitential' educational initiatives and dietary labelling proposals, nutrition experts and governmental agencies have sought to expunge consideration of olive oil's taste, its 'nutraceutical' (nutritious and pharmaceutical) properties and its ecological value (olive oil having a low carbon footprint), to say nothing of its fundamental contribution to creating pleasure at the table.[1]

The olive tree in mythologies and Mediterranean monotheisms

Religion, mythology, literature and theatre are the ways through which every culture transmits its values, knowledge and beliefs from one generation to another. In this sense, Mediterranean food as we know it today is the outcome of constant development, implementation, cancellation, hybridization and change. In particular, olive oil and its history present a stratification of features which are worth summarizing here so that we can understand more clearly the wealth of this cultural ingredient.

Athena, goddess of Reason, born from Zeus' head by parthenogenesis, gave man the olive tree together with democracy. For the Greeks, these are two emblems of the *polis*. The myth tells that when the goddess and Poseidon were contending for possession of Attica, Zeus announced a competition to settle the question and designated the King of Athens, Cecrops, as arbiter. Poseidon touched the land with his trident and an absolutely new animal, the horse, appeared out of nowhere. It was a technological revolution of extraordinary significance. Athena the blue-eyed goddess, with Olympian calm, struck the earth with her magic javelin and an olive tree (*elaia*) sprang from the ground. Since then, the plant has been designated by the same name as the chaste goddess: 'sea-grey-eyed' (*glaukopis*) (Euphor., *frag.* 57).[2] Cecrops unhesitatingly gave victory to the Virgin goddess, by reason of her greater farsightedness. Her tree yielded edible olives, oil to nourish and to provide light at night, and wood to warm oneself and to make tools, while the horse encouraged men to conquer lands and go to war (Apollodorus 3.14.1; Sophocles, *O.C.* 694–705; Cicero, *de legibus* 1.1.2; Hyginus, *fab.* 164; Pausanias, 1.24.2, 27.2).

Borrowing Claude Lévi-Strauss's famous distinction, we might say that the goddess's gift was a sign of peace and was suited to a 'stationary history' that aims at a balance between man and territory, while the horse is a tool of conquest suited to a 'cumulative history' (1967). Two antithetical models of development: using current terminology we might say that one is frugal and sustainable, while the other is Promethean and unsustainable. The mythical contest is immortalized in Phidias' marble frieze on the west side of the Parthenon as a kind of permanent warning for all future generations that might find themselves having to choose between these two options: two visions of the world analysed outside myth but inside history by Plato in the dialogue between Socrates and Glaucon on the *anankaiotate polis*, the city of strict necessity (*Republic* II, 372 D).

The sacred olive tree of Athena is regarded as an immortal plant. So much so, that, according to many legendary witnesses, it reflowered prodigiously from the still warm ashes of the burning acropolis, set alight by the Persians led by Xerxes in 480 BCE (Herodotus, 8.55). Just like the Palladium, it is a symbol of *civitas graeca*, to the point that the ephebes – the Athenian youths leaving childhood and entering adulthood – swear to defend the homeland, calling as witnesses those very *moriai*, the consecrated olive trees. In addition, the oil pressed from the fruits of these prodigious trees surrounding the Parthenon, were used to fill the decorated amphoras awarded to the athletes who won the Panathenaic games. This oil was regarded as so precious that it was kept by the treasurers of Athena (Scarpi 1989: 130–1). The value of the olive plant was such that in the ancient world uprooting even a single exemplar was punished with death (Aristotle, *Ath. resp.* 60.2).

According to Herodotus the Greeks identified civilization with honey, cereals, wine and olive oil (*History* I: 1–5). Indeed, the sustenance of the Achaeans camping on the island of Delos as they waited to leave for Troy was magically procured by three sisters, known as *Oinotrópoi*, literally those who transform water into wine. Their individual names give us a further glimpse into the sacred value of the Mediterranean triad. One was called Oinò, the second Elaìs and the third Spermò, evoking wine, oil and cereals respectively (Scarpi 2005: 38). Herodotus and Lycophron – also cited by Virgil – tell of the three 'mythical vivandières' receiving from Dionysus the gift of transforming everything they touch into wine, oil and the seeds of wheat, respectively (*Aeneid* XXI). But the link with the god of wheat did not end here, because, as descendants of Dionysus through Anius, Rhoeio and Staphylus, the three maidens were directly related to the god of Bacchanalia. According to the religious historian Paolo Scarpi, this genealogy indicates, through the figurative language of myth, that Dionysus had jurisdiction over the products symbolizing what the Greeks saw as the superiority of their civilization: a more dynamic and open system of trade than that of other peoples. Thus the god's real gift to his three great-great-grand-daughters was trade itself (2005: 38).

And so, mythology and history give us an image of the olive and its juice as having political as well as dietary value. In this sense, olive oil is an emblem of the Mediterranean in the art of cooking, but also in the art of government, as a symbol of private lives and public virtues, of loyalty and fidelity. It is no accident that Ulysses' nuptial bed was carved out of an olive trunk whose roots were still in the ground (*Odyssey* XXIII, 188), symbolizing his indissoluble marriage with Penelope. Symbol of eternity and tenacity, partly due to its resistance, the olive is, in short, a binding agent, both literally and metaphorically.

The olive was also central to the founding myth of the Roman Empire: in his *History of Rome* (I: 3–4), Livy claims that Romulus and Remus were born under an olive tree (Carandini 2016; Giardina 2011). And perhaps we owe to these legendary details the belief, widely held in popular European cultures, that extra virgin olive oil – derived from traditional cold mechanical extraction without use of solvents or refining methods – protects children from the dangers that threaten them. Indeed, the birth of a child was accompanied by the planting of an olive tree. And oil-fed lanterns were lit beside newborn babies to keep away evil spirits (Cattabiani 2017).

For the Jews, the olive was a symbol of justice and wisdom. In the Old Testament the tree is cited no fewer than seventy times. In the first book of Kings we read that, while the first Temple of Jerusalem was being built, Solomon 'made doors of olive tree … The two doors also were of olive tree: and he carved upon them carvings of cherubim … So also made he for the door of the temple posts of olive tree' (1 Kgs 6.31-3). In the book of Judges we are told that one day the trees decided to choose a king. They all went to the olive tree and asked if it wanted to be king, but it modestly refused such an honour, as it would no longer be able to perform its prime, natural task of producing oil for gods and men (Judg. 9.6-15). The Bible also recounts that, after the Great Flood, a dove brought Noah an olive branch to announce that heaven and earth were at last reconciled. From then on, the olive assumed a dual sense: it became the symbol of *rebirth*, because, after its destruction, the earth once again flourished; it became a symbol of peace, because it certified the end of punishment and the reconciliation of God and man (Gen. 8).

In the Christian festival of Palm Sunday, the olive represents Christ himself, whose name means *the anointed*. Through his sacrifice, the son of God becomes an instrument of reconciliation and peace for all humanity. The symbology of the olive is ubiquitous in the Gospels: Jesus is greeted by an enthusiastic crowd waving palm leaves and olive branches (Mt. 21.1-11); he spent the final hours before the Passion on the Mount of Olives (Mt. 26.39-44). The olive garden where Christ prepared himself for martyrdom is known as Gethsemane, which means literally 'olive press'. This garden, symbol of the Messianic consecration of God incarnate is also described as 'the blessed olive, from which has been pressed the oil that has freed humanity from its sins'. The very name

Messiah derives from the Hebrew *masiah*, which means 'anointed' (Scarpi 2005: 76). Olive oil was from the first a consecrated, ritual fluid for Christians and was used in the liturgies with the name of *chrism* and in the sacraments of baptism, extreme unction, confirmation and the ordination of new priests.

While ancient Greece sacralized the creation of the olive tree, ascribing it to Athena, and while Christ is considered the Lord's anointed, the other civilizations of *mare nostrum* took the olive no less seriously. The oil trade dates back to the most remote past, as is proved by the Babylonian Code of Hammurabi held in the Louvre. The Hammurabi Code, 2,500 years before Christ, regulated the production and sale of olive oil, decreed sanctions for adulterating or stealing it, and presents the most ancient set of rules on the subject.

In Jewish tradition, the first olive seed actually fell from the Earthly Paradise and landed on Adam's tomb, as if to say that the history of this tree and of humanity are one and the same (Cattabiani 2017). In the same tradition, oil is regarded as sacrosanct and an instrument of consecration, being used to anoint kings, priests, prophets and all those who are invested from above, the so-called 'anointed of the Lord'. That olive oil is often connected in the oriental world to the origin of things and creation is borne out by the Hebrew myth of Jacob's anointed stone. When Jacob anointed a pillar with oil that had dripped down directly from heaven, God set the stone so deeply in the earth that the pillar was called the 'foundation stone' and it came to represent the centre of the world, on which the temple of Solomon was built (Graves and Patai 1980).

In Islam, too, the olive is the tree of the cosmos, the pillar of the world, the blessed plant. It symbolizes universal man and the Prophet Mohammed. The sacred status of the plant with the silver leaves, on which it is said the name of Allah is written, is directly proportional to its importance as food. The *Koran* says this clearly in *Sura* 24, known as the 'Verse of Light', which compares God to a 'blessed olive tree, neither of the East nor the West, whose oil would almost glow even if untouched by fire' (Bausani 1978; Brosse 1994: 231). One particularly strong popular belief held in Morocco in the early twentieth century was that a glass of oil could increase male procreative capacity (Westermarck 1926, I: 80). We can also see how precious this vegetable liquid was from the fact that in Mediterranean cultures breaking an olive jar is a sign of ill omen, and to ward off such an eventuality people in this corner of the world are taught from one generation to another to handle all receptacles containing this oil with great care.

All three monotheisms, in fact, share the material culture of the Mediterranean, to the point that all three consider olive oil as holy, uncorrupted and radiant, as an emanation of the divine spirit. Its extraordinary capacity to create light has always been surrounded by a supernatural aura: in popular European traditions, it was thought that to find treasures hidden in the depths of the earth one must dip a child's index finger in olive oil. Darkness would be made light and mountains would become transparent, thanks to a 'seasoned finger'. This is also why in Old French the term *huilé* not only meant 'anointed' but also 'illuminated'. The word *huile* also indicates a person able to allay disagreements, who can make any situation fluid, make everything go 'as smooth as oil'. In the eighteenth century, according to the Littré etymological dictionary, the term *chrism* still indicated a secret tie or particular way of building a relationship.[3]

One account of the thaumaturgic powers of oil comes from the secular intellectual Antonio Gramsci, founder of the Italian communist party. Gramsci describes his recovery at the age of four after three days of haemorrhages and convulsions: 'One of my aunts claimed that I came round when she rubbed my feet with olive oil from a lamp dedicated to a Madonna, and so when I refused to perform religious acts she rebuked me sharply, reminding me that I owed my life to the Madonna – which, to tell the truth, worried me not a little' (1973: 479).

Apart from factors of diet, taste and health, the symbolic success of olive oil in all Mediterranean cultures can also be explained by the physical characteristics of the oil itself. It connects and separates, it binds and at the same time prevents the ingredients from sticking to each other or being dispersed. Its very nature as a lubricant led to its cultural status as a 'metaphorical emulsifier' (Niola 2012). Thus, oil is found in many rites of passage and separation, such as baptism, confirmation and extreme unction. In short, the oil joins and disjoins precisely because it greases (Moro and Niola 2017; Niola 2012). These may seem rigid dogmas and bewildering abstractions, but such beliefs and practices derive in fact from the concrete, daily experience of someone who greases a receptacle or oils an ingredient to make it slide better. In a sense, it is the human flavour of theology. Today olive oil has become a secular decalogue and it sacralizes the virtues of the Mediterranean diet (Moro 2014).

Nutritional scientific evidence

The Mediterranean diet is the most widely studied and tested nutritional model in the world. Teams of experts periodically revise the scientific research investigating the various aspects of the relation between this particular way of eating and health. For decades the result has always been unfailingly the same. The Mediterranean diet encourages better conditions of health, it prevents non-transmissible illnesses such as diabetes, hypertension, heart attacks and cancer, and prevents degenerative cardio-cerebrovascular diseases whose onset begins at an advanced age (Boccardi et al. 2018; Keys 1987).

From the start, the study of the Mediterranean diet has also concerned the role of extra virgin olive oil, which is used daily as part of this diet and as the main form of fat. Ever since the earliest research on diet in Mediterranean countries was carried out in Crete by the Rockefeller Foundation in the 1940s, this fat was examined attentively by experts. The 1940s researchers reached the conclusion that olive oil was a fundamental food and key factor in explaining the longevity of the islands' inhabitants. With his biochemist wife, Margaret Haney, Ancel Keys took part in this research and shortly after became one of the most celebrated nutritionists in the world thanks to his identification of a genuine pattern of eating that he and his wife christened the Mediterranean diet. On the basis of data collected by the international team of the Seven Countries Study, Keys and Haney, in their bestselling *Eat Well and Stay Well* (1959), related high longevity with low consumption of animal fats and daily consumption of extra virgin olive oil. Keys went so far as to write: 'From many surveys in Crete, starting in 1957, I have the impression that centenarians are common among farmers, whose breakfast is often only a wineglass of olive oil' (Keys 1987). Their findings gradually trickled down to the general public as well as to doctors, through books, scientific articles and an incessant campaign of communication involving TV networks such as CBS, BBC and RAI, and periodicals such as *Time*, *Oggi* and many Anglo-American and European newspapers (Moro 2014). The results of the Keys research on the benefits of the Mediterranean diet and its main fat were gradually confirmed by innumerable studies, including the famous PREDIMED Study, to which we add the findings of one of the most recent scientific articles by Luis Serra-Majem et al.: 'Besides the health benefits associated to the type and proportion of fatty acids (Garcia-Martínez et al. 2018), the use of olive oil is associated with a high consumption of vegetables when used as salad dressing for raw or cooked vegetables AND legumes. Despite their lack of knowledge about the effects of olive oil on health, the inhabitants of Mediterranean countries always cited olive oil in oral culture as being responsible for the longevity of the population' (Serra-Majem et al. 2019: 2). In addition, numerous studies on the effects of extra virgin olive oil, published in scientific journals, and made known generally by the mass media, particularly in Europe, the United States and Canada, have shown the positive influence it can have on health, not only due to its lack of cholesterol but also because it contains so many elements that can prevent cardiovascular disease, degenerative pathologies of the brain, inflammations, metabolic syndrome, cancer, diabetes and obesity (Boccardi et al. 2018; Pintó et al. 2019; Yubero-Serrano et al. 2019).

Invention of the 'traffic light diet'

From the sacred to the profane: I now turn to an analysis of how extra virgin olive oil has been toppled from the highest summits of Mediterranean theological thought by its most recent excommunication from the ambit of food education. I focus here on how a relatively recent educational model – known as the 'traffic light diet', sometimes called the 'stop light diet' – has modified the image and the narrative around this ingredient. This nutritional and educational model was conceived in the 1970s by the American paediatrician Leonard H. Epstein and his research group, a team specializing in the study of overweight and obese children, at the Faculty of Medicine, University of Buffalo, United States (Epstein and Squires 1988). The need to develop new tools for combating obesity, which is both a sociological and medical phenomenon, led the research group to summarize the complex thinking of medicine in an immediately understandable formula for adolescents and their families. The choice fell on an object of daily life, the traffic light, with its unequivocal signals to 'go ahead' in the case of a green light, and 'not to proceed' in the case of red, with yellow signalling a moderate warning 'to take care'.

To explain the programme for learning the basics of a balanced diet, Leonard Epstein and Sally Squires developed an itinerary of food education, concentrated into eight weeks, set out in the popular work *The Stop-Light Diet for Children. An Eight-Week Program for Parents and Children*. Published in 1988, it categorizes ingredients by their calorie content. Foods with less than twenty calories per unit get the green light and can be eaten regularly. As in the case of fruit and vegetables, most foods are given the yellow light, signifying that they should be consumed with moderation, while ingredients or dishes with high fat content, along with those with simple sugars, are given the red light, and their recommended consumption is limited to a maximum of four times a week.

The authors encourage parents to eliminate all foods marked with a red light from their pantries. As may be guessed, these include extra virgin olive oil for its high calorie content. The food itinerary includes many other precepts, such as physical activity and psychological counselling, that will not be considered here as they are not relevant for our purposes.

In Epstein's clinical practice, reading the book was accompanied by consultations with experts and supervision by a dietician or a psychotherapist. The results varied considerably. In an article published in 2000, Epstein describes how one intervention of his group reduced the weight of obese children treated with the 'traffic light diet' by 25 per cent. This article was enthusiastically taken up again by Dr Ryan D. Brown of Oklahoma University and cited in an article entitled 'The Traffic Light Diet Can Lower Risk for Obesity and Diabetes', published in 2011 in the peer-reviewed journal the *NASN School Nurse*.

The traffic light diet does not however seem to have led to extraordinarily successful results, even according to Epstein's own studies. The website of the University of Buffalo Jacobs School of Medicine and Biomedical Sciences presents the invention of the traffic light diet as a milestone in treating child obesity, yet avoids triumphalism. In a general remark quoted on the web page, Epstein confesses to having learnt that in the end a diet works best when it involves the whole family and not just children – because 'kids model their parents … They learn healthy as well as unhealthy behaviors from them'.[4]

Recent research carried out at Harvard University (Seward et al. 2016) on students who use the university's cafeterias is decidedly less optimistic, however. Many students appreciate the appearance of the traffic light on food labels and dishes on display, but their eating behaviour is not actually influenced by colour coding and does not significantly improve as a direct result of its implementation.

Meanwhile, the food pyramid, conceived by the American Department of Agriculture in 1992 and later developed by the non-profit organization Old Ways, WHO, FAO and Harvard University with the collaboration of internationally renowned experts in nutrition (Kovacs and Orange-Ravachol 2015; Willet et al. 1995) has more or less monopolized communication on food education in both North America and Europe. Recently, however, the pedagogical model of MyPlate (ChooseMyPlate.gov) has gained ground in America after being launched by the Department of Agriculture in 2011, though it is still little known in Europe. Like a pie chart, the visual image of a plate indicates the portions of fruit, vegetables, cereals, proteins and dairy products to consume each day, and also promotes the golden ratio of the Mediterranean diet, as indicated by the government's dietary guidelines. However, unlike the pyramid, the MyPlate visual does not indicate the foods which eaters are expected to favour. Consequently, in this case, too, the health advantages of extra virgin olive oil disappear from view. Very probably, this sort of censorship of fundamental information about the value of daily use of olive oil can also be read as a lack of economic interest in promoting the consumption of an ingredient that the United States mostly imports from the Mediterranean, since local production there is recent and extremely limited.

Several decades after the traffic light first appeared in public health policy in the United States, the UK and Europe have dusted off the now dated system, while introducing a significant difference. The red/yellow/green code has now become a communication tool rather than a model for dieting. The traffic light rules are no longer to be learned as a whole but read directly on the labels of foodstuffs and prepared meals.

It was the UK that led the way in the early 2000s, in an attempt to tackle increasing obesity, especially among the young. The colour-coded system was relaunched with the publication of the book *The Traffic Light Diet* by Judith Wills (2004), a leading British health expert. The text is simple and basically little more than a tutorial on healthy eating for beginners.

Turning the image of the traffic light into a genuine logo was, however, the work of the Food Standards Agency (FSA), a non-ministerial government department that is politically independent and was put in exclusive charge of public health until 2010, guided by experts in the field. In 2006 it commissioned Initials Marketing to restyle the traffic light for inclusion in the educational and commercial system in the UK.

UK traffic light labelling

British traffic light labelling colour-codes food products as red, yellow or green according to their content of fat, saturated fat, salt or sugars per 100 g of the products. As with the traffic light diet, if one of the components of a particular food item exceeds an acceptable level, the item will be marked red; yellow is used if the level is close to being reached; and the product is marked as green if it presents no problem. These labels were introduced in the UK in June 2013 and are voluntary, but they are recommended by the Ministry of Health and have been widely adopted by many supermarkets (an estimated 98 per cent), though studies disagree on the pedagogical effectiveness of these colour-coded labels (Borgmeier and Westenhoefer 2009; Johnson et al. 2014).

The British traffic light labelling was introduced after approval of EU regulation 1169/2011 on Food Information for Consumers; alongside 'mandatory' food information, this regulation allows for 'voluntary' information. Article 35 of the EU regulation states: 'To facilitate the comparison of products in different package sizes, it is appropriate to retain the requirement that the mandatory nutrition declaration should refer to 100 g or 100 ml amounts and, if appropriate, to allow additional portion-based declarations.' Essentially, the EU has so far opted for neutral, objective and measurable information, without suggestions, promotions or bans. The debate on labelling is indeed wide-ranging and complex, as Kornelia Hagen (2010) explains; Hagen considers traffic light labelling as an indispensable tool for combating the spread of obesity in Germany. Hagen discusses the different positions of policymakers on both sides of the Atlantic regarding communication with consumers. She also shows how, in the face of growing demand for information on food and health from consumers, the food industry continues to disapprove of requirements to specify the nutritional value of their products on labels. The industrial food lobby, in short, remains averse to any kind of information that may make the consumer more aware of the kind of food he or she is buying and that may in some way lead to reduced consumption.

Traffic light labelling and olive oil: Key issues and controversies

On 12 April 2016, the European Parliament voted against adopting the traffic light labelling that the UK had sought to render mandatory for all foods produced and sold in the EU. The parliament questioned the 'nutritional profiles' on which the colour coding was based, not the British system as such. The Strasbourg Parliament also asked the European Commission to 're-examine the scientific basis, utility and feasibility' of the 2006 regulation regarding the nutritional and health indicators supplied on food products, as well as 'possibly eliminating the concept of nutritional profiles'. This was not a direct, explicit dismissal of the traffic light labelling already in force in the UK, but an indirect questioning of such labelling. The case arose from the need to define nutritionally correct profiles which could be extended to the European market so as to prevent health claims being attached to nutritionally questionable products (Article 4 of regulation no. 1924/2006). The problem, however, is that ten years later, the European Commission had still not established common rules for these profiles. The result was and still is a general confusion over product labelling, which considered objectively seems incorrect and unbalanced from a nutritional standpoint.

In October 2014, the European Commission had already opened infringement proceedings against the UK for alleged violation of the principle of free circulation of goods. The goal of the commission was not to call into question the aim pursued by the UK in informing consumers and protecting their health, but to contest how it was being done through traffic light labelling. The 12 April 2016 resolution approved by the European Parliament is therefore the direct consequence of this proceeding. But if the provision is not binding for the various member states, it will be even less so for the UK after Brexit.

The European Parliament vote was 'a strong signal to the Commission regarding any form of labelling like the British traffic light system', according to Paolo De Castro, Italian Democratic Party Euro MP and former Italian minister for Agriculture, Food and Forestry Policies. De Castro was himself one of the originators of UNESCO's recognition of the Mediterranean diet as an intangible cultural heritage of universal significance.

On 1 June 2017, Euro MP Mara Bizzotto raised a parliamentary question to address the issue of traffic light labelling as discriminatory towards high-quality products of the Mediterranean diet. Bizzotto observed that as a result of the traffic light labelling system, many Italian products (including Parmigiano Reggiano, Prosciutto di Parma and extra virgin olive oil) certified with the labels protected designation of origin (PDO) and protected geographical indication (PGI) are considered unhealthy foods and given a red sticker, whilst certain fizzy drinks are given green stickers. Bizzotto stressed the fact that the traffic light labelling system, in force in the UK since 2014, is supported by large multinationals in the food sector whose products are in competition with traditional items of the Mediterranean diet certified according to the labelling system based on the geographical indication of origin. Bizzotto pointed out that associations of Italian producers oppose the traffic light labelling system because it impinges on trade and industry, provides incomplete and misleading nutritional information, distorts the image of genuine foods, and prevents consumers from making informed choices. Bizzotto presented two parliamentary questions seeking guarantees for impartial and correct information on food products: she requested the Commission's support for a consolidated labelling system instead of the traffic light system and for measures to protect top-quality Italian and European PDO/PGI foods from attempts to distort the market. The Commission's reply was soon given: on 17 July, Vytenis Andriukaitis, food policy expert, wrote a response reminding that producers are free to indicate all nutritional information they regard as useful on the front portion of labels, while the back of the label is bound by current European regulations. It should also be borne in mind that Great Britain has been accused by the European Commission of infringing upon regulations regarding the use of the traffic light system.[5]

Although the European Parliament to all intents and purposes rejected the traffic light system in 2016, it was later introduced in an adapted form and on a voluntary basis in France. The French Minister of Health, referring explicitly to the UK educational model, has created a special traffic light labelling system, using five colours ranging from green to red, with light green and orange-amber intermediate shades. This labelling has been named the Nutri-Score. In this case too extra virgin olive oil is included in the category of foods to limit, on par with saturated fatty acids, sugar and salt (Julia et al. 2014). Olive oil is placed in the general category of 'energies', if not simply that of fats, as if the consumption of butter and oil had the same consequences for health. In addition, the red labelling of this vegetable fat contradicts the recommendations of the WHO to use extra virgin olive oil as the main fat in one's daily diet.

The traffic light system was put forward again in the summer of 2018 to the United Nations (UN) and the WHO, both currently involved in public health anti-obesity initiatives to reduce the incidence of non-transmissible disease by 2030. On 27 September 2018 an intergovernmental meeting was held in the New York offices of the UN to reconsider the possibility of introducing the traffic light in the labelling of all products sold in the European market and elsewhere. In the months before the meeting, a new alarm was sounded in public opinion and in the press, exemplified by the headlines in Italian dailies: 'UN, Italian Farming in the Dock, Oil and Parmesan Not Wanted' (Cappellini 2018) and 'UN War on Fats and Salt: Parmesan under Attack' (Pini 2018).

The Italian food industry criticized these proposed UN provisions. Through Assica, the Association of Meat and Salami Industrialists, obviously concerned that their products might be given the red light, Italian food industry representatives drew attention to the fact that 'there are no good foods and bad foods when there are incentives for a moderate, varied diet, as the Mediterranean diet itself indicates' (Pini 2018). In a tweet, the president of the Italian association of food producers (Federalimentare), Luigi Scordamaglia, strongly objected to the presence of danger warnings on the packaging of

Italian products: 'Parmesan, ham, pizza and oil can seriously damage your health, like a cigarette. #WHO and #UN declare war on diabetes and cardiovascular disease with an unacceptable attack that has undeclared aims' (Pini 2018).

Were a UN resolution of this kind to be adopted, no regulation would be imposed on any country, as national governments would be under no obligation to recognize it. Nevertheless, immediately after the news, President Franco Verrascina of the Confederation of Agricultural Producers (Copagri) noted: 'Though no member state is obliged to recognise a resolution of this kind, it would cause considerable harm to the image of the nation's food industry. One need only think that wine, olive oil, parmesan and Parma Ham could be affected – products that symbolize the country and are known and appreciated the world over' (Pini 2018).

'Who, on the other hand, would benefit from such a resolution from the United Nations?' Micaela Cappellini, a journalist for *Il Sole 24 Ore* wondered.

> To understand that, one need only look at what happened in Europe when the UK first, and then France, adopted the colour-coded food labelling, which was in many respects similar to what is now being discussed by the UN. As the Italian farmers' union Coldiretti noted in a recent press campaign, this method gives a green light to Coca Cola Light, for its reduced sugar content, and a red light to 85% of Italian products with Protected Denomination of Origin, a sort of copyright for food specialities. And if all you have to do to be in order is replace sugar with aspartame, it means the winners are the chemical industry and all the producers of chemical substitutes for food. (Cappellini 2018)

This alarmist scenario which would have potentially penalized typical products of the Mediterranean diet was in fact avoided. In the end, during the third high-level meeting of the UN on the prevention and control of non-transmissible diseases held in 2018, any reference to dissuasive tools, such as colour labelling of certain foods, was rejected. The final document includes a general invitation to promote healthy lifestyles.

Paradoxically, in my view, ostracism on the part of certain dieticians towards extra virgin olive oil has led both entrepreneurs of quality food and those defending the virtuous model of the Mediterranean diet to find themselves on the same side of this debate. The forming of this coalition once again proves that the olive retains its evocative symbolic value in at least equal measure to its nutritional value. While their actions are guided by different motives, industrial actors and defenders of the Mediterranean diet are united in their opposition to a message so far removed from the food culture of the Mediterranean and its healthy lifestyle. In their view, reductive schematisms such as the traffic light and its variants sacrifice the cultural and cognitive wealth represented by food. Still worse, such simplified nutritional models regard the main instrument for opposing obesity as the reduced consumption of a product that is little known and consumed, on a global scale: only 3 per cent of the world's population consume olive oil. Such models also fail to take into account the specific micronutrients and antioxidants characteristic of this natural fat that have been proven essential in slowing the effects of the ageing process. The fluid that has extended the life of the Mediterranean population and that has flavoured the culinary history of the

Mediterranean cannot be defined uniquely by the calories it contains, and so cannot be put on the same plane as other ingredients such as single cream, soft margarine, light mayonnaise and low-fat dressing. Yet this is precisely what the Department of Health & Human Services in the United States does, as for example in a nutritional table published by Rayan Brown of Oklahoma University in his essay 'The Traffic Light Diet Can Lower Risk for Obesity and Diabetes' (2011). It should be said that olive oil is not included in this schema, as was feared in some quarters, among red-light foods, which include butter and bacon, hot dogs and hamburgers, cakes and cheeses. But it is in the yellow column, along with biscuits, ice creams, sugared fruit juices, ham, tuna in oil, eggs and peanut butter, and has been declassified from the 'healthy food' category to be listed as a food one should be careful of. And so, *pace* the great goddess of democracy Athena, her precious gift is associated with foods that are probably much less healthy and quite without its thousand-year history. Exiled, like a pagan god, from the tables of '*Homo dieteticus*' (Niola 2015), olive oil has been vilified for the diet-conscious global citizen, often unaware of or uninterested in gastronomical values.

The Mediterranean Diet Virtual Museum (www.mediterraneandietvm.com), which I run with the anthropologist Marino Niola, published an interview in 2018 with the nutritionist Antonia Trichopoulou of Athens University.[6] Starting in the 1990s, together with Walter Willet of Harvard University and Anna Ferro-Luzzi of the Italian *Istituto Superiore di Sanità* (Willet et al. 1995), Trichopoulou has promoted the Mediterranean food pyramid. In this interview, she explains that when the international medical and nutrition vulgate began demonizing the calorie levels of extra virgin olive oil and promoting alternative fats like margarine and different seed oils, in the 1970s and 1980s, this had a completely unexpected effect in Greece. Not only did the per capita consumption of Athena's elixir diminish, but at the same time there was a marked reduction in the consumption of vegetables and pulses. Trichopoulou points out that traditional Greek cooking is wholly based on an abundant use of extra virgin olive oil, not only for seasoning purposes but also for the flavouring of dishes. Thus, nutritional indicators that were apparently useful for improving public health had the effect of leading to rejection of the Mediterranean diet in favour of less healthy models of eating. This historical change, she claims, also interrupted the transmission of a thousand-year-old gastronomic culture in her country, damaging an immense heritage made up of practices, techniques of preservation, strategies of taste that had been handed down from generation to generation. Tested over the centuries, such practices were regarded as the basis of the Greeks' extraordinary longevity. Trichopoulou also told me, in a recent conversation, of the general mistrust of extra virgin olive oil that she has always found in non-Mediterranean scientific communities, which have often shown a lipidic prejudice against olives and their juice.

Conclusion

No message in the realm of public communication is without consequences for the ideologies and behaviour of different communities. The transition from the complexity of traditional eating systems to the simplification of contemporary models not only risks errors of misinterpretation but also penalizes the cultural wealth of various nations, by promoting reductionist nutritional schematism. The end result is to reduce well-being and lifestyle to a kind of bio-dogma, turning the pleasure of taste into a sin to be expiated, and declassifying traditional cuisines as obsolete practices to overcome. If nothing else, the case of Greece teaches us that, before putting our clumsy hands on the labelling of products and, hence, on the imaginary and practices of ordinary people, we need to listen to the lessons of history. We need to think back to Athena and Jesus Christ and forget the traffic light. We need, in short, to remember with Hippocrates, Feuerbach, and Ancel Keys and his wife Margaret Haney that we are what we eat. And everything we make into a taboo becomes the shadow of our selves. Because *edere*, the Latin term from which derive words such as educate and education, in the ancient world meant simply *eat*. Nourish the body and the mind.

Notes

1. The present writer has studied the Mediterranean diet from a social and anthropological viewpoint for more than ten years, during which she has written extensively on the subject, including numerous academic articles, research papers and popular books (such as Moro 2014, 2018). In 2012, she founded a centre for social research on the Mediterranean diet called MedEatResearch at the Università Suor Orsola Benincasa of Naples. Since 2015 she has been a consultant for the Italian Ministry of Agriculture for safeguarding the heritage of the Mediterranean diet. In 2018 she became Ambassador for the Culture of Italian Food in the World for the Ministry of Culture and the Ministry of Agriculture. Since 2019 she has worked with the Italian representatives of the Food and Agricultural Organization in a campaign to make decision makers aware of the cultural and nutritional values of the Mediterranean diet. She notes that she does not find herself in any conflict of interest.

2. August Meineke, *Fragmenta comicorum Graecorum*, Berlin, G. Reimeri, 1839–57, vol. 1, page 150. Luigi Leurini, Euphor. *fr.* 57-v. Groningen e Callim, hymn, 3, 46ss, Lexis 9–10, pages 145–53, Amsterdam, Adolph M. Hakkert, 1992.

3. See the etymology of the French word *chrême* (chrism) in the online *Dictionnaire Littré* (1863–77): https://www.littre.org/definition/chrême (accessed 15 October 2021).

4. University of Buffalo, 'Traffic Light Diet for Overweight Children', available online: http://www.buffalo.edu/ub2020/archives/strategic-initative-archive/strengths/health.host.html/content/shared/smbs/research_highlights/traffic-light-diet.detail.html (accessed 6 February 2020).

5. Regulation (EU) 1169/2011 on food information to consumers allows member states to recommend or food business operators to use, on a voluntary basis, additional forms of expression and presentation of the nutrition declaration on the front-of-pack or other voluntary nutrition information, provided that specific requirements are met. Article 35(5) of the same regulation requires the commission to submit by 13 December 2017 a report to the European Parliament and the council on the use of front-of-pack nutrition labelling schemes, on their effect on the internal market and on the advisability of further harmonization in the area. The conclusions of this report will serve to inform the further debate on how consumers can best be provided with nutrition information and on whether a common approach across the

EU should be considered in this context. Concerning the UK traffic light schemes, following complaints, the Commission launched an infringement procedure in 2014 against the UK which is still pending. No indication can be given at this stage on the outcome of this procedure. In the case of foods marketed as PDO or PGI, the related Union symbols must appear on the labelling. The indications 'protected designation of origin' or 'protected geographical indication' or the corresponding abbreviations may appear on the labelling. All such foods are listed in a publicly available commission database (OJ L 304, 22 November 2011, p. 18, available online: http://ec.europa.eu/agri culture/quality/door/list.html), which includes information about their qualities and characteristics, helping consumers to make informed choices.

6. Interview with Antonia Trichopoulou, 'Do Not Betray Tradition', available online: https://mediterraneandietvm.com/en/antonia-trichopoulou-do-not-betray-tradition/.

Strategies for disseminating dietetics: The health regimen as medical book genre in seventeenth-century France

Justine Le Floc'h

Introduction

In the seventeenth century, medicine was still based upon the Galenic humoral system. In Galenic medicine, ingestion of food is considered essential for maintaining a proper balance of the four basic fluids called humours (blood, phlegm, yellow bile or choler and black bile or melancholy). Eating is seen as responsible for renewing humours, and therefore as crucial for staying healthy. In the words of Guy Patin, dean of the Faculty of Medicine in Paris and author of the *Traité de la Conservation de santé* (Treatise on the conservation of health), eating enables man to 'repair the solid substance of his body, which endures perpetual dissipation'.[1] This 'mechanics' of the body considers food not only for its medicinal properties but also as necessary 'to maintain our stoutness and keep our strength for a better use and integrity of our actions'.[2]

Dietetics, also called 'hygiene',[3] was at that time considered a minor branch of medicine, alongside physiology, pathology, semiotics or prognostics, and therapeutics. Dietetics taught people how to adapt their life choices according to their own temperament and needs. Its area of expertise included not only nutrition but also extended to other areas regarded just as essential for preserving health as food and drink: sleep, physical activities and environment (Hill 2003: 16). In more precise terms, in the seventeenth century, dietetics dealt with six groups of phenomena: air, food and drink, motion and rest, sleep and waking, bodily evacuations, emotions or passions. In accordance with Avicenna's distinction (Mikkeli 2000: 59–68), these six categories constituted 'non-natural things' (the *res non naturales*), neither good nor dangerous in themselves, as opposed to 'contra-natural things', which led to pathologies. In other words, dietetics as a field of medical knowledge concerned itself with objects that guaranteed the proper functioning of the body when present in moderation in daily life, but that could create disease in the case of either excess or deficiency.

In the early modern age,[4] attempts to promote dietetics gave rise to an increase in the publication of books belonging to a medical genre called 'health regimens' or 'living regimens'.[5] Authors of such works sought to disseminate good health practices among their intended readership, including practitioners, apothecaries, medical assistants and also volunteers and non-professional readers. Print technology made these works more accessible to a broad public.[6] Given this wide-ranging audience, authors developed communicational strategies to contribute to public information and education about dietetics: pleasing and accessible language and eloquent discourse were adopted as the key traits of popularization.

In this chapter, I present the medical book genre and explore its communicational characteristics. This analysis follows studies carried out by early modern scholars such as Heikki Mikkeli (Finland), Ken Albala (USA), David Gentilcore (UK), Marilyn Nicoud and Magdalena Koźluk (France), who have drawn attention to the circulation and reception of dietary advice through popular publications. At the intersection of the history of medicine and the history of food, this study aims to characterize how dietetics was disseminated in the early modern period.

Methodologically speaking, this study is based on a corpus of vernacular treatises which participated in the diffusion of dietetics in France in the seventeenth century. Most of the works are listed in Charles Sorel's bibliography *La Bibliothèque française* (1664), an inventory of the major French publications of the early modern period. Among the medical writers whom Sorel cited for their renown and whom I have included in this corpus are Nicolas de La Framboisière, André Du Laurens, Philippe Guybert, Guy Patin and Joseph Du Chesne. The selection of works discussed in this chapter is also mentioned by the bibliographies of the Medic@ collection,[7] which provides access to over twenty thousand medical documents. Also included are publications identified by the scholar Henri-Jean Martin, author of *Livre, pouvoirs et sociétés à Paris au XVIIᵉ siècle*, whose extensive research on the numbers of editions of individual texts constitutes a crucial reference work for French early modern studies.

Medical history is here examined through a discourse analysis perspective, in order to explore writers' communicational strategies, that is, the conception of dietetics that they promoted, the image that they gave of themselves (*ethos*) as experts and the rhetorical choices which aimed to make the reading experience both pleasant and instructive. Understanding how these books tried to popularize good health practices requires paying attention to their paratextual materials, including prefaces, dedications and 'warnings' to the readers, which are usually placed at the beginning of individual works and are intended to incite readers to read the book while creating a positive image of the author himself.

The first part of this chapter discusses physicians' assertions, in prefaces and dedications, regarding their intentions as writers. Our analysis shows that dietetics was promoted as a universal and useful field of knowledge, so much so that health regimen authors described themselves as having 'charitable' motivations. This proclaimed intention should not be considered without taking into account certain macro-contextual factors: these publications were used to promote medical expertise in the context of the rivalry between professionals and pseudo-professionals, and between doctors and apothecaries. The second part of this chapter focuses on generic and stylistic considerations, in order to highlight some of the formal characteristics of this medical literature. Health regimens sought to disseminate knowledge about dietetics by making reading both easy and pleasant, in accordance with the well-known Horatian adage that instruction combined with delight makes learning agreeable while facilitating memory processes (Horace, *Epistle* II, 1, v. 356; II, 3, v. 343).

The promotion of preventive medicine

Universally useful knowledge to be adapted to character types

In the early modern period, dietetics was not of much interest to physicians, who were generally more concerned about curing the sick than preventing illness in healthy people (Céard 1982: 24). The three branches of medical knowledge, medicine itself, the art of the apothecary and surgery, do not mention dietetics. However, in the sixteenth century, following the model of Hippocrates, author of the treatise *On Regimen*, physicians began to give greater consideration to this field of expertise (Grmek 1995: 257). For instance, Pierre Pigray, author of an *Épitomé des préceptes de médecine et chirurgie* (Epitome of the precepts of medicine and surgery), written for his fellow physicians as well as medical students, praised the natural character of dietetics, and suggested that this virtue proved its therapeutic excellence:

> Diet, which is the most gentle and familiar remedy, can be regarded as the first part or the first remedy in curative medicine (although its main function is to conserve health) because it is so much an ally of nature that it will not alter it at all, so that if man can heal a disease only by diet or living regimen, there is no need for other remedies.[8]

Maintaining a healthy regimen was thus presented as the best remedy and protection against diseases, as it helps to avoid recourse to any other curative measure 'but out of obligation and extreme necessity' (Pigray 1609: 73).

In the sixteenth century, the great surgeon Ambroise Paré regarded dietetics as a therapeutic specialty and as a way of healing sick people. At the beginning of the seventeenth century, some doctors asserted that it had the advantage of being universal and easy to practice (Koźluk 2012: 171–2). Nicolas Abraham de La Framboisière, dean of the University of Reims and one of the king's physicians, promoted this view. In his ambitious instructional guide to medicine (1613), a table of contents featured at the beginning of the volume clarifies the structure of medical matters in the early modern period. The discipline of medicine, just like surgery and the art of the apothecary, is situated above nature and below grace, as a reminder that human beings are between beasts and angels: medicine is divided into two branches: therapeutics, dedicated to the cure of sick people, and dietetics, called 'self-government'. This political analogy suggests that diet represents the control of reason over the body and submission to medical laws dictated by reason to ensure a long life. The term 'self-government' also conveys the idea that dietetics is useful for everyone, including healthy people, as a kind of prevention. In the author's opinion, such knowledge should thus be widely disseminated, since 'of all the goods that God gave us, none is greater or more excellent than health'.[9]

But even though dietetics claims to be universally useful knowledge, this does not imply that its principles can provide universal rules. On the contrary, La Framboisière recommends diversifying diets according to age, complexion, geographic area and season. In terms of food, a balanced diet requires regulating quantity, quality, habits, as well as the order, duration and time of meals (1613: 181). The reader is advised to follow natural tendencies and to avoid excess or deficit, while taking into account temperament and humoral characteristics. La Framboisière proposes for instance that phlegmatic people, easy to identify by their flabby, moist skin, should not eat much. Bilious people, with their hot temperament, should avoid red meat and wine, which might increase their natural heat. The ability to determine an appropriate diet for oneself thus depends on self-knowledge: 'He who knows himself must assess which things are harmful or salutary'.[10] The use of vocabulary linked to salvation and self-knowledge establishes a continuum between medicine, morality and theology.

The *Traité de la Conservation de santé*, written by Guy Patin, offers another example of this preoccupation, with chapters on food providing detailed recommendations about the choice of foods and sauces and how to cook them:

> Melancholic and bilious people need more boiled food than roasted food, phlegmatic people on the contrary need more roasted food than boiled food, sanguine temperaments benefit from everything, as long as it is with moderation. Wine cools down melancholic people …, bilious people have no need for it …, sanguine individuals must get into the good habit of putting a half volume of water in it, if they don't want it to cause them harm.[11]

Patin warns readers against the temptation to seek universal laws in a field of knowledge that is subjected to diversity and variability, according to changes in temperaments, time and circumstances. For Patin, renouncing the desire for universality is precisely the basis of excellence in medicine (Patin 1632: 68). Although the use of diet is universally advisable, its application must be adapted to character traits and must avoid the prescription of general rules.

A useful and charitable undertaking

At the French king Henri IV's request, La Framboisière wrote his volume exclusively in French. This choice participated in the work's success and recognition as a medical reference book in the seventeenth century. Choosing a vernacular language not only illustrated a new perspective on dietetics amongst scholars in the early modern period but it also responded to the keen interest of readers for this domain as well as demonstrating the author's conviction that this knowledge should be a common good (Gentilcore 2016: 22–6):

Some physicians, more interested in their profit than about common interest, will disapprove that I wrote the principles of our art in vernacular language. But those who have right intentions prefer the public good instead of their own, because by doing one's best to benefit everyone, one gets closer to God, who takes care of everybody, and away from beasts, which only care about themselves.[12]

Even though such assertions are mainly rhetorical, reference books are often introduced as the work of 'charitable physicians' who offer recommendations, recipes and remedies to their readers. Some authors took into consideration the material and financial realities of expected readers (Fouquet 1678; Patin 1633: 519–26). Joseph Du Chesne, sieur de La Violette, a king's physician and author of *Portrait de la santé* (Portrait of health),[13] mentions his wish to be read by a wide audience and to include people who do not have medical knowledge (1606: 'Au lecteur débonnaire'). He justifies this ambition by his strong attachment to the duty of charity, which he judges to be superior to any 'personal benefit', a motivation which he assumes to be held by many doctors:

It will be a general health regimen, adaptable and adjustable to any kind of disease, either severe or minor, useful for any gender, any age, anyone, for both adults and children, the wealthy and the poor, and even true physicians, as the Asclepiads were, keen on people's health, charitable and more interested in their neighbour's good and in their honour than in their personal advantage, will be able to learn from it. The reading and communication of my book will, as much as I can, be denied to all mercenaries, conjurers, charlatans, theriac sellers, empirics, and any kind of inept people who dare to interfere in medicine without any legitimate vocation.[14]

Le Portrait de la santé expresses the attributes of the ideal figure of a benevolent physician, who practices his art out of a sense of duty. The vulgarization of medicine thus coincides with the assertion of medicine as a *pro bono publico* field of knowledge (Koźluk 2012: 35).

At the end of the seventeenth century, the same reasons seem to have encouraged Mme Fouquet, mother of the financial superintendent Nicolas Fouquet, to write her own regimen: she dedicates her volume to the 'pious and charitable ladies' who like her, volunteer to serve poor and sick people. A devout Catholic, she believed in the missionary ideas of Vincent de Paul and participated in the activities of the Daughters of Charity, providing – like other noble ladies – personal care to the sick and helpless. Saint-Simon called her 'mother of the poor' and Mme de Sévigné described her as a 'saint' who could 'work miracles' (Lafont 2010: 166–7). Her book was one of the bestsellers of the seventeenth century: over fifty editions were produced between 1676 and 1757. The volume enumerates a series of remedies which are easy to prepare at home. In the 1712 edition, the editor explains his wish that people should be given the means to prepare remedies themselves and to become the authors of their own healing (Fouquet 1678: 'Aux âmes charitables'). The advice that Mme Fouquet gives in her book takes into account the material and financial constraints of the assumed readership: recipes for medications are inexpensive and easy to administer without professional equipment (Lafont 2010).

The interests of the medical corporation

Alongside the virtuous motivations expressed in paratextual pieces, these popular books are also very much aligned with the preoccupations of the medical corporation and its desire for self-promotion. Guy Patin's *Traité de la Conservation de santé* provides an interesting example of this ambivalence between charitable and self-serving motivations. It was published in 1633 as a chapter of *Le Médecin charitable* (The charitable physician), a voluminous book written by Philibert Guybert, whose purpose, as the title suggests, is to offer a useful and charitable medical guide. On the one hand, it is meant to help readers heal themselves, while following the safe and wise advice of a legitimate doctor; on the other hand, it is proclaimed to be charitable because it reveals the secrets of unscrupulous apothecaries. Far from being allies of physicians at that time, apothecaries were considered to be charlatans who practised questionable medicine. A short passage in the treatise, in which Patin presents the virtues of the lemon, helps to demonstrate the implications of this conflict of interest:

> Among the fruits that people bring us here from Provence, I have a great deal of respect for the lemon, which I value more than any cardiac drugs available in the shops of our time, which most of the time are drugs in name only, and which are brought across the sea, only to be sold at a higher price. Because to tell the truth, for any kind of malignant diseases and rotten fevers, simple or not, and even for the plague, a half-dozen good lemons is a better remedy and more reliable than all the oriental Bezoar brought here, which is nothing but a counterfeit stone made by the Jews of Constantinople and elsewhere, and useless to cure diseases, even unworthy of being considered a remedy ... than theriac or mithridate, whose merits against poisons are praised by a whole bunch of ignorant empirics and charlatans,[15] because those drugs only make those who sell them richer and heat up or burn the guts of the unfortunate sick people who let themselves be deceived.[16]

The lemon is offered up as a highly effective and sufficient remedy which can spare the need for any other treatment such as those used by apothecaries and other charlatans. Moreover, wine is presented as almost as powerful 'as all the other remedies put together'.[17] As these recommendations illustrate, dietary literature is a means to limit the influence of charlatans and empirics, that is, pseudo-professionals who do not follow the academic curriculum and whose health recommendations remain suspect. The discourse on bloodletting offers another example of this concern: The author, who recommends this practice, sets one condition: bloodletting must be 'ruled and moderated by the advice of a cautious and wise physician ... and not by the appetite of a bunch of weaklings or charlatans and ignorant empirics'.[18] Targeting Paracelsians in particular (Patin 1632: 55, 60), who fell into disrepute in the seventeenth century, Patin seeks to establish the authority of the physician for medical advice. He thus recommends that readers 'never do anything, nor initiate anything, nor change from their first prescriptions', unless 'their regular physician approves of it'.[19]

But while denouncing charlatans, Patin also promotes dietetics as a way to keep one's health without using medicines, a fact which cannot be fully understood without mentioning the institutional conflict between doctors and apothecaries. In the early modern period, apothecaries were not allowed to deliver any drug without a prescription from a doctor. Their shops were inspected by representatives from the medical faculty and their examination jury was composed of physicians. Such control was highly contested by apothecaries in the sixteenth and seventeenth centuries; this contestation triggered a reaction from physicians who sought to preserve their institutional superiority. This dispute led to an agreement in 1631, which was in fact an 'act of unconditional submission of apothecaries to physicians' (Lunel 2008: 47–53).

Philibert Guybert, author of *Le Médecin charitable*, was involved in the campaign against Parisian apothecaries; his controversial publications include *Le Prix et la Valeur des Médicaments* (The price and the value of medicines) and *L'Apothicaire charitable* (The charitable apothecary). His treatise teaches his fellow physicians and his readers how to dispense with apothecaries, whom he considers thieves concerned more about trade than about health, as we find in his criticism of powdered mixtures such as theriac and mithridate, and his extolling of the virtues of the lemon. Apart from the pious intentions claimed in the title, the dissemination of medical knowledge through this manual thus also serves corporatist interests. The book was unsurprisingly unfavourably received by Parisian apothecaries, who saw it as an attempt to deprive them of their expertise and authority on drugs and remedies.

As these considerations drawn from analysis of health regimens have highlighted, several converging factors in the early modern period explain the desire to promote dietetics. On the one hand, this book genre disseminates medical expertise that is useful not only to cure the sick but also to prevent disease. These works also claim to help practitioners and volunteers improve their skills, and even to allow the poor to protect or cure themselves. In this sense, such publications are of 'charitable' intent. On the other hand, this genre acts as an instrument in a professional rivalry. By disseminating apothecaries' recipes while protecting physicians' prerogatives with regard to the treatment of disease, such treatises reinforce the legitimacy of physicians and their knowledge of the human body. Charlatans are strongly condemned and apothecaries are portrayed as useless, greedy tradesmen of whom one should be suspicious.

In promoting dietetics, writers of health regimens developed writing strategies in order to facilitate the widespread circulation of their books. This communicational objective is fulfilled through rhetorical means, including arrangement of material, selection of examples and anecdotes, and the use of eloquence to impress information upon the reader's memory and to persuade him to follow dietary advice. The second part of this chapter examines the rhetorical and stylistic characteristics of the medical book genre.

Erudition, eloquence and pleasure
as means of popularization

Dietetics as an academic field suffered from two disadvantages in the early modern period: in addition to not being necessary or vital (since it did not claim to cure disease), this knowledge was perceived as unpleasant (since recommendations about food, drinks, activities, environment and the like implied constraints on everyday living habits). The dissemination of knowledge in dietetics thus required discourse which could be both accessible and engaging for readers. Most health regimens were written in vernacular language. Their authors used a pleasant style: they illustrated their principles with many examples taken from medieval casuistry and ancient anecdotes passed down through historical and moral literature.

Using vernacular language

Physicians had to adapt their writing to the expectations of non-professionals. Their first concession was writing their works in French instead of Latin. Vernacular language was required not only for the author's fellow physicians but also for apothecaries, surgeons or readers who did not master scholarly language. In this respect, physicians' wish to promote dietetics converged with publishers' economic interests and the need to ensure that their printed books could reach a wide audience, including non-specialist readers (Brockliss and Jones 1997: 99; Koźluk 2012: 97–8). In 1641, Théophraste Renaudot, a doctor and author of a treatise on poverty, created the *Bureau d'Adresse*, dedicated to helping poor people find work. Soon this organization expanded its services and started offering medical advice and scientific lectures. One of these public presentations was devoted to the question of whether or not French was an appropriate language to learn all sciences. A verdict was reached: French was declared as having enough relevant vocabulary, whereas 'using other languages in a speech is more vain and conceited than solid'.[20]

Such defences of the vernacular can be understood when we consider that choosing French in the early modern period was not an obvious communicational strategy. Indeed, some physicians resisted the use of the vernacular, considering that widespread dissemination of medical knowledge posed a threat to their expertise and prerogatives. However, this objection was quickly dropped when it became apparent that health regimens remained inaccessible to non-specialists lacking mastery of medical vocabulary and basic notions. Using the vernacular was in fact recognized as insufficient for the true democratization of medicine and dietetics (Renaudot [1632–42] 2004). A variety of other motivations led scholars to make the audacious choice to write in the vernacular. The use of vernacular language could for instance be considered more consistent with the expression of philosophical conceptions, or a way to break with tradition.[21] But mostly, by illustrating the capacity of the French language to deal with scientific knowledge, authors took part in the Renaissance debate about the hierarchy of languages and were able to show the *'génie de la langue'*, namely the excellence of French as against Italian, as part of a political competition (Argaud 2009;

Defaux 2003). When Richelieu created the *Académie Française*, it was precisely with the aim to enhance the vernacular and to 'make it pure, eloquent and able to deal with arts and sciences'.[22]

Placere and *docere* through narratives

Aside from the fact that authors of health regimens chose French instead of Latin, they developed several writing techniques that explain the success of their books. One such technique was the use of narratives inherited from history and mythology.

Indeed, authors used their erudition to make reading both pleasant (*placere*) and educative (*docere*). Joseph Du Chesne's treatise is presented as a '*Dieteticon polyhistoricon*' (1606: 3). The full title is enlightening: *The Portrait of Health, Where Is Lively Represented the Universal and Particular Rule to Live Very Healthy and Long. Enriched with Several Precepts, Reasons and Good Examples, from the Most Famous Greek and Latin Physicians, Philosophers and Historians.*[23] By categorizing his work as a 'portrait' and a 'lively representation' the author follows the trend of *images parlantes* (or Imagines). Renewed by the modern translation of Philostratus, this kind of writing is a variation of ὑποτύπωσις (hypotyposis), a vivid description aimed at helping readers imagine what is described. The eloquence of the physician is highlighted as a stylistic ornament that makes the reading experience more captivating. The excellence of modern medical recommendations is also confirmed through references to Ancient knowledge. Du Chesne frequently introduces scholarly references in his dietetic treatise when dealing with controversial issues such as the Paracelsists versus Anatomists debate. He successively refers to Pliny, Caelius, Olympiodorus, Plato, Albertus Magnus, Aristotle, Apollonius and others, to denounce the anatomists' mistakes (Du Chesne 1606: 195). Scholarly erudition therefore offers several advantages: it is useful not only to make the author's discourse more pleasant but also to reinforce his ethos and to increase the force of his argumentation.

For his *Traité de la Conservation de santé*, Guy Patin also mixes discourse on dietetics with exemplary narratives. In the section about fruits, and especially melon (Charbonneau 2002), he starts by explaining how this fruit is recommended for bilious people, who have a hot temperament, since it helps them cool off and moisten their bodies. On the contrary, phlegmatic and sanguine people are warned against the grave dangers of consuming melon, as Patin asserts by citing an anecdote taken from papal history:

Platina in his *Papal History* informs us that Paul II suffered apoplexy around the second hour of the night, which made him suddenly suffocate, alone in his room, complaining of no pain the day before, a death for which no one could find any apparent reason, except that at his last supper he ate two heavy melons in their entirety, all of which happened in 1471. Several emperors and other great figures died for the same reason. *Münster in Chron.* recounts that Albert II, emperor of Germany, weary and tired during his travel in Hungary, ate a melon to quench his thirst, after which he suffered from a stomach flux that caused his death. For the same reason two other emperors died, namely Frederick III and Henry VII.[24]

The author then denounces a rumour claiming that melon is harmless when it is served with wine, which is considered naturally hot: according to him, such a mistake is a severe sin against one's health (Patin 1632: 19). Patin concludes: 'Therefore everyone must find out from their regular physician the temperament and strength of their stomachs, as well as what is good for them.'[25]

The use of academic references and quotations as well as historical, philosophical and classical knowledge aims to captivate readers' attention through arguments enriched with examples and eloquence. As a consequence, in health regimens, erudition paradoxically appears to be a way of popularizing knowledge. Although these treatises may seem relatively homogeneous in their medical recommendations and conceptions, due to the dominance of Galenic medicine, they reveal a variety of stylistic choices. Telling narratives is not the only way to hold the readers' attention. Pierre Jacquelot (1630), author of *L'Art de vivre longuement selon Médée* (The art of living long according to Medea), uses the ancient feminine figure of Medea as an allegory of medicine.[26] The Medea he refers to is not Jason's wife, unfairly betrayed and forsaken, who murders her two children in revenge, but the sorceress with magical abilities: thanks to a herbal potion that she prepares in her cauldron, she rejuvenates Aeson, Jason's father, and proves that she masters the art of 'long living'. But when Pelias' turn comes, Medea deceives his daughters and has them kill the king of Iolcus (Ovid, *Metamorphoses* VII).[27] In Jacquelot's health regimen, allegory is a common thread: just as Medea sometimes uses her art not to heal but to kill, dietetics, neutral in itself, can either reinforce or harm, depending on the physician's ability to determine what is best for the specific temperament of his patient.

The functions of erudition

Connecting medical knowledge with classic texts thus reminds readers that the academic field of medicine is inherited from the Galenic tradition in which 'the best doctor is also a philosopher'.[28] The fact that medicine and classics are woven together can be explained not only by the authors' humanist approach to knowledge but also by virtue of the medical training they receive. Like their fellow physicians, La Framboisière and Joseph Du Chesne follow a tradition which held that learning medicine first requires cultivating the mind: the *cursus studiorum* includes Greek, Latin, rhetoric, philosophy, long before medical studies, and even then, pedagogical content is mainly theoretical. Coursework for physicians mainly requires the practice of critical interpretation, learning the classics and mastery of eloquence and dialectic (Lunel 2008: 41).

In addition, references to philosophy, history and mythology in health regimen treatises allowed medical writers to highlight the value of medical knowledge. Pierre Jacquelot assures his reader for instance that medicine constitutes the culmination of all other fields:

> Grammar was the masterpiece, the others after it were created in the following order: History, Rhetoric, Dialectic, Mathematics, Physiology, and finally Medicine, the princess of human sciences, to which all the Asclepiads devoted themselves, sharpened by the knowledge of the other arts, namely Philosophy.[29]

Called 'the princess of human sciences' since it focuses on human nature, medicine is placed under the aegis of philosophy. Humanist erudition is thus an asset for health regimens and allows the medical book genre to compete with moral literature. Dietetics, which constitutes a minor field, thus accedes to the dignity of immanent wisdom.[30]

The use of adorned writing styles also aims to persuade patients to accept allopathic treatments to balance their temperament. Dietetics is dedicated to non-natural objects, in other words, to questions that entail making a decision from among several options regarding foods, environments and behaviours. In this respect, it seems relevant to bear in mind that the early modern period is highly influenced not only by the Galenic system but also by Augustinian anthropology, which holds that human nature suffers from the consequences of original sin and that man is unable to use his faculties, such as reason and will, rightly and freely. In this theological perspective, human weakness makes rhetoric necessary to combat false desires and to help individuals see and follow what is right. For this reason, dietary literature, more than any other medical book genre, needs to use rhetoric and a deliberative style as an instrument to persuade the readers to live healthfully and with moderation: common sense and rational recommendations are considered insufficient to obtain this effect (Nicoud 2012). The doctor-philosopher who uses wisdom and ancient knowledge as therapy is thus also an orator who uses discourse as a professional tool in the treatment he delivers. For this reason, rhetoric, that is, the ability to use persuasive discourse, is, like history, considered necessary to practice medicine.

Conclusion

In the early modern period, health regimens thus addressed several communicational concerns. Regarded as a public good, they aimed to prevent disease through recommendations intended not only for the sick but also for healthy people. This explains why they are presented as charitable works. But as has been mentioned, by emphasizing how excellent and necessary medicine is, these works also promote a professional branch presented as the only reliable one.

Among the strategies used to make such books both accessible and pleasant, the choice of vernacular language is not entirely unambiguous: this first step towards popularization is insufficient to allow non-professionals to read medical texts easily. In addition to the choice of the vernacular, health regimen authors' writing features clear arrangement of materials as well as stylistic efforts to avoid jargon. Referring to classic texts is one way to make medical discourse more appealing. Narratives from the Ancients form a foundational basis of medical knowledge which physicians master along with other domains. Erudition and popularization are thus not seen as opposed, especially when one considers that, for economic reasons, health regimen books were probably read in this period by people who lacked medical training, but who did not lack education.

Notes

1. 'Il est nécessaire à l'homme de manger pour réparer la substance solide de son corps, qui endure une perpétuelle dissipation' (Patin 1632: 10).
2. 'Nous ne parlerons pas ici du médicinal, mais seulement du pur et simple aliment, lequel n'est pour autre chose que d'entretenir notre embonpoint, et conserver nos forces en leur être pour une plus grande facilité et intégrité de nos actions' (Patin 1632: 11).
3. Initially, the word 'hygiene' referred to the theoretical part of the curriculum for medical students, while 'dietetics' indicated therapeutic considerations in order to cure patients, but in seventeenth-century treatises, the two terms tended to be used interchangeably.
4. Ken Albala (2002: 25–47) distinguished three periods in the Renaissance: first, a dietary literature targeted the courtiers (1470–1530), next came a 'Galenic revival' (1530–70), when the corpus of Greek medicine was printed in Venice, in reliable editions, and then came a divergence of opinions amongst regimen writers, 'the breakdown of orthodoxy' (1570–1650). See also Mikkeli (2000: 69–72).
5. In accordance with the medieval tradition of *regimina sanitatis*. The *Regiminen sanitatis salernitanum* published during the Middle Ages (eleventh to twelfth centuries) by the medical school of Salerno is still an important reference. See the new translation and reading by Le Long (1637).
6. David Gentilcore (2016: 24–5) discusses the extent and the nature of this readership in England and asserts that not only elites read regimens but also tradesmen, although accessibility to preventive medicine mostly depended on economic means.
7. Digital library Medic@: www.biusante.parisdescartes.fr/histoire/medica/index.php (accessed 15 October 2021).
8. 'La diète, qui est le remède le plus doux et familier, peut être dite la première partie ou premier remède de médecine curative (encore que son principal office soit de conserver la santé) parce qu'elle est si amie de nature, qu'elle ne l'altère aucunement, de sorte que si on peut guérir une maladie par diète ou régime de vivre seulement, il n'est besoin des autres remèdes' (Pigray 1609: 7).
9. 'Car entre tous les biens que nous tenons de Dieu, il n'y en a point de plus grand, ni de plus excellent que la santé' (La Framboisière 1613: 112). This health regimen was first published in 1600, in a separate edition entitled 'The Government Necessary for Everyone to Live Long and Healthy' (see La Framboisière 1600).
10. 'Qui se sait connaître soi-même doit juger des choses qui lui sont nuisibles ou salutaires' (La Framboisière 1613: 74). See also Albala (2002: 79–114).
11. 'Les mélancoliques et bilieux ont plus besoin de bouilli que de rôti, les pituiteux au contraire de rôti que de bouilli, aux sanguins tout est bon, pourvu qu'ils en usent modérément. Le vin refroidit les mélancoliques … les bilieux n'en ont guère besoin … les sanguins y doivent mettre par bonne coutume plus de la moitié d'eau, s'ils ne veulent qu'enfin il lui nuise' (Patin 1632: 67–8).
12. 'Quelques médecins plus curieux de leur profit que du commun trouveront mauvais que j'ai décrit les règles de notre art en langage vulgaire. Mais ceux qui ont le cœur bien assis préfèrent le bien public à leur particulier, attendu qu'en s'étudiant de bien faire à chacun, on s'approche de Dieu, qui a soin de tout le monde, comme on s'éloigne des bêtes qui ne se soucient que d'elles-mêmes' (La Framboisière 1613: 'Réponse de l'auteur aux censeurs de ses œuvres'). La Framboisière aimed at delivering a book that would be both useful and charitable. Somehow, he anticipated the trend for 'charitable'

books such as *Le Médecin charitable* (Guibert 1623) and Madame Fouquet's ([1678] 1712) *Recueil des remedes faciles et domestiques choisis, experimentez & trés-approuvez pour toutes sortes de Maladies internes & externes, & difficiles à guerir.*

13. Joseph Du Chesne (Quercetanus) is also well known for defending alchemy in the antimony quarrel and for promoting iatrochemistry in the early seventeenth century. On iatrochemistry, see Gentilcore (2016: 30–7). See also Grmek (1995: 37–59), Kahn (2007), and Giacomotto-Charra and Vons (2017).

14. 'Ce sera un régime de vivre, général, qui pourra s'adapter et approprier à toutes maladies et grandes et petites, servant à tous sexes, à tous âges, et à toutes personnes, aux petites aussi bien qu'aux grands, et aux riches aussi bien qu'aux pauvres, et dont même tous vrais Asclépiades médecins, amateurs de la santé des hommes, qui sont charitables et plus curieux du bien de leur prochain et de leur honneur que de leur profit particulier en pourront tirer quelque utilité. Bannissant autant que je puis de la lecture et communication de mon livre, tous mercenaires, tous prestidigitateurs, charlatans, vendeurs de triacles, empiriques, et toute telle sorte de gens ineptes qui s'osent mêler de médecine sans légitime vocation' (Du Chesne 1606: 9).

15. In the seventeenth century, there was a competition between professionals and non-professionals in the field of medical advice. Among the latter, a distinction can be made between charlatans, who traded as stallholders to sell miraculous drugs to naive patients, and empiric physicians, who pretended to be professionals, although they neither followed a training course nor obtained a degree.

16. 'Des fruits que l'on nous apporte ici de Provence, j'en estime particulièrement le citron, lequel je prise plus que tous les remèdes cardiaques des boutiques de ce temps, qui n'en ont le plus souvent que le nom, et auxquels on fait passer la mer, pour nous les vendre plus chers. Car à vrai dire, en toute sorte de maladies malignes et fièvres pourries, simples ou non, et en la peste même, nous pouvons tirer plus de secours et de soulagement de demie douzaine de bons citrons, que de tout le Bezoard de Levant qu'on nous apporte ici, qui n'est qu'une pierre contrefaite par les Juifs de Constantinople et ailleurs, et du tout inutile à la guérison des maladies, indigne même d'être mise au rang des remèdes … ni que de la thériaque ou du mithridate, qu'un tas de charlatans et empiriques ignorants vantent ici tant contre les poisons, vu que ces drogues ne sont bonnes qu'à enrichir ceux qui les vendent, et à échauffer ou brûler les entrailles des pauvres malades qui s'en laissent abuser' (Patin 1632: 20–1).

17. 'Presque autant que tous les autres remèdes ensemble' (Patin 1632: 91).

18. 'Régi et modéré par l'avis d'un prudent et judicieux médecin … et non pas à l'appétit d'un tas de femmelettes, ou de charlatans et ignorants empiriques' (Patin 1632: 31–2).

19. 'Ne jamais rien faire, ni entreprendre, ni changer de ses premières ordonnances', unless 'le médecin ordinaire l'approuve' (Patin 1632: 99).

20. 'Ce que l'on emploie les autres langues dans un discours tient plus de la vanité pédantesque que du solide' (Renaudot [1632–42] 2004: 121).

21. R. Descartes (1637), *Discourse on Methode*: part 6. On this matter, see Bruno (2009: 20–34).

22. 'Lettres patentes pour l'établissement de l'Académie Françoise', Paris, janvier 1635, art. XXIV: 'La principale fonction de l'Académie sera de travailler avec tout le soin et toute la diligence possibles à donner des règles certaines à notre langue et à la rendre pure, éloquente et capable de traiter les arts et les sciences.'

23. *Le Portrait de la santé où est au vif représentée la règle universelle et particulière de bien sainement et longuement vivre. Enrichi de plusieurs préceptes, raisons et beaux*

exemples, tirés des médecins, philosophes et historiens, tant grecs que latins, les plus célèbres.

24. 'Platine nous apprend *en son histoire des Papes* que Paul second fut surpris sur les deux heures de la nuit d'une apoplexie, de laquelle il étouffa soudainement, étant seul en sa chambre, ne se plaignant d'aucun mal le jour auparavant, de laquelle mort on ne trouva aucune cause apparente, sinon qu'à son dernier souper il avait mangé deux grands melons tous entiers, ce qui arriva en l'an 1471. Plusieurs empereurs et autres grands personnages sont morts pour une même cause. *Münster in Chron.* rapporte qu'Albert d'Autriche, empereur d'Allemagne, se trouvant las et fatigué en son voyage d'Hongrie, mangea d'un melon pour étancher sa soif, en suite de quoi il tomba en un flux de ventre duquel il mourut. De même cause moururent deux autres empereurs, savoir Frédéric III et Henri VII' (Patin 1632: 18). He refers to Bartolomeo Sacchi, known as 'Platina', the first librarian of the Vatican Library and the author of *Vitæ Pontificum* (1479). He was also the author of *De honesta volptate*, a successful cookbook. See Albala (2002: 27).

25. 'C'est pourquoi chacun doit apprendre de son médecin ordinaire le tempérament et la force de son estomac, avec ce qui lui est bon' (Patin 1632: 19).

26. See also Koźluk and Pittion (2009).

27. For a study of the figure of Medea as sorceress, see Mimoso-Ruiz (1978). See also Grmek (1997)..

28. *Quod Optimus Medicus Sit Quoque Philosophicus* is the title of a short essay by Galen (2017).

29. 'La grammaire fut le chef-d'œuvre, les autres après furent inventés par ordre, l'Histoire, la Rhétorique, la Dialectique, les Mathématiques, la Physiologie, et enfin la Médecine, princesse des sciences humaines, à laquelle s'adonna toute la lignée des Asclépiades, conduite et aiguisée par la connaissance des autres arts, nommément de la philosophie' (Jacquelot 1630: 34). See also Du Chesne (1606: 3).

30. Another interesting hypothesis suggests that, on the contrary, the use of ancient commonplaces in the medical field was a way to revitalize ageing knowledge (Koźluk and Pittion 2009: 199).

Projecting *savoir-faire* in the French classroom: Nutrition filmstrips, 1930–70

Didier Nourrisson
Translated by Samuel Trainor

From the moment it was put in place at the end of the nineteenth century, France's universal public school system taught rational and moral dietary practices. Gluttony was to be a thing of the past while war was declared on hunger or malnutrition: pupils had to learn to expand not merely their minds but also their palates.

In the 1880s, primary schools began to put this theory into practice on site, in the form of the *cantine scolaire* (school canteen), a term that was first used during Paris city council debates. Primary schools had a whole toolbox of pedagogical strategies to teach nutrition, a required subject in the new syllabi. The traditional tools available to pupils (textbooks, wall charts, etc.) were supplemented, as technology advanced and a visual culture developed, with a large number of educational filmstrips for projection before the whole class.

In this essay, we analyse a largely unknown corpus of filmstrips relating to diet and nutrition. How did filmstrips come into favour? What do filmstrips indicate about diet and about pedagogical methods? As we will see, the corpus shows an intent to provide scientific information but also to moralize, and it illustrates as well a clash between economic and public health interests.

Canteens, textbooks, blotting paper and other traditional teaching aids for promoting healthy eating

School canteens were set up in France during the second half of the nineteenth century (Chachignon 1993; Nourrisson 2002a). The first opened in 1844 in the Breton town of Lannion in a *salle d'asile* (literally asylum room) – they were not yet called *écoles maternelles* (nursery schools or kindergartens) – in order to provide pupils a bowl of hot soup for lunch. The first medical doctoral thesis about school canteens (Gosselin 1908) mentions that in Pont-Audemer in Normandy around 1860, 'the Bon Secours sisters cooked hot food to be delivered to the children at the town's three schools'. These services aimed to help three types of pupils: children living far from school, those whose parents were absent all day and those whose parents were poor. In fact, though, the vast majority of nineteenth-century children had nothing else to eat but what they had in their satchels. In Paris and a handful of other major cities (Lyon, Marseille, Bordeaux), however, students could enjoy a hot meal cooked on the premises. But the menus were quite monotonous: from Monday to Saturday, nothing but soup, vegetable purée and bread (Moll-Weiss 1906: 151–61).[1] The first canteen networks were established much later, in the 1920s, and menus began to vary a little: 5,217 school canteens in France in 1925–6, expanding to 7,634 in 1930–1, offered a range of different meat- and fish-based menus throughout the week (Moll-Weiss 1931). French primary schools, then, initially began teaching about nutrition not by providing healthy food, but by demonstrating it in the classroom (Baumert 2013; Rosset 2017; Stengel 2012).

The 1880s saw the codification of the free, compulsory and secular French education system; the Jules Ferry Laws of 1882 defined its school subjects. From the outset, school syllabi planned for teaching 'home economics', 'hygiene', 'moral and civic instruction' and 'exploring the natural world', allowing institutions to demonstrate principles of healthy eating and good table manners. In order to do this, certain pedagogical materials were made available to teachers, or were even directly imposed on them.

Specific subject disciplines were defined by the Jules Ferry Laws of 1882 and official textbooks became mandatory in France in 1890. The 'dietary curriculum' was initially formulated in textbooks. One early example, *Le savoir-faire et le savoir-vivre*, was published by Larousse and reissued twenty-five times over a period of fifty years. This textbook went into detail about the 'diet', defined as 'a set of rules on how to feed oneself' (Freyssinet-Domingeon and Nourrisson 2009; Frioux and Nourrisson 2015):

> Generally speaking, a mixed diet is the best for everyone; it involves making use of a specific quantity of animal and vegetable substances. Eating only meat or vegetables can have a detrimental effect on health; it is therefore important to alternate or to eat both in the same meal. (Juranville 1879: 120)

Meal planning and table manners also made up part of the curriculum: pupils were taught about the importance of taking meals at fixed and predetermined times, no more than six hours apart; of limiting the dishes in a meal to a reasonable number; and of eating slowly and only 'moderate amounts of easily digestible dishes' (Juranville 1879: 119–20). Interwar manuals began to give more explicit advice about good hygiene and morality. For instance, the book *Morale pour l'enseignement primaire supérieur* (Faye 1932) promotes 'sobriety and temperance':

> We drink whenever the opportunity arises … Are we sponges? … We eat more than necessary. Are we nothing but a mouth and a belly? … The mind is the master and the body is the servant.

As dietetics developed during the interwar period, primary and secondary school syllabi began to include nutritional science in their curricula. Lessons on healthy eating became more precise as a result, offering content on how to determine proper serving sizes in a rational way and how to distinguish between lipids, carbohydrates, proteins and vitamins. But textbooks featured few images and explanations were often pedantic. By the end of the 1950s, however, textbooks had become more colourful and attractive, containing many more illustrations. A good example can be found in the work of Marcel Orieux (a primary school teacher), Marcel Everaere and Henri Braillon (teachers in the recently created secondary school system, the *collège*) (Everaere and Braillon 1954). In the chapter on 'Man' in their junior high school textbook, *Leçon de choses. Cours moyen*, they include a double page spread titled 'Our nutrients and digestion': on the left-hand page are three highly realistic drawings (a meal laid out on a table, a cross section of the stomach and another of the intestine shown in the process of digesting); while, on the facing page, the text presents both 'Nutrients that keep us healthy' and 'Stages of digestion', followed by a set of questions and exercises. In their next book, *Sciences appliquées* (Orieux, Everaere and Braillon 1959), aimed at boys in the final year of study at rural primary schools, five of the twenty-six chapters are devoted to nutrition: 'Nutrients', 'The digestive system and digestion', 'Our diet', 'Drinks. Alcoholism' and 'Dangerous foods'.

An even more useful tool for teaching through images was the wall chart. These were developed alongside textbooks and allowed the entire class to be taught at once. An early example of a wall chart explaining the principles and practices of good hygiene was produced by Dr Galtier-Boissière in the 1890s. Les Éditions Rossignol, a publishing company set up by a husband-and-wife team of primary school teachers in 1946, produced an extensive collection of wall charts on dietary practices throughout history and around the world (Frioux and Nourrisson 2015).

After the Second World War, school blotters, used for soaking up stray drops of ink, took on a distinctly pedagogical role by presenting advice about what and how to eat and drink, and why. For example, the blotter series 'When life revolves around milk' (*Quand le tour de la vie se fait autour du lait*) prepared the groundwork for the introduction of free milk to schools by Prime Minister Pierre Mendès-France in 1954. During the same period, however, commercial advertising also proliferated on school blotters, undermining considerations of hygiene or healthy moderation. There were adverts for products such as: wine, 'le vin des Célestins réchauffe et rafraichit'; mineral water, 'l'eau minérale Parot naturellement'; fizzy pop and beer, 'demandez une limonade Alméras et une bière Sodibra, celle que j'aime'; biscuits, 'Lu et approuvé'.

Among other visual aids on dietary subjects we also find reward coupons – picture cards designed (like 'gold stars') to reward pupils for good work or behaviour. One series, published by the Aiguebelle chocolate company in the early 1900s, warned about the dangers of alcoholism, while another series published by Badoit in the 1920s, provided pupils with a lesson on the history of the company's mineral water (Frioux and Nourrisson 2015).

But these pedagogical tools, even when used in combination, were deemed insufficient. School textbooks tended to be too wordy; wall charts were often oversimplified; blotters were too commercial; and reward coupons remained vague. Educational filmstrips seem to have been chosen as the solution to this problem, considering how widely they were distributed by the fifteen educational film offices (Les Offices du cinéma éducateur) that served each of France's academic regions.

The arrival of educational filmstrips

Educational filmstrips first appeared in French schools in the wake of the First World War, a period in which many children had gone hungry. Those who had been debilitated by the privations of war, in both Belgium and France, were in desperate need of nutritional support (Guiot 2018). Pupils were famished.

Technology was already available for projecting images in class: 'magic lantern' slide shows (known in France as *vues sur verre*) had been developed by the Musée pédagogique, founded in 1879 by Ferdinand Buisson. The need for images in the rather closed-off world of the primary school had prompted a drive, at the end of the First World War, to provide classrooms with a range of new, comprehensive photographic sequences.[2] The solution was found in the form of filmstrips, a much less labour-intensive format than cinematography. Educational film libraries were established around the country, which were responsible for putting these visual aids into circulation, from 1920 up until the 1970s.[3]

Filmstrips had no soundtrack and were projected frame by frame to the entire class, accompanied by the teacher's personalized commentary (Jeunet and Nourrisson 2001). An accompanying booklet created by the publisher Éditions Nouvelles pour l'Enseignement, called *L'alimentation humaine*, points out some of the pedagogical advantages:

> The visual method – teaching by projecting carefully designed images while providing informed commentary – can be a precious teaching aid in any classroom where active teaching methods are applied.

The booklet also takes pains to underline the indispensable role of the teacher:

> Because these are still images, they can be kept in the children's gaze for as long as the teacher sees fit. The projection time is extremely variable because the teacher is free to choose his own commentary; the images are under the teacher's direct control and have a very clear educational value.

The corpus used for this study consists of one hundred filmstrips about food and nutrition.[4] The Office du Cinéma Éducateur de la Loire (OCEL), a former department of the education authority for the Loire academic region, circulated the filmstrips among the regional primary schools. They appear to have been used extensively, because the majority of the filmstrips catalogued by the OCEL exist in duplicate (with sometimes up to twelve copies). Production dates of these filmstrips have often been difficult to establish (Borde and Perrin 1992; De Pastre-Robert et al. 2004; Freyssinet-Domingeon and Nourrisson 2009; Wagnon and André 2014).

Only five of these filmstrips were produced before 1940. The oldest is probably a filmstrip published by Mazo, a company already supplying magic lantern slides before 1914. The filmstrip *L'alcoolisme* (Alcoholism) reuses a number of old documents, such as a drawing comparing a 'healthy liver' to an 'alcoholic liver' and a map of France indicating local alcohol consumption (by *département*) dating from 1920. We also know that two filmstrip publishers were active before the Second World War, namely les Éditions de la Photoscopie (*L'œuf et le lait* (Eggs and milk), *Vivre sainement* (Healthy living)) and Filmostat (*Le vignoble girondin* (Bordeaux vineyards)). The filmstrip *Le vignoble girondin* (Bordeaux vineyards) is notable for having been produced by the local section of the primary school teachers' union, the Syndicat National des Instituteurs, which had close ties with the radical modern educational reformer Célestin Freinet. The only specifically dated filmstrip from the period, produced in 1935, is the film *La viande* (Meat) published by Alfred Carlier. Carlier was a close associate of Freinet's and a co-founder in 1931 of the *Bibliothèque de travail* (*BT*), the well-known educational periodical. Carlier launched his filmstrip publishing company in 1934. *La viande* reproduces images from the *BT* on the filmstrip.

All of the other films were published between 1948 and 1965. Traditional textbook publishers took to producing filmstrips: Hachette bought up Filmostat (*L'histoire du pain* (The history of bread)); Hatier created Les Éditions Nouvelles pour l'Enseignement (nine films about food and nutrition);[5] Larousse, under its own name, produced a long series on 'Applied sciences' (nine films). There were also several newcomers, which were often specialized and did not necessarily have any prior link to the world of education: Office Scolaire d'Etudes par le Film, Fédération Nationale du Cinéma Éducateur, Centre Audio-visuel de l'ENS Saint-Cloud, Les Éditions filmées (eleven films), Editafilm, Comité de Défense Contre l'Alcoolisme, and so on. The clear leader in the field, however, was the Office de Documentation par le Film (ODF), which published 40 per cent of the filmstrips in the corpus.

Credits are provided at the end of the filmstrips. In the Éditions Nouvelles pour l'Enseignement collection, for example, Paulette Delessaux, a home economics teacher, is listed as author of the texts, while Mademoiselle Sourgen, Home Economics Inspector General, is credited for the presentation, and the educational specialist Raymond Bettembos has credits for the accompanying documentation (Amalvi 2002). This collection includes two filmstrips about water as well.[6] As explained in the accompanying booklet, home economics curricula had to be intensified because 'changing customs and developments in household appliances entailed preparing young girls for the conditions of modern domestic life'. Home economics was intended to be 'liberating for women, and for all family groups, providing all the comforts of better living, safety and happiness'. Beyond the lyrical grandiloquence, such instruction was above all meant to initiate pupils into consumer society, leisure activities and visual culture.

The demand for filmstrips came directly from the French national education system. On the one hand, official directives were calling for increased use of visual images in teaching practices. On the other hand, the old-fashioned term for domestic science classes *enseignement ménager* (household teaching) had been updated with the more scientific-sounding *enseignement de l'économie familiale* (domestic economy),[7] in response to wartime shortages and rationing (Brison 1982).

Meanwhile, private companies were becoming involved in the filmstrip market in order to promote consumer activity, but also with an eye on their own commercial interests. One need only look at the list of businesses that financed the new filmstrip publisher the ODF: the Alsace breweries, led by Kronenbourg; major dairy industries such as Nestle; mineral water companies like Evian; alcohol retailers like the wine merchant chain Nicolas; producers of confectionery and sugar derivatives (such as La Pie qui Chante, Banania, Ovomaltine, Lefèvre-Utile biscuits). Also involved in filmstrip production were some of the major trade associations for French producers of food and drink (vintners, cider makers, distilleries, ice-cream makers, seafood canners, the French coffee board, etc.). This was the thirty-year postwar period of economic prosperity in France known as the *Trente Glorieuses*. Advertising was given a position of privilege in the new screen-based teaching activities. Adolescents, described by the American term *teenagers*, had become a new specific target market. Street billboards, the local cinema, classroom screenings: these precursors to the TV ad combined to influence consumer behaviour (De Iulio 2009; Nourrisson 2002a, 2002b).

The government, for its part, sought to promote French produce. The Ministry of the Colonies championed rice from French Indochina, while the Ministry of Agriculture, via its flour and bread information committee, supported cereal farmers. Healthy eating was seen as one of the keys to developing the nation's economic strength.

Preoccupation with commercial and productivity concerns did not mean, however, that social problems and health issues were neglected. An increasingly protective French state developed a new communication strategy, which included ongoing public health campaigns (Nourrisson 2002b; Thénard-Duvivier 2012). The school system contributed to carrying out this 'bio-policy' through health education (Berlivet 2010). This approach especially characterized the Mendès-France administration in the 1950s (Nourrisson 2014). Public health bodies, in keeping with their remit, promoted hygienic behaviour. The Caisse nationale de sécurité sociale (national health insurance system) funded a filmstrip made by the Fédération nationale du cinéma éducateur called *La digestion et l'hygiène alimentaire* (Digestion and food hygiene); it also financed a filmstrip by the Comité universitaire de prévention des toxicomanies (University committee for drug addiction prevention) called *L'alcoolisme* (Alcoholism). In addition, the national committee for the prevention of alcoholism (Comité national de défense contre l'alcoolisme or CNDCA) – created in 1950 and funded by the family benefits service, the Caisse d'allocations familiales – tackled what it saw as the 'French disease and social scourge' of alcoholism by producing no fewer than six educational filmstrips over a period of twenty years. This is deeply ironic considering the cognitive dissonance between the filmstrips shown in class, which insisted on the dangers of alcoholism, and the ubiquitous street billboards, which promoted the benefits of drinking wine (Nourrisson 2017a).

According to prescriptivist educational strategies, 'the image prompts and leads the viewer both to think and to act' (Éditions Nouvelles pour l'Enseignement booklet). In our corpus, over five thousand frames (roughly fifty frames per film) – at the time they were referred to in French as *photogrammes* – were designed to encourage thinking and action.

What messages do filmstrips convey about food and nutrition?

The filmstrips cover every area of the dietary field. One need look no further than the list of titles in the series of fifteen films published by the Éditions Nouvelles pour l'Enseignement (OCEL catalogue no. 4051–65): Diets around the world; A balanced diet; Wheat, rice and their derivatives; Milk and dairy products; Meat; Fish; Vegetables; Fruit; Drinks; Condiments and seasonings; Cooking equipment; Various cooking methods; Pastries and baking; Jams and conserves; Well-prepared meals.[8] These topics combine elements of history, geography and the earth and life sciences.

All cooking techniques, food groups and types of drinks were broadly covered by the educational filmstrip. Our thematic classification of the corpus of filmstrips includes first, a general category on diet and nutrition, and second, individual categories for the various types of food and drink described. A clear majority of filmstrips (60 per cent) fall into the second grouping on individual foods, with films on the following: rice, bread and pastries (9); seafood (4); fruits and vegetables (4); meat and eggs (4); sugar (3); jams and conserves (3); condiments and seasonings (3); and ice cream (1). Filmstrips about drinks outnumber quite significantly those dealing with solid foods: topics include distilled spirits and alcoholism (17); other alcoholic drinks (wine, beer, cider) (14); milk and dairy products (12); coffee, tea and hot chocolate (5); and drinking water (only 4). Rather curiously, there is one missing category – fizzy drinks (or soda). Indeed, in France, a veritable fascination with sodas developed among young people and advertising professionals alike during the 1950s, the golden age of the filmstrip. Coca-Cola's highly successful entry into the French soft drinks market in this period was achieved through an extremely active advertising campaign, using huge posters, merchandising and brand tie-ins to their best advantage. The company probably had no need to rely on filmstrips to build its notoriety (Nourrisson 2008).

This corpus of filmstrips also reveals evolving educational methods. A comparison, for example, of two of the filmstrips, both produced by the Swiss company Ovomaltine (Ovaltine)[9] and published by the ODF, is highly instructive. Both films are about the same subject – nutrition – but were produced fifteen years apart. The first, *La nutrition*, was published in the wake of the Second World War, around 1950, during a period in which food shortages were still a concern. It is an extremely long (eighty-five-frame) black and white filmstrip with three primary messages: first, 'the human diet varies according to the flora and fauna of different geographical regions'; second, 'the amount of food and drink consumed must provide a quantity of energy sufficient to meet the body's daily needs'; finally, and above all, the perfect all-round product to provide all this is the chocolate malt mix Ovomaltine. On frame 58 we read: 'The laboratory has profited from the great wealth of knowledge in nutritional science to create a product that can both maintain a healthy diet and make up for a lack of nourishment.'[10] The film even refers to the Ovolmaltine factory as an 'institute of food hygiene', staffed by 'nurses'! The second filmstrip, Eating well (*Bien se nourrir*) was made fifteen years later, by which time Ovomaltine had become a regular fixture on the French breakfast table; its forty-three frames offer a much more scientific appraisal of nutrition with only eight of these dedicated to pure advertising.

Dietetics had become the guiding principle of nutrition, all the way down to the primary school level. Instruction on the subject was provided to students of the *Ecole Normale* teacher training school and to university bursars. Priority was given to promoting sensible, balanced diets, even in schools. The precepts of a proper diet were clearly applied in the new 'school restaurants' created in the 1950s and 1960s to replace and update school canteens. (Nourrisson 2002b). Ovomaltine was forced to take this fact into consideration by reducing the commercial content of its filmstrips.

Filmstrips began to put science in the spotlight in earnest. For example, the ODF used the anatomical specimens provided to medical schools by the Parisian company Deyrolle to demonstrate digestion.

The pupil's diet is conceived in these filmstrips in terms of the daily reference intake (*ration*) or the amount of nutrients an individual should consume in a day in order to remain healthy. The work carried out at the beginning of the century by pioneering nutritionists such as Augusta Moll-Weiss is, however, never mentioned. Louis Pasteur is the only scientific figure to appear on screen, peering into a microscope to illustrate the process of pasteurization (*Pasteur et ses découvertes*, Larousse).

The daily ration had to be varied and the diet balanced, because this was the only way to provide the body with all the nutrients it needed. The filmstrips emphasize that daily food intake should include the five basic food groups:

1. Group 1 (fresh and preserved meats, fish, eggs, nuts) which provide proteins and amino acids
2. Group 2 (dairy products) which provide proteins and amino acids, fat and vitamins
3. Group 3 (fats)
4. Group 4 (carbohydrates) which are the body's principle sources of energy (calories)
5. Group 5 (fruit and vegetables) which provide the following: sugars, and thus energy; vitamins, particularly when eaten raw (salad, onion, parsley, fresh fruit, etc.); cellulose (dietary fibre), which aid the function of the intestine and prevent constipation.

In this model, the body is presented as a machine that burns energy and that needs regular refuelling. 'Energy-boosting foods, when transformed into heat, keep the biological machine running. This heat is measured in calories' (*La nutrition*, ODF). A sedentary man requires 1,650 calories per day; a manual labourer requires 4,000 calories per day; to carry out intensive sporting activities (filmstrip images show a race on an athletic track and a volleyball match), the body needs 4,500 calories per day.

Yet, starting from the first half of the twentieth century, dieticians had pointed out the poor quality of French children's diets. They observed 'a regrettable excess of meat', 'an almost total lack of fresh fruits and vegetables' and more often than not a 'failure of imagination' in the meals that school canteens provided to pupils.[11] In Lyon, although the city ran a network of school canteens, the menus suffered from repetitiveness: soup, meat, vegetables (essentially starchy carbohydrates); any drinks or desserts had to be brought by the pupils themselves (Brison 1982). The war obviously aggravated these deficiencies (Nourrisson 2002a). The filmstrip *L'alimentation dans le monde* (Éditions Nouvelles pour l'Enseignement, around 1948) shows a shelter for refugees (frame 5) accompanied by the comment:

Once the wars had ended, governments found themselves responsible for feeding the masses of people who had inevitably been displaced and had lost their homes. Considering the number of children, in particular orphans involved, this measure seems indispensable.

The 'rules' of dietetics are also hammered home. In the filmstrip Healthy eating (*Se nourrir sainement*, ODF), sponsored by the hot chocolate company Banania,[12] we find the following rules:

1st rule: Daily intake should provide the amount of energy necessary for the body to function.
2nd rule: Daily intake should also provide the body with other, non-energy-based elements that are essential for life: minerals, vitamins, fibre, water.
3rd rule: A good balance among the components of daily intake is necessary.

The films offer plenty of advice: pupils are warned against eating too much fat or meat, whether fresh or preserved, and against eating too much bread because of the risks of digestive problems. Other risks and dangers are pointed out as well: poisonous mushrooms and spoiled or contaminated products which can cause food poisoning, cooked foods which lose their vitamins and so on. Suggestions vary especially with regard to drinks, depending on the historical period. Prior to 1950, all kinds of drinks were permitted, except for alcoholic spirits. The composition of a standard meal around 1948 was as follows: bread 200 g, meat 100 g, fresh vegetables 100 g, butter 15 g, wine 200 ml (*Vivre sainement*, Éditions de la Photoscopie). Wine is even considered 'hygienic', in the Pasteurian sense: its ingredients make it 'the healthiest and most hygienic of drinks' (*La vigne et le vin*, Office Scolaire d'Enseignement par le Film; *Le vin*, ODF, produced by the wine merchants Nicolas). In the 1950s, however, the message changed: any fermented drink contained alcohol and could cause alcoholism. This became policy in 1956 when a circular issued by the education ministry prohibited serving of wine in school canteens (Nourrisson 2017a).

Children are directly called upon to be actors of their own diet in the filmstrips, through expressions of nutritional advice: 'food gives me the elements necessary for bodily subsistence ... I know how to live a clean, healthy life and I intend to help those around me do the same' (*Vivre sainement*, Éditions de la Photoscopie); 'throw out dirty water, a source of germs and sickness' (*L'eau*, Les éditions filmées); or through overtly commercial messages, 'always keep a bottle of Evian in reserve' (*Grande sœur*, ODF).

Moralizing messages abound in the filmstrips. 'Good manners for a pupil' entail 'living a clean, healthy life' (*Vivre sainement*, Éditions de la Photoscopie). Pupils are advised to exercise self-control and to pass on the principles of 'good' behaviour to others. 'Where the common drinker swigs, gulps and guzzles, the man of taste savours with poise and moderation', we are told by the filmstrip *Le vin* (ODF). Historical figures are also summoned to deliver messages of gastronomic wisdom. The filmstrip *La cuisine à travers les âges* (ODF) quotes from the pioneering book *La physiologie du goût* (1826) by Brillat-Savarin, the inventor of French gastronomy: 'you are what you eat'; while *Cuisines et coutumes* (ODF) gives us Epicurus, the third century BCE philosopher: 'The wise man does not seek the largest quantity of food; he cares only for the food that is the most delicious.'

As it is explained in the filmstrips, days should be organized around meal times. French pupils are sometimes encouraged to follow foreign examples: 'many people in the Anglo-Saxon world avoid this energy dip around 11 am by taking the time to eat a full meal at breakfast' (*Se nourrir sainement*, ODF). Following the example of the Oslo breakfast, which was very fashionable in the post-war period, filmstrips emphasize the importance of a substantial breakfast 'to stay "in form", to eat healthily, etc., but most importantly to get the day off to a good start' (*Se nourrir sainement*, ODF). On the other hand, the filmstrip *Cuisines et coutumes* (ODF) demonstrates various foreign diets while strongly promoting French culinary culture: 'we can see, then, that rice is the staple of the Chinese diet'; [next slide] 'and mutton is the most important meat for Arabs'; [next slide] 'Methods of cooking and preserving food reflect the cultures of different ethnic groups'; [next slide] 'today, in France, production is organized according to scientifically proven techniques, saving a great deal of time without sacrificing the quality of prepared dishes'. This paean to culinary technology is sung by the Arthur Martin company, the leading producer of home cooking appliances in France in the 1960s.

Filmstrips also promote temperance and a philosophy of life: 'taken in moderation, wine is a friend' (*Le vignoble et le vin*, Éditions de la Photoscopie); and more surprisingly, 'eat your fill, but adjust your menus to what you spend' (*Vivre sainement*, Éditions de la Photoscopie).

One filmstrip in particular provides a lesson in social morality that takes on an extremely innovative form for the 1950s. *Prosper Laberluche*, produced by the Christian publisher La Bonne Presse, is the first filmstrip to feature comics from start to finish. It tells the story of an alcoholic. Paul de Combret, a well-known illustrator who contributed to the *Bibliothèque de Suzette* series (249 titles between 1919 and 1965), depicts the tale of a country postman, Prosper Laberluche. A notorious alcoholic, he makes no bones about this and says: 'clocking up the miles doesn't help you lose weight, but it gives you a real thirst'; 'alcohol warms you up in winter, in summer it cools you down'; 'a drink soon gets used up when you're striding along. One little sweat and it's all gone. The throat gets a hankering for another.' He samples an array of different alcoholic beverages in the course of his delivery rounds: a 'piccolo at the Gentet house', a 'pastis at the Quatre-Chemins', a 'drop at old Rollin's', 'the famous white wine of the Perron slopes' and 'even the cheap piquette at the Larousses'. This ecumenical approach to alcohol is the source of his misery. 'A drinker's house is a house of woe' (*Maison de buveur, maison de malheur*), according to one temperance slogan. Everything in Prosper's life (note the heavy irony of his name) is a catastrophe that lends further weight to the nineteenth-century theory of moral degeneration. His family life is shaken by the untimely death of his sons. The family does ultimately grow, thanks to his daughter Claire, who manages to survive and even marry. But, alas, her first baby is born with a cleft lip. The postman attempts suicide. At this point, the story could have become very dark, like that of the Rougon-Macquart family in the novels of Zola, producing successive generations of alcoholics. However, the second half of the twentieth century was a more optimistic period, so – under the influence of Disulfiram[13] – the postman finally agrees to seek help for his alcohol problem and his grandson has an operation to treat his disability. This filmstrip therefore brings together two innovations to teach pupils about acceptable behaviour: the first is formal – the comic-strip format; the second is thematic – the happy ending for a repentant alcoholic.

(Good) Taste and sweets

Filmstrips make it clear that abstinence is not enough to live well and that one should also learn to eat well and to have good taste. One of the filmstrips is in fact called *Le goût* (Taste); with its sixty-nine frames of photographs, drawings and explanatory diagrams, this filmstrip effectively sums up the key issues of the entire corpus.

The filmstrip was published by the ODF and produced by the confectionery brand La Pie qui Chante, which was undergoing a period of rapid expansion at the time. In 1960 the brand was given the coveted national product award 'le Diplôme du Prestige de la France' and began to sell its products in Belgium and Germany, under the Common Market, even making inroads in the United States.[14] As Soazick Carré and Jean-Watin Augouard note in their study of the La Pie qui Chante company:

> Associated with reward and comfort, the sweet is initially something offered to very young children by adults, first and foremost by the mother. The sweet then becomes a means of self-affirmation for the child, who begins to buy his own sweets on the way to school. This is how he discovers the market economy, both via his purchase and when he uses the sweet for bartering. When the child can decide on his own what to buy in a bakery, this choice allows him to transgress the limits of parental authority. Meanwhile, for the adult consumer, the sweet will always have a flavour of regression, of a return to early childhood. (Carré and Watin-Augouard 1995)

Efforts were thus made to target youngsters (*jeunes* was the word used at the time) with advertising. The expansion in school enrolment numbers (740,000 children in the age group eleven to eighteen attended school in France in 1946, rising rapidly to 1.8 million in 1961) explains this strategic approach. Following the success of its school blotters depicting famous movie stars to advertise its 'Hollywood' caramels (trademarked in 1925), La Pie qui Chante became a producer of filmstrips in its own right.

The ODF, which had a good deal of experience and *savoir-faire* when it came to interlacing science, art and technology, cleverly handled the sequence of slides in *Le Goût*:

1. In the first few slides, the figurative sense of the expressions 'to have taste' and 'to appreciate beauty' are explained, finishing with (on frame 8) a reproduction of the painting *The Allegory of the Five Senses* by David Téniers the Younger (1610–90) and the rhetorical question, 'Is taste the best of our senses?' Passing mention

of gastronomic pioneer Brillat-Savarin 'demonstrates the importance of taste in social lives'.

2. A reminder of 'the taste of primitive peoples', then of animals, follows.

3. A diagram of the mouth, tongue, taste buds and sensory organs in the gustatory system follows, providing a lesson in natural science: 'sensitivity to taste is increased by tongue movement, abundant salivation and especially suitable temperature' (frame 29). The film also underlines the importance of olfaction, explaining that the combination of taste and smell gives us the ability to appreciate a flavour. A photo (frame 34) depicts the 'satisfaction' of someone sampling wine, at a time when the oenologist Jacques Puisais was establishing the principles of wine tasting, in the first systematic taste education programme, as wine producers were doing their best to increase quality while also struggling to sell off their surplus stock.

4. Much of the film, however, centres on 'the search for sweetness' (frame 36). Sugar, it is explained, 'has a high energetic value' (frame 39), and should be used 'in many culinary products'. Let us not forget that the Coca-Cola company, with its extremely sugary fizzy drinks, was entering the French market at the time, and that the Beghin sugar company in northern France was supplying the La Pie qui Chante's sweet factory. A brief history (in seven frames) follows, of Western appropriation of oriental confectionery, served in the form of 'caramels and candies' at the court of Versailles. In this way, children are encouraged to develop a sweet tooth in school under the guise of a history of 'high society'.

5. The film ends with the expected hymn to modernity. 'Let us pay a visit to a factory and see how they make these delicious sweets' (frame 50). In 1960 the company opened a production unit in Villeneuve d'Ascq that was supposedly the most highly automated and modern in the world. Consequently, La Pie qui Chante was able to demonstrate to pupils both 'the greatest pleasure of gourmets' (frame 67) and exciting modern technology and *savoir-faire*.

Conclusion

This chapter highlights the importance of the educational filmstrip: an information and communication technology that was a novelty in French classrooms in the 1930s but that became widespread after the Second World War, at a time when visual culture and consumer society emerge triumphant. This new pedagogical technology – by projecting thousands of images in various formats (photos, drawings, diagrams, tables) – on screen before an entire class completely revolutionized teaching methods for several academic subjects, including life sciences, history, geography, as well as 'domestic science' and civic education. With their didactic scenarios, these filmstrips offered a more active method of communication than textbooks or wall charts, training pupils to learn from images and to interpret them as media. The films drew in the pupils' gaze, followed a storyline and initiated pupils into a new way of seeing, memorizing and learning. While not offering practical education in diet and nutrition, like in the canteen, filmstrips nevertheless made a strong appeal to one of the key senses involved in taste, sight.

Educational filmstrips, following school curricula and dominant ideas of nutrition, provided an overview of different types of food and drink as well as dietary advice. More generally, filmstrip producers and the teachers who used these resources sought to implement a dietary educational project with strong humanist values: teaching pupils how to eat and drink with good manners. They also defended the principles of quality food and community welfare through instruction on living and eating well with others.

Filmstrips also offered food industries and private companies a foothold in the French school system, known for its hostility to advertising. Such filmstrips prepared children for their entry into a new brand-oriented consumer society. While ostensibly serving public health needs while improving the efficacy of classroom teaching, dietary filmstrips sought to influence pupils to choose certain brands of confectionery and junk food, to which they gave an official stamp of approval. We have no way of knowing how these advertising images were received. However, we can say that schools – places of constant repetition – were inundated with these filmstrips. French children in the 1950s certainly took to eating La Pie qui Chante sweets, Lu biscuits, Nestlé chocolates; they licked La Basquaise ice cream cones and perhaps even drank Kronenbourg beer or Nicolas wine. 'Voltaire said of the bubbly foam in a glass of Champagne: It is the image of the French people', according to the filmstrip *Scènes de la vie champenoise* (ODF, Comité interprofessionnel des vins de Champagne).

Notes

1. Augusta Moll-Weiss (1863–1946) was one of the first dieticians and the founder of *L'école des mères* in Bordeaux, the first school in the world to teach young women how to take care of a baby. She was the author of numerous articles in medical and educational journals and of several books, including: *La cuisine rationnelle des malades et des bien portants* (Rational cookery for the sick and healthy), *L'alimentation de la jeunesse française* (The diets of young people in France) and *L'alimentation rationnelle* (Rational nutrition), which won the Académie de médecine's national book prize. She was also founder of the Goûter de l'écolier parisien, which offered an after-school snack to underfed children in Paris.
2. It is worth noting that the French military film service, Service cinématographique des armées, came into being at the same time and provided heavily censored views of the war.
3. The 'Filmathèque stéphanoise', established in 1921, later became the office for educational cinema for the Loire region. We are indebted to this archive for providing access to the vast majority of the 10,000 filmstrips that have been rediscovered.
4. We built this corpus by consulting the digital database *L'Ecole dans la Loire d'hier à aujourd'hui*, a catalogue of 10,000 filmstrips belonging to the Association stéphanoise. The majority of the educational filmstrips was issued by the Office du Cinéma éducateur de la Loire (OCEL), a former department of the education authority for the Loire academic region. The success of these filmstrips, which were lent out to

schools by the OCEL, is clearly evident from the number of copies retained by the archive: between three and twelve copies of each film.

5. A brochure outlining all of the food-related publications by the Éditions Nouvelles pour l'Enseignement mentions fifteen filmstrips, but we have been able to find only nine.

6. For a more complete list of filmstrips about water, organized by school subject, and relating to the multiple uses of water (other than drink), see Nourrisson (2019: 337–54).

7. After 1968, home economics classes were phased out in favour of technology courses and classes in tertiary industrial methods (Baumert 2013). Coincidentally, no more educational filmstrips were produced after 1970.

8. Translator's note: These titles are given in English for reasons of clarity. The original French titles are as follows: *Alimentation dans le monde; Alimentation équilibrée; Blé, riz et dérivés; Lait et produits laitiers; Les viandes; Les poissons; Les légumes; Les fruits; Les boissons; Condiments et aromates; Matériel culinaire; Différentes cuissons; Pâtes et pâtisseries; Conserves et confitures; des Tables bien preparées.*

9. The Wander company first started selling Ovomaltine – a product made from malted barley, skimmed milk powder, cocoa and yeast – in 1904. (Translator's note: the product was introduced quite early in Great Britain, under the name Ovaltine, in 1913.) It was widely sold internationally from 1937 onwards and arrived in France after the Second World War in the form of a soluble powder for an 'instant' breakfast or a chocolate bar as a 'break time' snack.

10. 'La science de la nutrition, riche d'enseignement, a été mise à profit (c'est le cas de le dire) par un laboratoire qui a réussi à préparer un produit capable, soit d'assurer une alimentation normale, soit de compléter une alimentation insuffisante.'

11. Augusta Moll-Weiss carried out an in-depth study of Parisian children's diet in the 1920s (Moll-Weiss 1931).

12. Banania, founded in 1914, had always advertised the health benefits of its product, which had supposedly been invented by a pharmacist in Courbevoie: 'children, adolescents, sportsmen, young mothers, businessmen, those with delicate stomachs, anaemics, convalescents, the aged – everyone can find health, strength and happiness in the beloved flavour of Banania, made with banana flour' (see Nourrisson 2002b).

13. The effect of Disulfiram was discovered by accident in 1948 by researchers Erik Jacobsen and Jens Hald, who were working in the Danish pharmaceutical laboratory Medicinalco. The drug was initially intended to treat intestinal parasites, but the researchers, who tested the product on themselves, experienced unpleasant side-effects when taking the drug in combination with alcohol. The product, which provokes a strong distaste for drinking, is commonly known as 'Antabuse'.

14. When it was founded in 1860, the company was just a local sweetshop in Lille, producing handmade confectionery. In 1925 it became La Pie qui Chante, taking its name from a former Montmartre cabaret. In 1955 it expanded into a national retail chain, investing in an extensive advertising campaign to be repeated on the radio and in the press.

Changing public health recommendations for older people: From curbing excess to battling undernutrition

Laura Guérin
Translated by Samuel Trainor

Introduction

In France, national health policy considers dietary care to be the utmost priority for older people. Providing balanced meals is seen as key for avoiding undernutrition and its associated health risks in the elderly. Efforts to prevent undernutrition in older people are so widespread that it is difficult to imagine a time when health policies on ageing failed to mention it. Yet at the end of the nineteenth century, undernutrition was not considered to be an age-related disorder. On the contrary, public authorities were in fact more preoccupied with the 'ills' of overeating among older people. Nor were the dietary needs of the elderly the object of medical research. In this chapter, I address the two following questions: What dietary recommendations circulate in the public sphere in the period before undernutrition becomes the primary focus in geriatric care? How have these recommendations changed since the nineteenth century? My discussion is based on the results of doctoral research in sociology conducted on the eating and dietary practices of older people in care homes. I show that the definitions of the dietary needs of older people, along with the public health policies supporting these definitions, have changed radically over the years. Until the 1940s, the main objective of health policy was preventing older people in hospitals and hospices from overeating.

Methodology

This chapter applies the socio-historical approach developed in my doctoral thesis on the diets of older people in care homes. The sources used are held at the archives of the Assistance Publique des Hôpitaux de Paris (AP-HP, the University Hospital Trust of Paris) and comprise documents showing how older peoples' meals and eating practices were described and planned across all public hospitals and hospices in Paris towards the end of the nineteenth century. The decrees and memoranda issued by the central administrative body for Parisian public hospitals are particularly useful in this regard; they reveal the main public health concerns of the period regarding elderly people who could no longer care for themselves. Other important sources include medical doctoral theses (a requirement to become a doctor in France) dealing with the relationship between diet and senility. While they were extremely rare at the beginning of the twentieth century, theses on such topics began to appear more often in the 1930s and 1940s and then greatly increased in the 1960s. The majority of these sources are held by the Bibliothèque Nationale de France (the French national library) and can be consulted online via the *Bibliothèque Interuniversitaire de Médecine* database (BIUM; a database shared by the country's medical universities).[1] Other sources include public health recommendations for elderly people. These documents reveal how tackling undernutrition has become a preeminent medical concern since the early 2000s. The corpus consists of texts establishing professional norms for elderly care, most commonly issued by France's national health authority, the Haute Autorité de Santé (HAS)[2] and its subsidiary agencies. Analysis of these textual sources shows a double evolution in the medical establishment's approach: on the one hand, a progressive medicalization of diets and dietary guidelines for older people; on the other, increasing importance given to undernutrition as an issue for elderly health.

Avoiding overfeeding the elderly

In France at the end of the nineteenth century, most dietary recommendations concerning older people were issued by the medical boards overseeing public hospitals. Yet the job of providing dietary support to older people fell, by and large, to family members. Historically, women were expected to feed the older as well as the younger generations. However, archival documents about private domestic care are virtually non-existent (Cribier and Feller 2013: 480), so much so that most of what we know about diets and eating practices of older people in the period comes from the French Hospital Trust. Discussions about *what* and *how* older people should eat were crucial questions for medical administrators and researchers. Yet the actual dietary needs of older people were considered as almost insignificant in quantitative terms and were seen as unworthy of attention.

Hospitals and hospices of the period provided care to older people whose limited financial resources did not allow them a decent quality of life. At the end of the nineteenth century, a clear difference was established between the functions of these two institutions: hospitals dealt first and foremost with the sick, while hospices were primarily reserved for the aged. The basic mission of the hospital was healing whereas the elderly poor, seen as a burden, were to be managed at a separate location (Guillemard 1981: 7). In practice, the distinction was not always strictly observed: 'Establishments exist which fulfil the double role of hospital and hospice, catering at once to the sick, the elderly and to children. This is especially true in small towns where meagre public finances do not permit the funding of two separate institutions' (Cros-Mayrevieille 1912: 348).[3] Between the second half of the nineteenth century and the Second World War, ten thousand elderly people were cared for in the hospices and care homes that fell under the auspices of the AP-HP, Paris's health and social security authority (Rossigneux-Méheust 2013: 47). In this context, it was the religious principle of Christian charity that justified providing food; hospital care was still reminiscent of that given in monasteries. Discussions about the dietary needs of older people centred primarily on the nature of assistance to be provided, and applied not only to elderly people classified as destitute but also to other categories of people cared for by the AP-HP including *vieillards* (the aged), *orphelins* (orphans), *incurables* (terminally ill) and *infirmes* (the infirm), to name a few. The charitable provision of food, then, was the same for everyone across the board. It was considered important to respect the dietary prescriptions of the Catholic Church, such as avoiding meat on Fridays and observing Lent. Beyond such religious considerations, hospital and hospice administrators aimed to provide enough food to live on, without actually encouraging people to rely fully on the AP-HP. The overarching concern was to rationalize food distribution in order to cut costs. The regulations that were in force in Paris hospitals between 1867 and 1902 laid out four different kinds of diets that could be provided to the people being cared for, depending on the state of their health: *diète absolue* (strictly limited diet), *diète simple* (minimal diet) consisting of nothing but broth, *régime de potages* (soup diet) and *alimentation solide* (solid food) (Séré 1936: 15). The medical establishment began to differentiate nutritional needs according to categories of the population towards the end of the nineteenth century. This approach expanded upon measures put into place in the early nineteenth century to quantify dietary requirements within institutions such as prisons, hospitals and the army (Depecker, Lhuissier and Maurice 2013). Daily menus were set up for different kinds of patients. However, older people's needs appear to have been completely side-lined when hospitals began to define nutritional requirements for their patients. In fact, there were almost no recommendations concerning their dietary needs. In 1901, for example, Dr Anatole Chauffard, professor of internal medicine, launched a reform of hospital meals which recommended diversifying the food served: 'Less wine, boiled meats and broth, more milk, eggs, starches and pasta: here, in a nutshell, are some of the healthy characteristics of this new diet' (Chauffard 1902: 209).[4] Seven specific diets were prescribed according to sex, age and pathology. For example, newborn babies, weaned infants, young children and older children were all put on different diets. Tuberculosis patients were given a 'hypernutritious diet' with supplemental eggs and meat. Older people's diet was a marginal concern and did not figure in the documents. The central administrative body for Parisian hospitals was significantly more interested in cutting costs than in providing elderly people with a nutritious diet. Caring for the old in hospices was not considered as important as caring for children or mothers in need (Nardin 2007). Hospitals and hospices often took in people considered to be 'indolent' (Borsa 1985: 50) – and the elderly were considered a notable example of this socially disparaged trait.

Hospital and hospice administrators, therefore, had to balance two fundamental goals when considering older people's nutritional needs. The first objective was that of meeting the elderly persons' basic needs, just like those of other beneficiaries of public assistance. The second objective, in light of the relative inactivity of the elderly and their inability to provide for themselves, was to rein in any excessive eating or drinking, considered morally unacceptable. On the rare occasion that sources mention older people's dietary needs as a health-related issue, the key criterion in determining nutritional requirements was the socially expected act of working. Working right up until one's death was considered the norm (Guillemard 1981: 6). Not working was therefore a kind of social deviance of old age. An article published by Professor Landouzy about the proper implementation of the 14 July 1905 law requiring aid to the incapacitated, to those with incurable illnesses and to destitute people over seventy years of age is a case in point. Landouzy argues that food for elderly people dependant on public assistance should be strictly limited in order to put government money to best use.

> How many people in their seventies, if their means allowed them to do so, would fall into the trap of eating copious amounts of food, believing that they need to maintain the ample diets to which they had become accustomed in their fifties? … The elderly man in retirement no longer needs his diet to provide the muscular energy that is indispensable to the manual labourer. His energy requirements can be reduced, on the one hand, to the needs of his internal functions (the systems of respiration, circulation and secretion) and on the other hand, to the energy expended in taking a stroll or in his daily activities around the home. (Landouzy and Joseph 1907: 10)[5]

According to Landouzy, the amount of money needed to meet the nutritional needs of the elderly is 50 centimes, which he considers good and frugal use of state funds. Here we find confirmation of a clear difference in approach to providing food to older people as compared to babies and working-age adults. In this context, work is the factor that determines the energy requirements of each individual. This way of thinking was not exclusive to the nineteenth century; the expression *rations d'entretien* (maintenance rations), used in a medical thesis by Arthur Bribing just before the Second World War, develops this idea by distinguishing between a diet for those who live a sedentary life and for those who do daily physical labour (Bribing 1939: 27).

For the elderly poor in hospices, the question of food is more often presented in the sources in terms of *chores* – for example, mandatory daily participation in vegetable peeling – or of *sanctions*, with food quality deliberately lowered, on the orders of an institution's director, as a punishment for rule-breaking. In this context, feeding older people was a form of rigid social control. The rules that were imposed during mealtimes make this abundantly clear. At the beginning of the twentieth century, meals were served in hospices according to a strict timetable, eaten in silence and prepared from scrupulously measured rations, as a powerful demonstration to the elderly poor of respectability. Regulations of the Parisian hospices and care homes administered by the AP-HP include numerous rules for refectory meals. Article 42 of the Sainte-Périne care home, for example, states:

> Residents must behave with decorum in the refectory. Men are required to take off their hats; all discussion is strictly prohibited. Any resident behaving in a

disorderly fashion is liable to be ejected from the refectory by order of the director and will be held accountable. (Tourtel, Favard and Napias 1900: 184)[6]

While meal regulations are specific to each institution in the early twentieth century, they also share some common points. In particular, elderly residents are often required to get out of bed and go to the refectory if they want to eat. The Galignani, la Salpêtrière, la Rochefoucauld and les Mesnages care homes all insisted on this rule (Tourtel, Favard and Napias 1900: 194).

Memoranda and orders issued by the AP-HP about feeding the elderly often mention two mainstays of these institutions' menus. The expression *vin d'âge* exemplified the notion that wine was good for older people,[7] and the popular saying *le vin est le lait des vieillards* (wine is old men's milk) (Loux 1997) captured this same idea of wine as the drink to nourish and comfort those who were not long for this world. This established idea was challenged at the start of the nineteenth century, when institutions began rationing the amount of wine they served to the elderly based on their sex and the severity of their infirmity.[8] The goal had now become to limit alcoholism.

By limiting the amount of wine they served, administrators began to create a hierarchy among the elderly they cared for, morally justifying their surveillance of alcohol consumption on the grounds of fear of alcohol abuse. Wine then became a major tool of social control of the elderly in the public care system. (Rossigneux-Méheust 2013: 48)

Drinking alcohol was increasingly disparaged, as it made these institutions appear badly managed. On the other hand, meat broth was lauded as an indispensable part of the older person's diet. The rare extant medical sources from this period do not consider undernutrition to be of clinical importance with regard to ageing. In his *Traité clinique et pratique des maladies du vieillard* (Practical treatise on the clinical treatment of age-related illnesses), Dr Maxime Durand-Fardel describes certain degenerative diseases at great length, including brain deterioration, circulatory problems, acute delirium and tuberculosis. In a chapter on gastroenterological conditions, Fardel argues that a loss of appetite in the elderly is not necessarily pathological:

Elderly people do not generally have a very big appetite. The majority of those who eat a lot do so merely because no other occupation is available to them to stimulate their senses; but we can be certain that none of them actually requires a large quantity of food. It is true that a patient's former habits should be taken into account, and that heavy eaters should not reduce their intake too rapidly from the quantities of food to which they are accustomed; but they must do so nonetheless, relative to their necessarily decreasing needs. However, we see a large number of elderly patients who lose their appetites, without there being any form of general or local morbidity in the major bodily functions. This is a kind of essential anorexia, which appears to be the result, not merely of inactivity of the stomach, but also of a dulling of the sense of taste and of the sensation that governs hunger. (Durand-Fardel 1854: 724)[9]

Thus, the high value society places on work is the main consideration whenever sources deal with the nutritional requirements of those physically unable to work, such as older people. The amount of food provided is defined in relation to what an active working man eats; such guidelines depended on measures of productivity and not on age-related infirmities, which were not thought at the time to warrant any special diets.

Fighting unhealthy eating

Medicalization of older people's diets began in the 1940s. As eating was increasingly correlated with life expectancy, any food habit running counter to prolonging life was condemned. Medical studies about diet in old age were published in increasing numbers. Such studies emphasize that older people often eat poorly, either too much or too little. Medical knowledge which circulates at the time contributes to normalization of guidelines for healthy eating among the elderly, and more broadly, contribute as well to normalization of a moralizing vision of ageing by focusing on avoiding excess. An elderly man, in accordance with this social hierarchy of ages, had to eat less than an active working man. Representations of old age during this period continue to be conceived and expressed in relation to childhood and adulthood.

In the 1920s, alcoholism is the only dietary disease requiring internment at the Asile départemental de vieillards et incurables (Bischwiller asylum for the elderly and incurable in Alsace). According to the documents, the principal reasons for admission between 1919 and 1924 are weakness of mind, imbecility, epilepsy, senile dementia, invalidity, cancer, blindness, paralysis and deaf-mutism (Gemmerle 1987: 94). This list of diseases, through its omissions, is particularly revealing of the fact that the dietary behaviour of the elderly was not considered to be a genuine medical problem in the early twentieth century. When doctors judge the diet of older people to be unhealthy they generally credit it to bad behaviour, rather than illness. The documents continue to reflect this point of view right up until the 1960s. More precisely, between 1920 and 1960, eating and dietary practices of elderly people become an increasingly important subject of medical research; however, studies focused more on prevention than treatment and worked to establish a set of nutritional principles to maintain health. Until the 1960s, undernutrition is not systematically mentioned in medical encyclopaedias. It is, for example, entirely absent from the *Petite encyclopédie médicale* (Hamburger 1950). When undernutrition is discussed at length, as it is in the *Guide d'alimentation pratique* (Practical dietary guide) of the Société scientifique d'hygiène alimentaire (French society for dietary hygiene), newborn infants are considered to be the main group at risk, rather than the elderly (Randoin et al. 1951). Various balanced diets for children, adolescents, pregnant women, and workers are described, but none specifically for older people.

For the first time, in 1939, in his book *Sur l'alimentation du vieillard* (On the old person's eating and diet), Dr Arthur Bribing laments that no comprehensive medical text had yet been written concerning the elderly: 'It seems to us that the subject is of genuine physiological and clinical interest, since the diet of the older man is almost always defective, and fails to meet his particular needs' (Bribing 1939: 12).[10] According to Bribing, overeating, systematic hyper-nutrition, bulimia and undernutrition are the most notable dietary disorders:

> Being deprived of other pleasures, the old man seeks to make up for this loss with culinary gratification, and while it is rare for him to be an alcoholic, it is quite common for him to be gluttonous and to have an especially sweet tooth. The quantity of sweets, chocolates and cakes that he ingests is not unrelated to the digestive problems he so often suffers: flatulence, auto-brewery syndrome, diarrhoea. Eating at the same table as his son or his grandson also encourages him to eat like they do, i.e. to overeat. (Bribing 1939: 17)[11]

The tendency towards overeating among the elderly is a recurring and central point in medical studies of the period. These studies call for curbing the older person's presumed excessive appetites. The authors seek to explain the dietary disorders of older people on moral grounds: the older person is described as one who irrationally or conceitedly imitates the eating habits of their juniors, attempting to consume as much as working-age men, with their higher nutritional requirements. When elderly undernutrition is considered, as is rarely the case, medical studies offer several explanations: poverty, miserliness, unbalanced diet and dental problems (Bribing 1939: 19). Three of these four explanations are moral judgements on behaviour, showing a clear tendency to proffer psychological reasons for food disorders. Dental problems are the only physical symptom of old age linked to undernutrition. In these medical studies, the three behaviours of overeating, undereating and poor dietary choice among the elderly are each mentioned and analysed, yet none predominates over the others. The social construction of age is expressed through dietary control, with aims to promote and to normalize restrictive eating regimens for the elderly. In this way, eating or drinking to excess is pointed up as deviant behaviour, a form of addiction, which is all the more morally reprehensible because it involves consuming more than the commonly accepted nutritional needs of the elderly. The central objective of medical theses on the subject of older people's eating behaviours turns to defining the optimal diet for meeting the lesser energy needs of older individuals. This is the idea put forward in the 1950s by Jacqueline François in her thesis 'Les bases physiologiques d'une alimentation rationnelle du vieillard normal' (Physiological principles for a rational diet for the normal elderly subject):

> In the elderly subject, we are thus presented with an organism that is not ill, but that has reached a particular kind of equilibrium, essentially a reduction of interactions, and thus of requirements. It has long been established, through experience and empirical observation, that an elderly person consumes less than an adult who expends energy by working. But we can easily fall into the trap of over-adjustment by restricting the elderly person to a diet that is very low in calories and made up of bland and unvaried foods. (François 1958: 29)[12]

In this way, dietary recommendations began to be determined less as a function of physical activity than of older people's specific needs; the elderly person's weakened metabolism, while not pathological, nevertheless required particular attention. The sources recognize that elderly subjects have diminished but persistent nutritional needs that must be consistently met on a daily basis (François 1958). Numerous foods are carefully studied in an effort to identify the perfect diet for the older person. Certain doctors warned against sausages and processed meats, cabbage and sorrel, for example, and discouraged chocolate (Lassablière 1941); while others considered alcohol's place in the diet 'extremely difficult to determine' (François 1958).

From the 1960s and 1970s onwards, attitudes started to change even further: the goal was no longer simply to describe the deviant dietary behaviours of older people and to prescribe the ideal diet. The texts reveal a new approach focused on characterizing these behaviours as specific medical conditions. Numerous studies from the period analyse cases of undernutrition, using expressions such as *maigreurs du vieillard* (elderly thinness), *maladies de privation* (illnesses of deprivation), *troubles nutritionnels* (nutritional disorders) and *alimentation erronée chez le vieillard* (incorrect diet amongst the elderly) to refer to this newly identified form of disordered eating. Medical texts from this period begin to use the term *dénutrition* (undernutrition) as one explanation for the elderly's health problems, although erroneous dietary behaviours were still considered to be the primary reason. *Sous-alimentation* (undernourishment) and *dénutrition* (undernutrition) were treated as equivalent concepts. General practitioners played a key role in diagnosing eating disorders, as Marie-Paule Robin explains in her 1975 medical PhD thesis: 'The Doctor must help every one of his elderly patients "age well". In order to do so, he should proactively and systematically look for major risk factors, not the least of which are undernutrition disorders, at every consultation, and eliminate them' (Robin 1975: 16).[13] Educating older people about nutrition and meal planning was an important aspect of the health education programmes the French government launched during the same period (Berlivet 2004).

The diets of older people became increasingly medicalized, as did geriatric care, a major feature of public policy after the Second World War. Before this period:

> Hospitals had been, to both doctors and the public, institutions where the poor and underprivileged ended their days. Medicine was therefore of secondary importance during the period 1840–1940; significant improvements in surgical methods and hygiene do not outweigh the lack of therapeutic solutions offered or the absence of effective medicines. (Hutet 2013: 350)[14]

With the publication in 1962 of the Laroque Report on ageing policy, followed by the government circular published on 24 September 1971 about sanitary and social amenities in care homes, providing medical care became one of the central missions of the French government. Care homes could use medical techniques and equipment that had traditionally been the preserve of hospitals, meaning that care homes were increasingly recognized as centres of medical expertise. This medical expertise gradually influenced every aspect of daily life, most notably diet, at these institutions.

Tackling undernutrition

At the end of the 1970s, the idea that good eating behaviours were the key to good health in old age gave way to the concept of undernutrition as a pathology of old age and as a problem to be treated in order to reduce morbidity. The hygienist approach to eating habits among the elderly was therefore progressively replaced by a medical conception of old age and ageing. The use of the term *dénutrition* (undernutrition) rather than *sous-alimentation* (undereating)[15] is a clear indication of the shift from concern about improper eating towards greater focus on bodily dysfunction. Geriatricians are not the only actors behind the medicalization of the eating practices of the elderly. The wider community, including retirement home workers – both medical and non-medical staff – and the families and friends of older people, are also responsibilized for the health of the elderly and encouraged to treat diet as an almost exclusively medical problem.

By the middle of the 1980s, undernutrition was increasingly recognized as the predominant dietary disorder suffered by older people, rather than one among many eating disorders. This process mirrors the scientific construction of Alzheimer's disease during the same period, which contributed to the emerging medical consensus about a distinct pathological category (Ngatcha-Ribert 2012: 6). Nevertheless, up until the 1990s, medical and dietetics literature on the nutritional needs of older people did not focus exclusively on undernutrition. Diabetes and obesity among the elderly are also studied, with specific diets developed and administered for each disorder. Different quantities of food for older people in hospitals or care homes are described in this early period (Vinit 1974). In her study on the diet of older people in care, *L'alimentation des personnes âgées en collectivité*, the dietician Françoise Vinit lists types of food to be prescribed and prohibited for older people suffering from obesity, diabetes and undernutrition (1974: 105). She highly recommends that potatoes, for example, be served to people suffering from undernutrition, carefully restricted for diabetics and strictly banned for obese people (1974: 105). Medical theses produced before 1990 on elderly undernutrition note that the topic had been unjustly overlooked by medical research to date and should consequently be further investigated.

Over the space of a century, the widely held conviction that older people needed to eat less than working-age adults evolved into a view that the elderly needed just as much, or, in the case of infectious disease, even more food. According to the geriatricians Alain Jean and Frédéric Bloch, 'The energetic requirements of older people are similar to those of young adults. The amount of protein needed is slightly higher than for a young adult' (Jean and Bloch 2005: 26).[16] Public health studies on the prevalence of undernutrition among older people became more numerous towards the end of the 1980s. According to the first European study, EURONUT-SENECA, only 4 per cent of elderly people living at home and in good health were found to be affected by undernutrition (De Groot et al. 1991). The reports increasingly draw distinctions between the levels of undernutrition amongst elderly populations depending on where they live: at home, in rest homes or in hospitals. According to an investigation carried out by the French Health Authority HAS, between 25 and 30 per cent of so-called dependent older people living at home or who rely on care workers while living at home suffer from undernutrition (HAS 2007). The epidemiological definition of undernutrition, or Protein-Energy Malnutrition (PEM), constitutes a decisive step towards medical recognition of the specific dietary needs of older people. Explanations for diminished food consumption are varied and take into account physical, physiological and psychological factors. The dominant approach to the problem is epidemiological: '[epidemiology] consists in studying the prevalence and distribution of undernutrition in the population, understanding its pathological state and determining its causes' (Pouyet 2015: 36).[17] With this disorder, according to the medical construction of undernutrition, the energetic and metabolic needs of the elderly subject are not being sufficiently met. When an elderly person's dietary intake is judged to be abnormally low, he or she must be placed under medical observation. Thus, just as with patients with impaired physical mobility, incontinence or a tendency to fall, 80 per cent of care homes in France (both the officially defined EHPADs[18] and other retirement homes) require that healthcare personnel follow medical protocols to prevent undernutrition (Marquier 2013: 11). In this context, 'meals at a care home [EHPADs] can no longer be considered in 2010 to be purely a "catering" service'"[19] (Agence Régionale de Santé 2011: 15). The public health literature identifies adjusting diet as the first course of action to treat older people in residential care (HAS 2007). The diet of dependant elderly people has become so medicalized that insufficient dietary intake has been analysed as both a cause and a consequence of neurodegenerative diseases such as Alzheimer's (Pouyet 2015). Older people are therefore systematically weighed when they move into French care homes, and from then on at monthly intervals, or sometimes even every fortnight. The key assumption underlying this medical conception of undernutrition is that bodily malfunctions related to the ageing process are the root cause of dietary disorders. The vast majority of undernutrition cases are thus explained through this epidemiological model by difficulties in chewing and swallowing, loss of smell and taste and the ability to use cutlery. Undernutrition has, therefore, now become a publicly acknowledged health risk.

The year 2003 intensified this medicalization of older people's diet in France. The significant increase in mortality due to the summer heatwave that year – reaching 15,000 additional deaths in France (Hémon and Jouglas 2003) – contributed heavily to the generalized understanding that hydration and nutrition in older people is a specific medical problem that needs systematic monitoring. The consequences of the 2003 heatwave led to drastic measures and practices in France regarding prevention and treatment of nutritional problems in older people living at home or in residential care. Government regulations increasingly dictated how to handle undernutrition in care homes and called on a variety of different experts and stakeholders: not only doctors but also frontline staff dealing with older people on a daily basis, and residents' families and friends. The health crisis caused by the heatwave thus prompted a new awareness of the dietary needs of older people, and led to the implementation of new regulations to fulfil them.

In the same year, the French ministry of health and social protection launched a national programme called Bien vieillir (Ageing well), focused on 'the promotion of health and well-being via diet, sport and physical exercise'. For the first time, then, food was a central plank of government policy on ageing. Between 2007 and 2009, under this plan and the national nutrition and health programme (Programme national nutrition santé, PNNS), nutritional recommendations were disseminated for the benefit of older people, aged sixty-five or over: 'This guide is distributed via the national health insurance network, the DDASSes,[20] and various associations and private health insurance providers. It is also available at a large number of pharmacies.'[21] Medical discourse on the nutritional disorders of older people which emerged during the 1970s are thus validated and popularized. The key recommendations to 'eat, drink, move' penetrate the private sphere and are relayed by television campaigns (Plan national 'Bien vieillir' 2007). The goal of the PNNS was to increase the disability-free life expectancy of elderly people through healthy diet and exercise, and thereby compensate for the growing numbers of dependent elderly in the general population. As the sociologist Bernard Ennuyer points out, starting in the 1990s, ageing policies established a dichotomy between 'a notion of *incidental* disability, whether congenital or related to illness or trauma, and *normal* disability, accompanying the *normal* process of ageing' (Ennuyer 2002: 187).[22] Beginning in the 2000s, undernutrition was represented as a common and widespread feature of this *normal* process of ageing; the combat against undernutrition was seen as a way to reduce public expenditures on dependent older adult care. A public and media consensus formed that undernutrition is a pathology in elderly people. Even when the media criticizes food services in care homes, as the French consumer association UFC-Que Choisir did in 2015, it explicitly acknowledges the medical paradigm:

> Even in our affluent societies, undernutrition can be a public health problem. This is particularly true of seniors. Around a third of those living in residential care (EHPADs) suffer from undernutrition. Which is not to say that entering a care home necessarily leads to this outcome. The issues are closely interwoven: age-related illnesses lead to both dependency and undernutrition. Cognitive impairment, in particular Alzheimer's disease, can make people lose their bearings when it comes to feeding themselves; difficulty chewing or swallowing, or poor dental hygiene, can create obvious physical obstacles to good nutrition; digestive problems or the alteration of taste caused by some medications only serve to exacerbate an anorexia that is often provoked by a more or less latent depression. (UFC-Que Choisir 2015: 46)[23]

The authors of the second French national nutrition and health programme (PNNS 2) express regret that undernutrition as a pathology is 'unrecognized in affluent societies' (Zazzo, Antoun and Basdevant 2010). Undernutrition is seen to be neglected, first and foremost, in favour of other illnesses, such as type 2 diabetes and cardiovascular diseases, but also because this disorder runs contrary to the fight against obesity in France. Public health authorities in France thus seek to increase awareness about undernutrition, especially in the case of older people in residential care, as a 'major problem of public health' (Zazzo, Antoun and Basdevant 2010: 5). Nutritional standards are now imposed on all medical institutions in France, and since 2011 a national day is dedicated to nutrition in hospitals, nursing homes and retirement homes. In this way, we can see how, from the end of the nineteenth century until today, nutritional recommendations regarding the elderly diet have changed quite radically.

The shift from an assumption of minimal nutritional requirements to one of great need – eating parsimoniously versus eating more – is remarkable. The bodily discipline demanded has been reversed: where the elderly were once seen as freeloaders in the hospice, they have become key beneficiaries and targets of public health policy in the modern care home.

Conclusion

At the end of the nineteenth century, the diet of older people in France was a private affair, confined to the domestic sphere, a domain that remains hidden to us and difficult to assess, particularly given the absence of material in the existing archives. Administrative documents from French public health institutions provide many examples of the dietary recommendations in circulation during the period. Until the 1940s, the primary motivation for providing free meals to destitute elderly people in France was charity. The key criteria determining the amount of food to be served to residents were financial and moral, and mealtime rules reflected the strict social controls over underprivileged ageing populations. When diet in old age became an object of medical attention, starting in the 1940s and 1950s, doctors generally explained excessive weight loss or increase as a result of abnormal or 'erroneous' dietary behaviours. The predominant medical consensus until the 1970s saw dietary problems in older people as being the result of poor choices on the part of patients. Morality was a prime concern here; older people were counselled to show restraint and avoid excess by eating less than a working man. Since the 1970s and 1980s, the term *dénutrition* (undernutrition) has come to describe a protein-energy deficiency. Today, undernutrition is considered in France as a common 'attribute of old age', in the same way as the concept of dependency. This problem is conceived as a specific form of dietary dependency among older people. A medical approach, and medical language, have been imposed as the only legitimate way to discuss the dietary needs of older people, and undernutrition in the elderly has become a key issue in French public policy on ageing. This medicalization of diet has been the cause of considerable friction and suffering in care homes, largely because this approach makes it difficult to interpret a refusal to eat as anything other than the symptom of a pathology. Refusing to eat can also be a deliberate and participatory act on the part of an older person (Guérin 2016, 2018). To dismiss this alternative interpretation is to view providing food as a medical treatment rather than as a service. This is tantamount to silencing all forms of dissent on the subject of food and eating.

Notes

1. The BIUM contains virtually every medical thesis presented in Paris since 1539.
2. Also the ANESM, *l'Agence nationale de l'évaluation et de la qualité des établissements et services sociaux et médico-sociaux*, but this medical oversight body has now been subsumed into the HAS.

3. 'Il existe des établissements qui revêtent le double caractère de l'hôpital et de l'hospice en recevant en même temps les malades, les vieillards et les enfants, et cela surtout dans les petites communes où l'insuffisance des revenus ne permettait pas de faire les frais de deux établissements.'

4. 'Diminution du vin, du bouilli et bouillon, augmentation du lait, des oeufs, des purées féculentes et des pâtes alimentaires: voilà, dans leur ensemble, quelques-unes des caractéristiques médicales de cette nouvelle diététique.'

5. 'Combien de septuagénaires, si leurs moyens le leur permettaient, ne manqueraient pas de se nourrir copieusement, s'imaginant avoir besoin de continuer l'alimentation forte dont ils avaient encore l'habitude à la cinquantaine? ... En retraite, le vieillard n'a plus à chercher dans l'alimentation l'énergétique musculaire indispensable au travailleur. L'énergétique dont il a besoin est celle que réclame d'une part, la vie intérieure (jeu de la respiration, de la circulation et des sécrétions); d'autre part, les dépenses qu'il fait à la promenade ou lors des occupations casanières.'

6. 'Les pensionnaires doivent se tenir convenablement au réfectoire. Les hommes ne peuvent y garder leur chapeau; toute discussion y est formellement interdite. En cas de désordre, le directeur peut faire sortir du réfectoire le pensionnaire qui serait en cause.'

7. Order issued on 24 December 1849, no. 5599. Archives of the AP-HP. Corpus of orders and memoranda. 'In order to make up for the increased cost of the lunch time meal, the following provisions shall be removed from the allocations currently in force: In the two Old-Age Hospices, wine, known as *vin d'âge*, included as one of the administered supplements, starting from 70 and 75 years of age.' 'Comme compensation de la valeur du déjeuner; les retranchements suivants auront lieu sur les allocations du régime actuellement en vigueur; Dans les deux Hospices de la Vieillesse, le vin, dit vin d'âge, qui s'accorde aux suppléments Administrés, à partir de 70 et 75 ans.'

8. The specific level of rationing varied from one institution to another.

9. 'Les vieillards n'ont pas en général un appétit très développé. La plupart de ceux qui mangent beaucoup le font surtout parce qu'aucune autre occupation intéressante n'est offerte à leur sensualité; mais on peut affirmer qu'aucun n'a besoin d'une grande quantité d'aliments. Il est vrai qu'il faut faire la part des habitudes antérieures, et que les grands mangeurs ne doivent pas réduire trop rapidement la quantité des aliments auxquels ils sont accoutumés; mais au moins doivent-ils toujours le faire dans la proportion du besoin, qui s'amoindrit effectivement. Mais on voit beaucoup de vieillards perdre l'appétit, sans qu'il existe aucun état morbide, général ou local, des premières voies. C'est une sorte d'anorexie essentielle, et qui paraît tenir à un simple état, non pas seulement d'atonie de l'estomac, mais d'obtusion du goût et de la sensation qui préside à la faim.'

10. 'Il nous semble que le sujet offre un réel intérêt physiologique et clinique, l'alimentation du vieillard étant presque toujours défectueuse, ne correspondant pas à ses besoins particuliers.'

11. 'Privé d'autres plaisirs, le vieillard cherche compensation dans ceux de la table, et si, rarement, il est alcoolique, souvent il est glouton et surtout très friand de sucreries. La quantité de bonbons, chocolats, gâteaux ingérés par lui, n'est pas étrangère aux troubles digestifs qu'il présente si souvent: la flatulence, la fermentation intestinale excessive, la diarrhée. Le fait d'être à la même table que son fils ou son petit-fils l'incite aussi à manger comme eux: à se suralimenter.'

12. 'Nous nous trouvons donc en présence, chez le vieillard, non pas d'un organisme malade, mais d'un organisme qui a atteint un équilibre particulier, avec pour caractère

essentiel une baisse des échanges, donc des besoins. On sait depuis longtemps, par expérience et empiriquement, qu'un vieillard consomme moins qu'un adulte qui dépense et travaille. Mais on est facilement tombé dans une attitude excessive en n'autorisant plus au vieillard qu'un régime très pauvre en calories, et constitué par des aliments monotones et sans intérêt gustatif.'

13. 'Apparaît la nécessité pour le Médecin d'aider chacun de ses patients âgés à "bien vieillir" et, pour ce fait d'entreprendre précocement une action de présentation par l'élimination des principaux facteurs de risque qu'il devra rechercher systématiquement à chaque consultation. Le dépistage des troubles de la dénutrition n'est pas l'un des moindres.'

14. 'L'hôpital reste pour les médecins et pour l'opinion publique un établissement dans lequel les plus pauvres et les plus déshérités achèvent leur vie. L'aspect médical est alors secondaire dans les années 1840–1940: les progrès de la chirurgie, de l'hygiène ne doivent pas masquer la pauvreté des moyens thérapeutiques, l'absence d'une efficace pharmacopée.'

15. At the end of the nineteenth century, the use of the term *dénutrition* (undernutrition) was largely limited to the animal kingdom in French dictionaries of medical science (Dechambre 1885).

16. 'Les besoins énergétiques des personnes âgées sont semblables à ceux de jeunes adultes. Les besoins en protéines sont légèrement supérieurs à ceux de l'adulte jeune.'

17. 'Elle consiste à étudier la prévalence et la répartition de la dénutrition dans la population, de caractériser son état pathologique et d'en définir les déterminants.'

18. Etablissements d'Hébergement pour Personnes Âgées Dépendantes are the most common form of institutions for the residential care of older people in France. EHPADs, like nursing homes, are considered to be medical as well as social institutions.

19. 'La nutrition en EHPAD ne peut plus être considérée en 2010 comme une prestation de service strictement "hôtelière." '

20. The health and social issues units of France's departmental local authorities: Direction départementale des Affaires sanitaires et sociales (DDASS).

21. 'Ce guide est diffusé auprès des réseaux de l'Assurance maladie, des DDASS, des réseaux associatifs et mutualistes. Il est également promu dans de nombreuses pharmacies.'

22. 'Une notion de handicap *aléatoire*, lié à la maladie, à l'accident, ou congénital, à une notion de handicap *normal*, qui serait la conséquence d'un processus *normal* de vieillissement.'

23. 'Même dans nos sociétés d'abondance, la dénutrition peut être un problème de santé publique. C'est le cas notamment chez les séniors. Pour ceux vivant en établissement d'hébergement pour personnes âgées dépendantes (Ehpad), sa prévalence est évaluée à plus d'un tiers. Non que l'entrée en maison de retraite mène fatalement à cette issue. Ce sont plutôt des phénomènes étroitement intriqués: les pathologies propres au grand âge conduisent à la fois à la dépendance et à la dénutrition. Le déclin cognitif, en particulier la maladie d'Alzheimer, brouille les repères sur les façons dont il convient de s'alimenter; les troubles de la mastication ou de la déglutition, la santé dentaire pas toujours optimale constituent des obstacles physiques évidents; l'altération du goût à certains médicaments ou les troubles digestifs ne font que rajouter à l'anorexie surtout amplifiée par la dépression plus ou moins latente.'

5

Food in the workplace, where productivity meets well-being: A contemporary question?

Elodie Sevin and Thomas Heller
Translated by Samuel Trainor

> *However, science cannot in the end be made into an all-purpose handmaiden either.*
> *At one moment it is supposed to rationalise firms and at another to create the*
> *cheerful mood that it has rationalised away. This is definitely asking too much.*
> Siegfried Kracauer (*The Salaried Masses*, 1998)

In today's corporate world, the twin goals of 'productivity' and 'well-being in the workplace' have become the focus of numerous practices and of a great deal of discourse. These two objectives are crucial to the context of late capitalism. In this regard, the issue of food and nutrition is particularly important and has become a burgeoning managerial concern. Sometimes food practices are seen as a problem – for example, when employees eat too much junk food (whether or not as a result of their working conditions); conversely, food can also be seen as a solution – something that can improve health, productivity, well-being and social bonding. Over the last few years new professions related to food and diet have emerged in the job market: personal coach, nutritionist, organic food producer, taste educator,[1] food designer, food manager and so on. In France, new philosophies of food and new dietary behaviours have also become prevalent, both in the workplace and in the community (such as vegetarianism, veganism, chrono-nutrition) and academic research in the area of food studies has increased significantly.

One might therefore assume the question of food in the workplace to be a contemporary concern arising in late modernity, a consequence of the acceleration of the economy and of our ways of life (Rosa 2013). However, historical research shows that the issue of food in the workplace has been a major economic and political consideration ever since the second half of the nineteenth century, as well as an important object of scientific research closely tied to questions about the development and the demands of industrial capitalism.

What does historical research tell us about the links between work and food practices in the Industrial Age? What questions were asked on the subject during that period?

How did scientific research and corporations explore and act upon these issues? How were these questions addressed in the workplace? Do these historical studies shed light on our current food practices in the workplace?

In this chapter we show that many of our current questions about food in the workplace, and its relationship to productivity and well-being, were already being raised 150 years ago. The precise nature of these questions obviously differs from one period to the next, as do the surrounding issues. Nevertheless, we believe their historical analysis can help us understand contemporary practices and can serve as a foundational and critical tool for the study of late modernity.

We have divided our historical approach into two main thematic areas. First, we examine the nature and quality of food in the workplace, that is, what workers eat. Second, we consider the social relationships surrounding the act of eating, that is, the social context of workplace eating practices. These themes are examined through the twin lenses of 'productivity' and 'well-being': two considerations that are obviously linked, but which also relate to distinct issues and practices. In the first part of the chapter, we explore the ways in which food and eating became a specific object of attention for industry in the late nineteenth and early twentieth centuries, and we consider how this heritage informs current trends. In the second part of the chapter, our historical reading focuses on the collective dimension of workplace meals, and the issues underlying this dimension. Our intention is to shed light upon current practices, and to examine what is at stake in the contemporary promotion of workplace food practices as a means of social bonding.

It is not the principal intention of this chapter to offer a historical reading of knowledge about food in the workplace context. Instead, historical considerations of knowledge circulation are used to illustrate our discussion. Contemporary representations, beliefs and practices related to food at work carry more or less explicit traces of the knowledge – scientific or otherwise – that shapes their development over time. The enduring relevance of such representations, beliefs and practices, from the late nineteenth century to the early twenty-first century, attests to the widespread nature of the knowledge that has influenced them. In this chapter, the work of historians informs our understanding of the present day and allows us to suggest precisely this kind of diachronic knowledge circulation. By attempting to counter the tendency to forget the past in favor of illusions of novelty, our aim is to provide a reminder of the past which has produced our present.

Food in the workplace: Productivity, social justice and well-being

We begin by detailing two situations which encapsulate present-day concerns about food in the workplace, as they are conveyed by the practices of food service providers in the corporate setting.

In 2017, the Maison Européenne des Sciences de l'Homme et de la Société (MESHS) of the Hauts-de-France region of northern France – a regional public research institute in the social sciences – asked us to participate in a meeting alongside other academics to discuss a project proposal made by a local businessman, the cofounder of a direct-delivery fruit company, Distrifuits.[2] This business, founded on environmentally friendly principles (local sourcing and distribution, quality organic produce, etc.), was initially set up to serve the needs of individual households. Distrifuits wished however to expand its activities into the corporate sector by offering workplace services and events highlighting its products (fruits). As part of this development project, the service provider sought academic partners willing to carry out a study which, as stated in the project framework document, would determine:

> whether a nutrition policy, promoting the consumption of fruit and vegetables, beyond its impact on an employee's physical health, might also play a role in the social dimension of an individual's health, on his human relations and therefore on his well-being and performance at work. (Distrifuits 2017: 43)

The cofounder of Distrifuits also emphasized the potential economic and managerial benefits of the project; his objectives were to: 'show that food management in businesses is not a liability but an asset. In short, respond to management concerns about the "bottom line" by demonstrating a measurable "ROI" [return on investment]' (Distifruits 2017: website).

The second example takes us to Belgium. In November of the same year, 2017, the Chamber of Commerce and Industry (CCI) of the city of Liège hosted a lecture and debate entitled 'Comment améliorer votre productivité grâce à l'alimentation?' (How can food and eating improve your productivity?). Approximately forty people were in attendance, mostly CEOs, human resource managers, training consultants and well-being consultants. The lecture, which we attended, was on the subject of nutrition and diet and was given by an independent dietician who also happened to coach the local professional soccer team, Standard Liège. The lecture focused first and foremost on dietetics and chrono-nutrition,[3] primarily from a health perspective. The question of productivity was only alluded to incidentally: food, as a result of its intrinsic qualities and depending on the time of day at which it was ingested (chrono-nutrition), could have an effect on sleep and fatigue, and thus on the ability to perform a given activity. The postprandial dip – the 'mid-afternoon slump' – was brought up as a particular concern. The speaker provided a series of tips on how to reduce or avoid it. The lecture was part of a broader programme focusing on sport and nutrition, organized by the CCI for local businesses, with a view to promoting the health and well-being of employees. The implicit suggestion here was that positive economic consequences (in terms of efficiency and performance) might be achieved by practicing a team sport, and by adopting an appropriate diet, overseen by a nutrition coach and a trainer.

These two examples illustrate, almost paradigmatically, the current concern with food in the workplace, and how this concern is embodied in practices meant to improve health, well-being and performance. The first example demonstrates the ambition to link such concerns to scientific (or scientific-economic) objectification via measurement and evaluation. The second example highlights how this concern comes to be inscribed in specific physical activities, overseen by experts and informed by advances in biochemistry which defines diet as either a catalyst or a hindrance to physical performance. It is in these two aspects – on the one hand, the measurement of the influence of diet on workplace performance and, on the other hand, fatigue understood as a hindrance to that performance – that present-day concerns echo those prevalent during the industrial development era of the middle and late nineteenth century. In his book *The Human Motor,* historian Anson Rabinbach makes a strong case for the combined study of these two issues. In the next section we discuss some of the salient elements of Rabinbach's argument.

Energy, fatigue and diet: Reconciling productivity and social justice?

In *The Human Motor,* Rabinbach shows how, from the 1850s to the 1930s, in France and Germany, knowledge of the laws of thermodynamics influenced thinking about industrial labour and how it might be organized and rationalized.

With the discovery of the law of conservation of energy, and later of entropy – its progressive dissipation – a new science of work was developed. Its primary object was the human body, seen only in terms of its productive force. The human body functioned merely as an engine. What Rabinbach reveals, through examination of numerous historical writings on the subject, most importantly those of physiologists, is a quest for balance between human energy, which literally generates work, and efficiency, as it comes up against the natural limit of human endurance, namely fatigue. Rabinbach notes that a classic moral approach to work, most obviously expressed as the condemnation of idleness, gave way little by little to a scientific approach, which examined the processes of expenditure and loss of human energy. In this sense fatigue was seen as an obstacle to the ideal of the unlimited productivity of 'the human engine'. Rabinbach explains that the notion of fatigue, to which scientists had previously paid very little attention, started to appear in medical research in the late 1870s, and that 'after 1900 the journals … overflowed with literature on every aspect of fatigue' (1990: 137). In certain cases, researchers sought to eradicate fatigue. In 1904 for example, Wolfgang Weichardt, a chemist from Heidelberg, announced the development of a vaccine against tiredness.

In this thermodynamic model of human activity, the concept of fatigue, as a manifestation of entropy, naturally led to the question of how the body might be used most productively, by economizing energy. This was not merely a question for individuals or businesses, Rabinbach points out, but for the nation as a whole. The power of a country, and in particular its economic power, would depend on its ability to optimize the management of the nation's energy and to provide the conditions for optimal productivity with minimal loss of energy, and therefore with as little fatigue as possible.

The importance of fatigue as a strain on productivity also required, within this conceptual framework, that provisions be made for workers to rest and to recover their ability to work. This meant taking breaks from work, having possibilities for entertainment, benefitting from reduced working hours and so on. Fatigue was thus seen as the natural limitation to what would otherwise be unbridled exploitation of the workforce. The concept of productivity became inextricably linked in the workplace to conditions designed to promote what we might refer to today as a kind of 'well-being'.

Thus, through the notion of fatigue, a link is established between productivity and social justice, insofar as fatigue limits the tapping of workers' energy and requires implementing modes of recovery. Rabinbach writes:

> The energetic calculus, which viewed fatigue as the objective boundary of the human motor, was not restricted to any single political doctrine or ideology: it represented a widely shared belief that conserving the energy of the working body held the key to both productivity and social justice. (1990: 18)

With such a thermodynamic approach to the body, based on the desire to conserve workforce energy that dissipates during physical exertion, it is easy to understand the importance of nutrition as a key area of research.

Nutrition is not central in Rabinbach's book, but he does provide instances of the type of questions that were being asked, and of the work being conducted on the relationship between diet and work. If, for example, we consider, as physiologist and engineer Étienne-Jules Marey did in 1867,[4] that 'a muscle is subordinate to two influences: one is reparative, requiring nutrition; the other exhausts and has a motor function' (quoted by Rabinbach 1990: 133), what diet might be best suited to optimizing a worker's performance? To what extent can the dietary habits of two different countries explain disparities in productivity? What are the calorie requirements of different social groups, in relation to their activities? It is in this light that Rabinbach mentions the work of Mr Gautier, a physiologist, who calculated that 'for a worker at rest 2,604 calories in 24 hours might suffice, whereas a worker working hard requires 3,556 calories' (1990: 130–1), and that 'only 25 to 65 percent [of calorie intake] was translated into useful work' (1990: 132). These areas of investigation, and the experiments designed to test them, reveal the importance of thermodynamics at that time, particularly when the calorie was introduced into the study of nutrition. Moreover, the late nineteenth century saw the nutritional concept of the calorie make its way beyond the confines of academia and circulate more widely in society (Scholliers 2020), increasing, little by little, its influence on food behaviours.

What conclusions might be drawn from these historical references gleaned from Rabinbach's work on the human engine (to which this brief overview hardly does justice)? First, we can say that current concerns relating to food in the workplace are not new, and that they do not result merely from present-day worries about either food or work. They are clearly little more than an extension and a rephrasing of concerns which have been prevalent throughout all the stages of industrial development. What we learn from this history is that thermodynamics makes it possible to consider a nation's power as an asset which can be managed. Within this framework, the worker somehow loses agency over his or her body, which becomes little more than a vehicle for energy, belonging primarily to the nation, to which its care is then entrusted. A strong link is thus established between productivity and social justice, through the mediating notion of fatigue; this link provides, to some extent, the science of work with a moral foundation. The rationale for this link is similar to the logic used in contemporary discussions of the relationship between well-being and productivity. This is of course not to say that thinking about work and its organization in terms of social justice is equivalent to thinking about it in terms of well-being. As Rabinbach notes, the hopes of many physiologists and social reformers seeking to establish a science of work that would promote social justice were dashed with the arrival in the workplace, and the adoption by industry, of the scientific methods developed by the engineer Frederick W. Taylor, who cared much less about economizing energy than he did about getting the most work possible out of the 'human motor'.

Exploring the link between well-being and productivity: The Hawthorne Studies

Rabinbach (1990) notes that, starting in the 1950s, the human engine metaphor, and the representation of work that it entailed, gradually became less popular. However, it can be argued that the first seeds of this obsolescence had been planted a few decades earlier, with the new psychological conception of the human experience at work, particularly after the pioneering industrial studies carried out between 1924 and 1932 at the Hawthorne Works of the Western Electric Company in Cicero, Illinois in the United States. We consider it important to mention the experiments carried out at Hawthorne because their conclusions, expressed in terms of social incentives, inspired businesses to begin conceiving of workers' engagement and efficiency in terms of well-being. We are certainly not claiming that the experiments revealed for the first time that for a subordinate to be efficient, his superiors should take care of him and not overwork him, and thus foster in him, from a subjective point of view, a kind of well-being. Roman slave owners were already well aware of this (Toner 2015). In the industrial context, however, and in relation to Taylor's scientific management theory and its conception of the individual worker, the Hawthorne Studies laid the groundwork for a meaningful correlation between 'well-being' and productivity, positing a rational link between the two concepts for the first time and disseminating this idea through research and management training. It is worth remembering that the initial goal of the experiments was 'to study the impact of fatigue, monotony and lighting on workers' productivity' (Geoffroy 2019). History has tended to portray these studies as a turning point in the way the worker's experience was understood, as they highlighted the role of social and relational motivations (sense of belonging, sympathetic management and recognition) in boosting productivity. The studies paved the way for a novel intellectual approach, known as the Human Relations Movement, which contributed to the development of research in the social sciences on the human factor in organizations. These experiments also ushered in a new era in management, which gave rise to most current managerial techniques and which led as well to the creation of the human resources function within organizations. Since the 1960s, many studies regarding these experiments have been published, shedding new critical light on the results. According to these analyses – synopses of which can been found in Lécuyer (1994) and in Geoffroy (2019) – further examination of the statistical data and careful reading of the first-hand accounts actually show that the principal determining factors of productivity are discipline, adequate break time from work and financial incentives. In other words, the results are shown not to diverge from Frederick W. Taylor's conclusions about the factors of productivity, rooted as they were in a thermodynamic theory of work. In the Hawthorne Studies, food plays a minor role, as evidenced in Geoffroy's statistical tables. It takes the form of snacks (fruit, sandwiches, soup, etc.) handed out during breaks, or else removed, according to the phases of the experiment. However, nothing in the statistical tables indicates that food was seriously studied as a variable; it seems to have been understood as a complementary benefit, available for a specific rest and recuperation period, rather than as a factor with a direct impact on productivity.

It is, however, quite surprising to think that the managerial techniques inspired by these experiments, and by the conclusions drawn from them, should have been founded on results that were scientifically erroneous, or at least exaggerated. This does not mean that the quality of social and human relations within an organization has no influence whatsoever on productivity, but it does mean that these relations were less important to the outcomes of the Hawthorne Studies than advocates of this relational approach have previously claimed. Over time, the promotion of this way of thinking has no doubt helped define the expectations and desires of managers and workers, just as the nature of work itself has been transformed, shifting 'from work centring on the physiology of muscles and nerves, to work of a "cognitive or semiotic" nature' (Rabinbach 1990: 298).[5] Whatever the case, the results of the Hawthorne Studies, by insisting on the importance of human and social relations in the workplace, clearly challenged representations of the worker derived from thermodynamics, which equated the body to an engine.

Food as fuel for a 'human motor' in search of well-being

The engine metaphor, nevertheless, is far from defunct, and can still be encountered in discourses related to food and physical activity in the workplace. No doubt this is a result of its evocative power, and the metonymic sense it creates of an obvious association between food (or exercise) and performance.

Hence the comments of the 'Mens sana in corpore sano' programme initiator at the CCI in Liège (see earlier) regarding work as an activity:

You need to be in shape to work hard. It's pretty hard to work for eight or ten hours a day. So, the healthier and more balanced your diet, the better the fuel in your body. A Formula 1 car doesn't use the stuff you get at a corner petrol station; it's not the same fuel. As for us, the only fuel we get is food. So it's just a matter of taking notice and saying, ok, my motor will perform better, and so will my brain. (interview with the author)

The dietician involved in the programme used the same metaphor in the PowerPoint presentation shown during his talk. One of the slides shows a silhouette of a petrol station pump alongside plates of food, in order to create a visual analogy.

In a similar vein, the worker is also sometimes considered as a (passive) piece of machinery. On 12 November 2019, Distrifruits, in partnership with a health insurance company (Apreva), organized an after-work event called *La joie dans l'estomac* (Delight in the stomach) at the Palais de la Bourse, which houses the Lille Chamber of Commerce. The event was hosted for various local economic stakeholders, and the exhibitors included a range of service providers in the field of health and well-being in the workplace. During the evening, time was set aside for short oral presentations by public figures concerned by this question of well-being (e.g. a local MP, a philosopher and the founder of La Fabrique Spinoza, a French association that focuses on citizens' happiness). According to a young CEO among the speakers:

> To keep things simple, I'm going to compare a business to a bike. A bike is made up of many parts and a business is made up of human beings who make it work. If the parts of the bike don't work properly, the bike won't go straight. A business is just like that! If the human beings aren't healthy, the business won't develop as it should. Can you see where I'm going with this? Today well-being is paramount, whether you are a business or an individual. So, we must ask ourselves how to make sure the parts don't deteriorate.

Without going so far as to consider the worker as a motor or a piece of machinery, the energy metaphor still plays a significant role in how professionals in the field talk about QLW (Quality of Life at Work) in general, and about food in the workplace in particular, thus demonstrating the persistent influence of thermodynamics in our conception of the individual worker. For example, Beecity, a French company that installs beehives on business premises and organizes presentations and events about honey production, states in its brochure that its mission is to 'inject energy and enthusiasm' into the workplace. As another example, the founder of Happy Quest – a business launched in 2018 which provides training in recognition, gratitude and active listening – explains in a YouTube video how he 'shifted from renewable energies to human energy to improve well-being at work'. In its handouts, Distrifruits promises something similar to prospective clients: 'We offer moments of congeniality and awareness-raising solutions which provide vitality and energy, thus boosting the well-being, health and performance of your employees.' Finally, at the event in Lille itself, the founder of La Fabrique Spinoza concluded his speech about the assessment of QLW by wondering if 'we might make use of QLW assessment as a means of generating happiness in the workplace, not as a mere academic undertaking, but to provide energy [*sic*]'.

These days it is more often well-being rather than fatigue that plays a central part in employers' conceptions of their workers and of productive activity. This is not to say that fatigue no longer matters (work-related stress, professional burnout and sleep disorders remain important subjects in French public health policy), but rather that fatigue can be subsumed into the broader paradigm of well-being.[6] Can we then say that well-being in the workplace now has the same status as fatigue did in the second half of the nineteenth century, that is to say that it represents a limit? Or, to put it more aptly, is the opposite of well-being (*mal-être*, literally 'ill-being') now seen as the key limitation to attaining the highest productivity possible, and is it thus an essential parameter for improving productivity? To a certain extent, it is possible to answer that question in the affirmative; at least this is what those who would profit from providing well-being in the workplace would have us believe. Just as the concept of fatigue inspired scientific research aiming to understand the mechanics of human work, a considerable amount of contemporary scientific research seeks to objectify well-being and to define and quantify its effects on performance (e.g. see Oswald, Proto and Sgroi 2015). This is also the core of Distrifruits' approach, which seeks to measure the links between the consumption of fruit at work, health, well-being and (indirectly) performance.

However, unlike the thinking about energy and fatigue in the nineteenth century, the conception of well-being in the twenty-first century, in terms of its link to productivity, is not – as far as we are aware – seen as a matter of social justice. The notion principally refers to individual and collective experiences, and to ways of improving them, rooted primarily in workers' bodies, minds and relationships. Its opposite, *mal-être*, is not seen as a barrier to the possibly unlimited exploitation of the workforce or a challenge to the principles of social justice. It is even quite likely that a focus on well-being is used to distract individual workers from larger issues of social justice, and to compensate for the social injustices inherent in the structures of neoliberal capitalism.

However, we should be careful not to idealize the concept of social justice that motivated certain work-related research in the late nineteenth century. Associated as it was with the idea of a 'nationalization' of the workforce's energy, social justice – such as it is described here – seems to come at the cost of a dispossession of the worker's body. When seen from this point of view, it might be argued that well-being, on the contrary, provides an opportunity for workers, via a wide range of practices, to reclaim their bodies. But nothing could be less certain. A concern for well-being, when businesses become responsible for its provision, and when it is seen as a factor in performance, can just as easily become an opportunity for employers to exert control over the lifestyles of their employees, particularly in matters of diet.

Food in the workplace: Relationships of sociability and authority

As we have seen in the work of Rabinbach (1990), in the second half of the nineteenth century, the issue of food and nutrition in the workplace was conceived in terms of the thermodynamics of the worker's body, whereby food provided energy to combat fatigue and boost productivity. As of the late 1990s and early 2000s, a group of historians specializing in the nineteenth century started focusing on the topic of food in the workplace – an area that had previously been largely overlooked – in particular in relation to the working classes. They studied it in the context of the emergence of industry and its influence on the allocation of time throughout the day for work, rest breaks and eating.

While these studies demonstrate, as did Rabinbach, that food was chiefly meant to (re)supply workers' energy, the majority also examine food in the workplace in terms of its 'social' dimension, by considering food in relation to the spaces and times set aside and organized for its consumption. In this second part, we shall continue to develop our examination of the link between food, productivity and well-being, but we will shift our attention to the social relations that are at play when people eat in the workplace, as these relations were shaped during the nineteenth century by paternalistic industries.

Food in the workplace: Social and symbolic functions

The working day is interspersed with breaks, both formal and informal, that are more or less tolerated. These breaks, which represent a time when work is suspended (Hatzfeld 2002), were originally considered by managers as moments for employees to recuperate, physically or psychologically. Such breaks are in general accompanied by the consumption of drinks and/or food, either alone or with others.

Food in the workplace was in fact first considered with regard to the restructuring of work rhythms, particularly in relation to the different types of breaks and their length, and the possibility (or not) for workers to return home during the longest breaks, depending on how far they lived from their workplace (Scholliers 1994).

In the context of the changing working conditions at the time, both in terms of the nature of work and of its temporal organization (Thompson 1967), historians have been concerned to show the political dimension of food and eating practices in factories in the nineteenth century. Businesses instrumentalized food and eating as a way of gaining further control over working time. Workplace canteens emerged and developed during the late nineteenth century, first in Great Britain and then in the rest of Europe, as the distance between the factory and workers' homes gradually increased. On the one hand, canteens correspond to a certain ideal of social progress through hygiene and good nutrition. The canteen represented a 'health benefit' imposing sets of prescriptions (zealous promotion of meat, dairy products and green vegetables, alongside bans on alcohol). On the other hand, canteens were also instrumentalized by companies to keep employees from leaving the workplace, to support ongoing efforts to rationalize working activities and to avoid any potential social conflict prompted by transformation of the rhythms of the workday. Workers were thus encouraged to avoid external socialization, perceived as potentially risky, as it allowed both the consumption of alcohol (Lhuissier 2007) and political discussion (Gacon 2014). With regard to the forms of control that employers imposed on employees' eating practices outside the home or the workplace, studies on the so-called *midinettes* (Albert 2013) – young Parisian seamstresses during the Belle Époque whose nickname derives from the observation that 'elles font la dînette à midi' (they snack/have tea parties at lunchtime) – reveal a very similar mindset. These female workers developed routines described by investigators at the time: they would eat bagged lunches in Parisian parks, eat at local restaurants or bring a ready-made lunch to the workshop. These practices were often condemned on grounds of health (an unbalanced diet) and morality (the risk of sexual encounters). As Bruegel notes (2004: 191), the first workplace canteen services (at the beginning of the twentieth century) aimed to take on a mediating role, promoting healthy food, reducing tensions in the workplace and fostering a 'family atmosphere' in the dining halls.

Yet workers show resistance to these changes. Far from general compliance, historians show that workers tended to eschew the canteen. The fact that workplace food services were symbolically linked to highly contested modifications of working rhythms meant that canteens were often deserted by workers in favour of a variety of alternative solutions outside the workplace. This historical account differs from that of historians concerned to show workers' efforts to remodel the canteen as the symbolic site of social interaction in the workplace (Gacon 2014). Historical readings thus differ starkly: some envision the canteen as an important site of sociability among workers, while for others the canteens actually only catered to a minority of employees. Whatever the case, workers always sought to make a clean break from work by distancing themselves from the workplace with symbolic gestures that might reconnect them, to a greater or lesser extent, with the domestic sphere (Gacon 2014), and they would re-establish personal structures of socialization (grouping by affinity and redistributing roles, identities and rules, in direct contrast to those constructed and fixed during periods of work). A similar observation was made by Hatzfeld (2002) in a study carried out at Peugeot's Sochaux plant. He notes that during snack breaks at the factory, workers seek to reclaim their agency.

If the most significant questions in the social sciences, particularly in the area of the sociology of work (discipline, rationalization, globalization, identity, etc.), can indeed be re-examined from the vantage point of a history of food in the workplace (Bouchet et al. 2016), we find that the canteen becomes the 'stage' crystallizing numerous issues arising from the transformations of work.

Food in the workplace within the framework of a new management theory

Starting in the late 1980s, dietary practices became the focus of a more modern form of management seeking to make employees feel more involved in the company by instilling a set of shared values and fostering conviviality as one of the key aspects of social relations in the workplace.

In the case of Peugeot's Sochaux plant, Hatzfeld clearly demonstrates that mealtimes and breaks are no longer seen by managers merely as moments of rest, health and comfort but also as opportunities to cultivate a convivial atmosphere by bringing their collective nature to the fore. Break times are synchronized (production lines are halted); break rooms become common rooms with glass partitions to allow public scrutiny and social control, while also making private conversations possible.

These questions of conviviality remain at the heart of managerial concerns today, and they still often crystallize around practices related to food in the workplace. This is illustrated by the example given earlier – the event called *La joie dans l'estomac* (Delight in the stomach) organized by Distrifruits. The event's organizers sought to convince participants that a business interested in the well-being of its staff must promote an atmosphere of conviviality surrounding food in the workplace and thus encourage employees to be more engaged.

In the meantime, managers seek to integrate break times more formally into the activities of production, to make them 'useful' and leverage them for economic gain. Thus, in many sectors, work does not always stop during the lunch break, as can be seen in the development of business lunches, formal catered lunchtime meetings or even informal ones where staff bring their own packed lunches.

Conclusion

This foray into the work of historians on the multiple links between food and work, as they have been elaborated since the mid-nineteenth century by various stakeholders in the worlds of business and industry, illustrates trends which still inform the contemporary management of food in the workplace today.

This leads us to the following considerations: first, the contemporary paradigm of 'well-being at work' now addresses questions regarding food in conjunction with both productivity and conviviality in the workplace. In this context, and as part of an economy that is now dominated by the service sector, we note – in addition to service providers already established at the beginning of the twentieth century, such as the institutional catering services described by Bruegel in 2004 – the emergence in the marketplace of new services leveraging the food aspects of well-being in the workplace for profit, and claiming to do so through conviviality and health (echoing notions influenced by thermodynamics).

Well-being has therefore become a 'catch-all' term, easily manipulated by modern managers and remaining relatively difficult for employees to challenge. It is worth noting how well-suited it is to the individualistic values of late modernity: personal development, fulfilment and self-actualization. It reveals as much about what businesses want for their employees as it does about any aspirations on the part of employees. It is also true that in certain countries, including France, the concept of well-being is directly related to specific provisions of labour law (e.g. Article L4121–1 of the French Work Code (Code du travail) states that employers must 'take the necessary measures to ensure the safety of employees and to protect their physical and mental health'; the French National Interprofessional Agreement of 2013 and the 2016 Rebsamen Law, both dealing with QLW issues; and, in Belgium, the law passed on 4 August 1996 which refers explicitly to the 'well-being of employees in the performance of their work'). But the practices associated with well-being are quite diverse and open to interpretation, and invariably synonymous with a kind of entrepreneurial humanism.

Well-being at work currently holds centre stage not only in the corporate world, where it informs a multitude of practices and discourses, but also in the media, and obviously in the practices and discourses of professionals in the field. However, the commotion that it creates, by invading the public arena, tends, as we have already suggested, to drown out, to cover up or to usurp a question that previously was much more central to the debates about work: the question of social justice (even though this idea obviously underpins the legal texts mentioned earlier). One of the most relevant benefits of this historical perspective is that it prompts us to examine issues raised by this well-being agenda through the prism of the notion of social justice.

Finally, if managers can easily manipulate the notion of well-being, so can various service providers with a vested interest in offering to boost it via the most diverse, unusual and unexpected sorts of products (such as, in the domain of food: introducing employees to beekeeping, getting them to ride 'smoothie bikes', awakening their sense of taste, teaching them to cook balanced meals, organizing convivial organic fruit themed get-togethers, introducing them to biscuits made of ground crickets or worms, etc.). This is only true because the term well-being – touted as a moral value in the corporate world, and having become the focus of a good deal of both academic and popular knowledge – is so perfectly suited to the marketplace. It carries precisely the kind of promise of a positive outcome for the individual that a product or a service should produce, a moral value readily translated into a market value. Social justice is a completely different kettle of fish. It cannot be submitted to this kind of instrumental rationalization, or to the logic of the marketplace, and remains inextricably political.

Notes

1. Translator's note: *éducateur du goût* – a French job title for a type of consultant who helps people understand and hone their sense of taste.
2. The name of the company has been invented to ensure confidentiality.
3. Chrono-nutrition is a diet based on the identification of specific types of nutrients (fats, carbohydrates, proteins, etc.) that should be ingested at specific times of the day.
4. 'Un muscle est soumis à deux influences, l'une réparatrice, la nutrition, l'autre épuisante, sa fonction motrice' (Marey 1868: 72). The translation here is the (somewhat flawed) one given in Rabinbach (1990: 133).
5. Rabinbach is quoting Pagès (1961: 110).
6. See e.g. the Lachmann Report. This was a report commissioned in 2010 by the then-prime minister François Fillon and co-signed by Henri Lachmann (chairman of the Supervisory Board of Schneider Electric), Christian Larose (vice president of the French Economic, Social and Environmental Council), Muriel Pénicaud (a former French Minister of Labour, but at the time executive vice president of Human Resources at Danone) and Marguerite Moleux (member of the French government's social affairs agency, L'inspection générale des affaires sociales). The report was called 'Bien-être et efficacité au travail: 10 propositions pour améliorer la santé psychologique au travail' (Well-being and efficiency at work: 10 proposals for the improvement of psychological health in the workplace).

Knowledge, information and mediations in tension:
A decade of food scandals and controversies

François Allard-Huver

The outbreak of bovine spongiform encephalopathy – commonly referred to as 'mad cow disease' – in the early 1990s is a founding event in the modern history of food scandals and controversies. The crisis marked generations of consumers, changed their habits and their expectations towards food and illustrated the fact that food could not be treated as just any commodity. This event also redefined the central focus of the European food system. Attention shifted from a food security approach – ensuring that everyone has enough food on their plate – to a food safety perspective – ensuring the best quality standards for food while enforcing animal health controls. Risk associated with food thus evolved from a quantitative to a qualitative issue, following the evolution of risk perception in postmodern society as described by Ulrich Beck (1986). Moreover, the mad cow disease crisis can be seen as a yardstick of modern food scandals, because it questioned the ways in which food system actors – scientists, industrial actors, retailers, consumers – construct, share and perceive food knowledge in times of crises and beyond. The last decade has witnessed an increase in food scandals and controversies, highlighting the fragility of a globally intertwined food system in which each new transgression casts doubt upon all actors. Indeed, not only do consumers demand more and more information about the food on their plate (European Commission 2012: 2), but they also show less and less trust in retailers, producers or food safety authorities to provide this information (IRSN 2018: 29). This paradoxical need for more information and distrust towards those who provide it is concomitant with other profound changes in the perception and attitudes of consumers towards food in a globalized market.

In essence we can say that consumers have a double-bind attitude when it comes to food (Bateson 1972):

1. They praise homemade cooking, yet the market share of fast food has never been higher in Europe (Aaron Allen & Associates 2018).

2. They are *neophile*, eager to try new things to eat – especially 'world cuisine' –but are, at the same time, *neophobe*, preferring tastes they already know or local products (Fumey 2016).
3. They trust farmers to provide good and reliable food (ANIA-TNS-Sofres 2013: 13) but also blame them for polluting soils, poisoning their children and jeopardizing future generations with GMOs and pesticides, leading to accusations of 'agribashing' (*L'Obs* 2019).

Media actors have also played a role in this evolution, blowing hot and cold about the food system: on the one hand, an increasing number of TV shows celebrate chefs or bakers, be they professionals (*Top Chef, MasterChef*) or amateurs (*The Great British Bake Off*), yet on the other hand, television documentaries abound which illustrate the 'dark side' of the food industry (*Cash Investigation*) or which investigate restaurants on the verge of collapse due to sanitary and business issues (*Ramsay's Kitchen Nightmares*). This ambivalent media coverage of food, running the gamut from food porn TV shows to food scare documentaries, not only leads to biased representation of the agri-food system but also indicates a certain nervousness and a growing concern regarding food in general in our societies. Indeed, in recent sanitary crises and food scandals such as the 2013 horsemeat scandal or the 2017 fipronil egg contamination incident, consumers as well as consumer associations criticized governments and industrial actors for providing confusing and incoherent data. Consumers were particularly critical of the lack of empathy shown to them, and of the minimal attempts made to reassure or at least to inform the public about the scale of the contamination and the risks to human health. Similarly, scientific experts struggle to provide trustworthy diet and nutritional guidance to 'eaters' as their studies are increasingly challenged by actors defending their own business and commercial interests. Thus, it is not only the way we perceive food that has changed but also the way we create, exchange and communicate information about food: what does it mean to be an 'eater' in these paradoxical times? Whom do consumers trust to provide healthy food? What reliable sources are available to inform consumers about the food they eat, the food they should eat or how they should eat? How is knowledge about food risk publicized, mediatized and commented on in the public sphere, especially in the context of controversies and sanitary crises?

In this chapter, we focus on three different food-related scandals which have marked the last decade. All three took place in the European Union, whose food safety system (from risk evaluation to risk management) claims to 'have the highest food safety standards in the world, based on solid science and risk assessment' (European Commission 2014). Ironically, this very ambition has exposed the European system to much criticism. Indeed, despite very strict control procedures, 'scandals' and 'frauds' have nevertheless occurred and been brought to light, with every mistake both amplified and severely judged by distrustful citizens: no less than 50 per cent of French consumers do not trust the EU and consider it unable to guarantee food safety (ANIA-TNS-Sofres 2013: 13)! Each case study questions particular aspects of food, its industry and its actors. The first crisis we consider is the 2011 *E. coli* outbreak which started in Germany and spread through Europe, causing the death of more than fifty people. The second is the so-called 'horse meat scandal' of 2013–14, a massive fraud involving various industrial actors across Europe. Finally, we focus on the 2017 fipronil egg contamination scandal. Each of these three examples illustrates a specific aspect of the way health issues regarding food are questioned in the public sphere, reported in the media and addressed by experts and food safety institutions. Using a historical and communicational perspective we explore four aspects of these scandals:

1. The first aspect is the info-documentary dimension of knowledge: food risks for health are expressed through various forms in the media including press releases, maps, speeches and the like. The actors who create, disseminate, comment upon or criticize these risks are equally varied.
2. Second, we examine the extent to which these events have not only modified the regulatory and risk assessment context but have also brought deep changes in the way food exists as a commodity in postmodern society.
3. Third, from a narratological perspective, we show how these controversies contribute to the creation of a specific discourse or a specific food narrative in the public sphere.
4. Finally, we address the emergence of new mediators who communicate during sanitary emergencies and whose discourses gain more and more publicity and trustworthiness in the public sphere, thus leading to a reorganization of the information-communication apparatus of food knowledge.

To conduct this analysis we draw on methodologies we have developed to question the circulation of 'texts' (documents, data, pictures, videos, etc.) during controversies in the ever-changing media environment (Allard-Huver and Gilewicz 2013, 2015). This methodology addresses several questions regarding the texts under study: '*Where* does the statement occur? *How* is the statement enunciated? *What* does the statement say? And *who* said it? These questions correspond to different levels of meaning: the medium, the document, the text, and the discourse, respectively' (Allard-Huver and Gilewicz 2013: 218). These questions guided our work from a methodological point of view. More precisely, for each case, we started by identifying temporal points of reference – the 'beginning' and the 'end' of the case – and by refining the choice of keywords, with the help of a search engine such as Google. After this first exploratory phase of analysis, we conducted a thorough search and selection of press articles through the press archive tool Europresse. We included French, German and English articles from national and regional news titles in our search, which allowed us to compare different narratives and cultural perspectives. After a preliminary general reading of the corpus we selected the titles most closely related to our research questions. In addition to this media corpus we also chose to include resources and documents produced by other actors involved in these controversies: third parties such as NGOs or agri-industrial actors; local and national governments; and in the case of the fipronil contamination incident, food safety authorities including the French ANSES or the European EFSA. Through this methodology, analysis of these three crises enables us to understand how, in a limited time frame and with regard to a specific issue, different actors exchange, comment upon and reconfigure food knowledge.

E. coli: Fears and foes

The 2011 *E. coli* outbreak presents all the classic 'ingredients' for successful media coverage of a sanitary crisis: a sudden disease outbreak, multiple countries and actors involved (each blaming the others), children's deaths, and just enough contradictions among officials to spread confusion or even panic among consumers. We assembled an initial corpus of more than three hundred news articles in French[1] directly relating to the crisis. On 19 May 2011, the Robert Koch Institute, Germany's national public health authority, reports the occurrence of a potential cluster of bloody diarrhoea and haemolytic uremic syndrome cases, linked to the *E. coli* O104 strain (enterohemorrhagic *E. coli*, EHEC) in the north of Germany. A wave of panic quickly spread through Europe: 'Fear Sprouts' (Sentker 2011), 'Killer Bacteria Alert' (ChassotVi 2011), 'A Mysterious Epidemic Linked to Raw Vegetable Consumption' (*NewsPress* 2011), 'Germany: A Dangerous Bacteria of Unknown Origin Causes Worry' (*La Croix* 2011). In the first week after the alert, most newspaper articles pointed out the lack of information as well as the authorities' difficulties in giving consumers clear instructions or strategies to prevent the disease. The tone of these first articles is mostly sensationalist; the focus is on the 'mystery' surrounding the first identified cases. Yet, after the initial surprise, we find an inflexion point in the last week of May 2011, when some journalists try to provide contextual information and scientific popularization about *E. coli*: what kind of bacteria it is, where it is most prevalent and the general symptoms following contamination. Soon after the beginning of the outbreak, the German Robert Koch Institute releases a new statement pointing out the possible role of 'raw vegetables', especially tomatoes, cucumbers and lettuce (RKI 2011). The institute thus recommends eating cooked rather than raw vegetables and emphasizes the importance of respecting basic *Küchenhygiene* – kitchen hygiene – rules such as washing products before eating them. These basic hygiene guidelines as well as the recommendation not to eat raw vegetables are quickly disseminated in newspapers across Europe, turning the outbreak into a vegetable paranoia: 'be wary of lettuce, cucumbers and tomatoes' (Lemaître 2011) or more precisely a cucumber scare – 'Cucumbers Blamed for 10 Deaths in Germany "Not on Sale in UK"' (Hickman and Paterson 2011) or 'Killer Bacteria Comes from Cucumbers' (*Le Matin* 2011).

While one potential vector of the disease is thus recognized, we also find that a majority (210 out of 310 French sources and more than 91 out of 230 other sources) of the newspapers focuses on the alleged 'Spanish' origin of the epidemic. Thus, the narrative shifts towards the search for a guilty party and blame is cast upon the country of origin of the presumed tainted cucumbers, Spain: 'Spanish Cucumbers from Malaga Are the EHEC Source' (Geisler 2011); 'Spanish Cucumbers Banned after *E. coli* Outbreak' (Govan 2011b); 'Spanish Cucumber Alert' (Echkenazi 2011). Several German state ministries consequently decide to ban Spanish cucumbers and encourage consumers to avoid them (Ministry for Food, Rural Affairs, and Consumer Protection 2011). What starts as a sanitary crisis quickly turns into a diplomatic feud between European countries: 'Spain has accused Germany of spreading alarm and needlessly damaging trade after blaming a deadly *E.coli* outbreak on cucumbers imported from Spain' (Govan 2011a). Yet while German authorities acknowledge the false alert regarding Spanish cucumbers as of 31 May (Hamburg 2011), French officials start to request 'complete information transparency' from both Spanish and German authorities and criticize the lack of accurate information (Lévêque 2011). Finally, as a conclusion to the mystery, the bacteria are traced back to a 2009 Egyptian *E. coli* strain and scientists suggest possible cross-contamination of products through a shipment of infected bean sprouts from Egypt (*Die Zeit* 2011). After Spanish cucumbers and other vegetables are cleared of responsibility for *E. coli*, retailers across Europe then try to reassure consumers about the safety of their products: 'Our Cucumbers Are Clear of *E. coli*, Say Supermarkets after 16 Die in Europe' (Govan and Wallop 2011). But the message was not well understood as the death toll of the outbreak kept rising in June and even affected children for the first time (*Spiegel* 2011).

While most of the four thousand cases were German, the majority of European countries were lastingly affected by the contamination and its aftermath (Frank et al. 2011). This case study illustrates several interesting points including the types of narratives that are created and disseminated during an outbreak. It helps us to comprehend how information circulates in the public sphere but also how food knowledge is reconfigured during a crisis. Our analysis shows that at the outset of the crisis some newspapers' attempts to make events understandable lead them to adopt codes and styles similar to those of fictional genres such as the detective or mystery story. Indeed, the crisis narrative starts with the mystery of the origin of the bacteria and evolves into a more complex story in which the search for a perpetrator catches the interest of newspapers. This evolution is coherent with the storytelling goal of creating an intelligible narrative out of the crisis (Quet 2015: 5). This alethurgical quest for the truth – where did the bacteria come from and how did it spread? – is soon swept away by a more trivial quest which we can describe using an actant model (Greimas 1966): Who is to be blamed? Who is the antagonist? From this point on, the need to represent and integrate the various actors and protagonists into the complex story of the crisis (Latour 1999) turns into a witch-hunt. The narratives are skewed; headlines and stories tend to over-dramatize and to stereotype, notably through the figure of the foreigner bringing disease, the 'Spanish cucumber'. Consequently, there are no heroes, only guilty and injured parties. As victims, consumers are both senders and receivers of a particular type of (food) knowledge: What can we eat safely? What should we avoid eating to be healthy? What enemies lurk in our refrigerators? This circumstantial knowledge sought by consumers during the crisis competes however with other long-term narratives related to food and health, such as those of authorities and food industry actors in their attempts to bring more vegetables to eaters' plates.

In the direct aftermath of the crisis, these narratives seem inaudible. Retailers try to reassure consumers and they propose special offers to foster sales (Bray and Faquet 2014). In France, the fresh fruits and vegetables interprofessional association (Interfel) launches a two-year communication campaign in 2012, in an attempt to change the narrative about these products through the slogan 'Envie de ...' (Desire for) promoting recipes and other positive contents (Interfel 2015). Similarly, in 2012 the British government tries to encourage vegetable and fruit consumption – the famous '5-a-day' – through a 'Responsibility Deal' with retailers (Department of Health and

Social Care 2012). Both initiatives share the same ambitions: to counter the food scare narrative but also to provide constructive elements to reassure the population. In the same way, one year after the crisis, the European Food Safety Authority issues a press release adopting the tone of a *satisfecit* and emphasizing the 'rapid response' of its task forces and their work (European Food Safety Authority 2012). Here, the authority tries to assert that, outside of the temporality of the crisis created by the media, the food safety response was appropriate and timely. Thus, two distinct narrative sequences can be distinguished here. At the beginning of the crisis, on the one hand, some media showed a clear inclination towards fearmongering and scapegoating in their treatment of the story, thus reinforcing the obtrusiveness of the issue in the public agenda. On the other hand, in the direct aftermath of the crisis, the food industry as well as institutional actors promoted more positive narratives in an attempt to mitigate the co-responsibility of all actors involved in the crisis. This first major sanitary issue of the decade shows up the fragility of public health discourse in a time of crisis and the long-term effort needed to recreate positive knowledge about food.

The horsemeat fraud: From commodification to 'food crime'

The second major food scandal of the decade was the 2013–14 horsemeat scandal. This European-wide fraud lastingly shocked consumers. It compelled the industry to reconsider food as a different kind of product, not to be defined by the logic of the capitalist market. The communication strategies rolled out by industrial actors during and after the crisis are of particular interest. In this case study, in addition to over 200 news articles,[2] we included the 'responses' and reports produced by institutional actors such as the European Commission or the Irish Department of Agriculture. Indeed, the horsemeat scandal starts in Ireland and the UK, in January 2013, when up to 30 per cent horse DNA is found in meat from hamburgers, lasagne and other frozen dishes during a regular DNA test (Department of Agriculture, Food and the Marine 2013). At the same time, fear that the meat is contaminated with phenylbutazone (an antibiotic sometimes used for horses but dangerous for humans) leads the European Commission to launch further tests: '7,259 tests were carried out by the competent authorities in the 27 EU countries … 193 revealed positive traces of horsemeat DNA (4.66%)' (European Commission 2013a). The tainted products are first found in discount stores in Europe (Aldi, Lidl, Tesco) sold under retailers' brands or, for many of them, under the Findus brand. Again, consistent with the need to find a guilty party in the crisis narrative and to present every crisis as if it were a police inquiry, some journalists from the BBC or *La Tribune* quickly name the fraud the 'Findus affair'[3]: 'Findus Affair: On the Trail of Suspect Horse Meat' (Torre 2013a), 'Findus Beef Lasagne Contained Up to 100% Horsemeat, FSA Says' (BBC 2013). However, the company is rapidly exonerated. The source of the fraud is determined to have been two 'dealers' who sold horse meat from Romanian slaughterhouses. This meat is later relabelled as beef meat with the complicity of a French producer, Spanghero. The latter then sells the tainted meat to

Comigel, a subsidiary producing different dishes for Findus, Aldi, Lidl or Tesco. At this point, the narratives of the scandal shift from a search for the 'perpetrator' to a 'denunciation' of the food production system and its excesses.

The info-documentary forms used to illustrate this story are also interesting; with the help of maps, lists, guides or illustrations, newspapers try to decipher and illustrate the intricacies and the complexity of the food industry: 'Agri-Food, the Strange Supply Chain of Findus' (Déniel 2013), 'Horsemeat Scandal: The Essential Guide' (Lawrence 2013) or 'Which Products and Distributors Are Impacted?' (*Tageschau* 2013). Others stress the crude reality of a globalized food market: 'For a Lasagne Dish, Two Traders, Four Companies, Five Countries' (Bran and Girard 2013) or the gloominess of the agri-food production processes: 'Ring of Steel, High Chimneys and Few Windows: Horse Meat Lasagne Factory Revealed … The huge Comigel food production plant in Luxembourg looks like a cross between a prison and a crematorium' (Collins 2013). The sordid nature of the frozen food business is underscored in multiple articles. Interestingly, these articles bring to light the 'newspeak' of the agro-food industry: 'mechanically separated meat' sold as 'frozen blocks of meat' or in the French industry jargon 'beef ore', *minerai de boeuf* (Observatoire des aliments 2013)! This deconstruction of meat, its transformation into a commodity like any other, is what made the labelling fraud possible. The commodification of meat inevitably 'obscure[s] the concrete reality of [its] production' (Watters 2015: 8) and provides fraud opportunities in a globalized food system where one lasagne dish involves more than five intermediaries. However, the institutional response is of a different nature and promotes an altered discourse about the scandal.

The response of officials to the horse meat scandal is in fact twofold: it consists, on the one hand, in reassuring the public about the sanitary issue and, on the other, in reducing the problem to a question of fraud. Authorities and European institutions seek in fact to reassure consumers as quickly as possible and to prove that the food is safe to eat: 'The Commission and national food authorities have, however, underlined that up to now there is no evidence of a health risk to consumers from horsemeat' (Sheil 2013). Following test results, the European Commission reaffirms the 'low concern for consumers' and asserts that the probability of developing health problems 'was estimated to range approximately from 2 in a trillion to 1 in 100 million' (European Commission 2013a). The Irish food safety authority, the first to have revealed the adulteration of meat, while stressing that the problem is not a sanitary one ('this is not a food safety or indeed a food quality issue') stresses the food market reputational issue: 'Food business operators have a responsibility not alone to place only safe food on the market but to ensure the quality and authenticity of the products it is selling' (Department of Agriculture, Food and the Marine 2013: 15). Furthermore, Minister for Agriculture Simon Coveney emphasizes the importance of consumers' trust and the responsibility of all agri-food actors in this process: 'Consumer confidence and trust is the most vital component of our policy relating to the broad food industry. Without consumer confidence and trust there is no future for any of the participants in the food supply chain whether they are retailers, processors, traders or primary producers' (Department of Agriculture, Food and the Marine 2013: 3–4). Moreover, for the European Commission spokesman, Frederic Vincent, the fact that the meat was safe calls for a completely different approach to the affair: 'We're not talking about a food safety issue ... Nobody got sick as far as I know. It's just a labelling issue' (McPartland 2013). Here, we have the second institutional response: an effort to frame the scandal as the result of a 'labelling' fraud or a 'mislabelling'. Just prior to the twentieth anniversary of the 'mad cow' outbreak, it seemed necessary to assert the efficiency and diligence of the different sanitary authorities. Occasionally, using a Q&A format, the European Commission tries to pin responsibility on 'large scale, cross-border fraudulent schemes that take advantage of the weaknesses of an increasingly globalized food supply' (European Commission 2013b). For some European officials, the entire scandal was to be considered a simple case of fraud committed by individuals outside the industry seeking to take advantage of loopholes; this explanation thus exonerates sanitary authorities as well as the entire agri-food business.

However, we also find dissonant discourse regarding this affair. In his report for the British government, Professor of Food Safety Chris Elliot denounces the emergence of 'food crime' while sharply criticizing the excesses of an industry rendered 'highly susceptible to fraudulent interference' by dubious products: 'The less fat visible in frozen blocks of smaller pieces of meat including "trim", the higher quality the meat trim is judged to be. Lower quality trim can be made to look like higher quality trim by the addition of lean meat such as red offal (e.g. heart, lungs), lean meat from cheaper species, or lean meat reclaimed from meat not suitable for human consumption' (Elliot 2014: 45). Hence, for some members of the European Parliament including Sophie Auconie, EU regulations are strong enough; the problem stems rather from industrial actors' fraudulent actions or the complacency of certain states: 'In reality the problem does not reside in a lack of rules but in the fact that they are not respected, and therefore a lack of control of the rules in certain member states. ... In the face of increasingly long supply chains within the agri-food business, it is absolutely essential to increase the means of control that authorities have over the food chains' (*Euractiv* 2013). The info-documentary forms chosen by European officials (reports, studies, statements, etc.) translate the way food is perceived in a risk management-oriented technocratic culture (Jasanoff 1986). Food safety is framed by European actors in a positivist perspective: there is no need to regulate the food production system, no need to amend its most incongruous practices because more tests, more science, more expertise can and will reduce risks (Sheil 2013). One cannot help but notice that this worldview – which regards food as a risk management question – is in utter contradiction with consumers' mistrust of the positivist ideology advocated by technocrats (Luhmann 2003). The official response, while exonerating risk managers, does not, however, ignore the need for a blaming narrative; responsibility is thus placed on industrial actors. How did these actors react to such accusations?

One of the most interesting communication strategies during the crisis was the one adopted by Findus. As one of the key protagonists in the scandal, Findus manages to take a stand not only as a victim of the fraud but also as a 'whistleblower'. Following the revelation of the presence of horse meat in its prepared meals, more than a hundred press articles across Europe directly associate the Swedish company with the scandal: 'The "Findus Affair" Frightens Consumers' (Bran and Girard 2013), 'Findus Leak Reveals Horse in "Beef" for Six Months' (Hickman 2013) or 'Horsemeat

Lasagne Scandal Leaves Findus' Reputation in Tatters' (Neville 2013). Nevertheless, the manufacturer publishes numerous press releases attesting that it was Findus's DNA tests that had helped uncover the fraud (Lentschner 2013). In an interview, Matthieu Lambeaux, Findus's South Europe CEO, stresses the injustice of the media treatment, and declares that Findus was 'pilloried' (Jullien 2013: 34). The manufacturer launches a website dedicated to 'transparency' and registers the 'Findus, in full transparency' brand as a response to the crisis. As suggested by the philosopher Gianni Vattimo, current postmodern society can be seen as searching for a 'transparent society', especially regarding the role of the media in the circulation of information (Vattimo 1992). By setting 'transparency' – repeated more than six times by Findus's CEO – as the axiological standard in its response to this crisis, the company tries to provide a positive discourse. Findus seeks as well to reaffirm this stance through multiple 'commitments' made to reassure consumers: the exclusive use of French beef (in France), promise of more DNA tests, creation of a direct contact line and so on. But the company also conducts more aggressive and paradoxical communication actions in order to 'clean' the web and restore its reputation. This leads some media to react in protest against the pressures from the company: '*La Tribune*, like many other digital media, was asked by the agency ReputationSquad to change three titles referring to Findus. We decided not to accede to this request. … We understand very well the inconvenience that information malleability can generate. Unfortunately, this is the necessary counterpart for respecting history, for refusing to rewrite it. Values for which we believe there can and should be unanimity' (Torre 2013b). Notwithstanding Findus's defense strategy, the food industry tries to restore consumers' trust by suggesting 'country of origin' labelling on meat products; if adopted, this proposal would reintroduce the geographic specificity of foods in a globalized world. Interestingly enough, when industry actors suggest this idea, the European Commission is the first to oppose it: 'The Commission wants to be clear that country of origin labelling cannot be considered as the tool to prevent fraudulent practices' (European Commission 2013b). Again, we find here the idea – seen as a superior axiological principle – that food is a commodity in a liberalized market requiring minimal state intervention. According to this view, the origin of composition of foods as commodities does not matter: only the 'brand' of the final product matters. Food is seen as a commodity whose success story should not be tainted by the mere 'hiccup' of a massive international and globalized fraud.

The 2017 fipronil egg contamination scandal: The rise of new mediators

In the summer of 2017, Belgium alerts its European partners to a possible contamination of eggs by a prohibited pesticide, fipronil. In this case study we focus on texts produced as part of the official and institutional responses of the French government and on the actions of one European NGO that is particularly active during the crisis, Foodwatch. Starting from a chicken farm in the Netherlands, the contamination quickly affects Germany and France as well as other European countries and leads to the withdrawal of several million eggs. Egg products such as waffles, pasta and other processed foods are also severely impacted by the contamination (IRSN 2018). While a first alert notification is issued in late June, authorities and industrial players, especially in France, take a long time to provide significant and transparent information about the scope of the contamination. In France, consumers wait until August to have access to the first official list of contaminated products, only published after multiple denials by the DGAL – the French Ministry of Agriculture and Food – claiming the absence of contamination in France. In addition, no risk assessment is conducted until mid-August to determine the potential hazards for humans consuming tainted eggs, even though fipronil belongs to a category of controversial pesticides. The DGAL's response to the crisis, difficult to find on its website, is hasty as well as sometimes confusing (DGAL 2017c). The first press release, dated 7 August, seems to exclude contamination in France: 'French authorities do not, to date, have information on contamination of eggs' (DGAL 2017a). However, one day later, a new press release contradicts the previous one and acknowledges that France is also affected: 'Five egg product establishments … received contaminated eggs from the Netherlands and Belgium' (DGAL 2017d). When the DGAL tries to minimize its responsibility by claiming that it was not aware of any contamination until 5 August, it creates in fact more confusion about the crisis and engenders doubts over the government's ability to protect consumers. Moreover, while everywhere else in Europe governments demand answers from the agro-food industry, the French government seems at best ignorant: 'The ministry was not able to say immediately if the products in question were found in businesses … "We are investigating", a ministry spokesperson told AFP' (*Le Figaro* 2017) and at worst, engaged in a cover-up: 'The Laying Hens Scandal Nipped in the Bud' (Daumin 2017). Even worse, when the French minister of Food and Agriculture speaks for the first time about the crisis, he shows that his priority is business before consumers: 'I wish to express my support for French companies which are victims of fraudulent practices. I agree to continue the investigations and to make all the information we have at our disposal available to consumers' (DGAL 2017b). Adopting a tone of reassurance for business actors, the minister addresses consumers using a strictly informative register.

The second aspect of the French officials' response is to transform what could be seen by the public as a sanitary scandal into a simple 'risk management story'. Work on creating an informative narrative is thus handed over to the ANSES – the French food safety authority. The ANSES is tasked by the government with analysing eggs, producing reports and reassuring consumers. The documents produced by the ANSES, although written in clear and comprehensible language, nonetheless require knowledge of food safety evaluation processes as well as scientific literature on risk: 'percentile', 'Quantity in g/kg body weight/day', or 'acute reference dose (ARfD)' (ANSES 2017: 2–3). Thus, while the media speak about a 'forbidden insecticide', raising the spectre of 'contamination' and 'potential neurotoxic effects', the food safety authority responds with 'scenarios' and 'maximal exposure limits': 'consumer exposure remains inferior to the acute reference dose based on a maximalist scenario' (ANSES 2017: 4). In its 2017 Annual Report, completely satisfied with this technical response, the ministry addresses itself a *satisfecit* regarding 'the fipronil in eggs case' stating that 'the management of this crisis has been marked by a concern for transparency towards the consumer' (DGAL 2018). This response is, however, in total contradiction to consumers' expectations: not only does the ministry try to spare industrial actors, providing outdated lists of tainted products (Rosenweg 2017) but is also inept at explaining the situation and offers completely inaccurate information to citizens: 'The authorities do not fully play transparency, since they do not communicate the [contamination] level observed for each sample analyzed' (Richard 2017). Here again we find a discrepancy between the chosen communication strategy and the target audience. In addition, this case illustrates how scientific institutions and experts struggle to popularize their discourse and how food authorities struggle as well to provide both transparent information and narratives that can reassure eaters.

Noting the government's inability to provide reliable information, consumers turn to other actors, new mediators to help them make choices during the crisis, such as the advocacy group Foodwatch: 'a non-profit campaigning organization that fights for safe, healthy and affordable food for all people' (Foodwatch 2020). Created in 2002 in Germany, the association has since opened offices in the Netherlands (2009) and in France (2013). Similar to other watchdog NGOs, Foodwatch aims at 'provid[ing] an important counterweight to the power of the food industry ... by conducting research, exposing scandals, mobilizing consumers and lobbying governments' (Foodwatch 2020). During the 2017 fipronil egg contamination scandal, the consumer association manages to push forward its narrative of an opaque and dishonest agro-food industry system in collusion with the authorities. The NGO also puts the question of transparency at the centre of the scandal and provides citizens with an alternative information source. First, in a succession of press releases, the association produces the narrative of a dishonest and secretive system: 'Does the fipronil egg contamination scandal spare France? Foodwatch asks the question and demands answers, on behalf of consumers who have the right to know' (Foodwatch 2017d), or '[French authorities] refuse to communicate the names of the companies concerned. An opacity denounced by Foodwatch' (Foodwatch 2017c). Then, in a letter sent to the DGAL, the consumer association pushes the idea that transparency is in fact not at the heart of the government's handling of the crisis: 'Foodwatch asks you again to communicate in a completely transparent manner all information about the measures taken, the extent of tests carried out, both by the administration and by companies, their detailed results, etc.' (Foodwatch 2017b). Finally, the NGO produces a two-pronged info-documentary apparatus to inform and mobilize consumers on this issue. On the one hand, it publishes and archives all tainted product lists on its website – the DGAL website showing only the latest version. On the other hand, it launches a petition – both an information medium and an empowerment tool – to request 'the truth' about the scandal. While disseminating information and communicating about the issue, the petition also places eaters in an active position: by signing and sharing the petition on social media, they are no longer passive consumers waiting to be 'spoon-fed' what little information others want to share, but they become actors of the system, requesting the 'truth'. With more than 50,000 signatures collected in a few weeks (Foodwatch 2017a), the petition was undeniably a success for Foodwatch, thus reaffirming eaters' willingness to make their voices heard.

Conclusion

Scandals have redefined the way we perceive and understand food and how we produce knowledge about food. In the last decade, these crises have brought to light the complex intricacies – and opacities – that link every actor in the food industry system from food safety experts to retailers, from media actors to eaters. In an increasingly complex and globalized system, where the commodification of food has been pushed to its limits, the slightest crisis quickly turns into a 'scandal'. The main question is no longer who will assess risks or co-construct knowledge for eaters, but who is at fault and who is to blame. Although not specifically part of our focus here, the posture of industry and mass retailers during these crises is often symptomatic of this growing mistrust. For instance, we noted in our corpus the harsh exchanges between retail actors such as Michel Edouard Leclerc, CEO of Leclerc retail group and Jean-Philippe Girard, head of the French agro-industry lobby ANIA, in which each makes himself out to be a victim of the crisis, claims to be a paragon of transparency and, of course, accuses others of opacity (ANIA 2017; Leclerc 2017). Thus, the lack of a quick and clear response from health authorities often amplifies the confusion surrounding the extent of the contamination and its real or supposed impacts on health. This has led many consumers to turn to other actors to obtain more 'transparent' information. These new knowledge mediators use and produce other info-documentary forms to alert and inform citizens. They exploit the potential of digital media and alternative means of publicization, such as petitions and social media, to provide alternative information but also to criticize institutional responses. The rise of these mediators sheds light on new and different processes at play in the production of food knowledge, just as it indicates the failure of institutional actors in this domain. The DGAL's response during the 2017 fipronil crisis provides a remarkable example of how, in a digital media culture focused on the rapid circulation and mediatization of information, and characterized by media buzz and virality, officials' old habits can become counterproductive. Indeed, in postmodern society, transparency has become both the heart of public demands and the axiology of institutional accountability. Moreover, in the post-truth era, mistrust is heightened by a 'context of growing suspicion of collusion between experts and industrial lobbies regarding food and agriculture' (IRSN 2019: 17). The loss of confidence in traditional food information mediators seems more pronounced than ever. The rise of the new mediators whom we have identified in this study and in other publications (Allard-Huver 2016, 2019) is the direct consequence of growing concern in public opinion reported by the media as well as a worrying lack of understanding between authorities and civil society actors such as Foodwatch. All of these crises show that producing fast and reliable information about food is a complex and difficult problem, giving rise to competing narratives attempting to win the battle of public opinion.

This decade of food scandals and controversies has intensified the divide between different visions, definitions, even *Weltanschauungs* of food. On the one hand, those upholding the idea that food is a commodity like any other. For proponents of this vision, food should be regulated, liberalized and commercialized like any other product such as a car or a television. When crisis strikes, the first reflex of these actors is to secure the trust of customers – not eaters – and to protect the reputation of the agri-food business. The best way to ensure the circulation of food as a standardized commodity is thus to create a techno-scientific system ensuring the safety of the products and guaranteeing standards for consumers. The economic system completely relies on a positivist risk management apparatus. According to this world vision, knowledge produced about food always takes on the info-documentary shape of reports, referrals, assessments, evaluations and similar technocratic totems. On the other hand, some actors defend the idea that food cannot, never has been and never should, be seen as a commodity. For these actors, food as well as cuisines are not products of an industry but carry the historic, geographic and symbolic weight of the culture from which they emerged (Levi-Strauss 1970). For these actors, country of origin labelling is not seen as an impediment to free market circulation but as a guarantee which shows the respect of standards inherited from practices steeped in local traditions of a given *terroir*. Even industrial actors and global players such as Findus understood the need to reaffirm this geographic reality. In this *Weltanschauung*, information mediators and civil society actors do not deny the role of food safety authorities but ask for more transparency in their risk evaluation processes – especially regarding controversial issues such as pesticides, endocrine disruptors or GMOs. They also ask for more mediators facilitating communication and playing the role of watchdogs. Finally, if each of these crises has redefined the way we *think* about food, they likewise have invited eaters to face the contradictions of the system in which they themselves participate. As some commentators of the horse meat scandal have pointed out, one cannot expect to pay 30p for a burger when its real price is closer to £1 (Lang 2013); one cannot expect the agro-food industry to protect the rainforest while still consuming Nutella hazelnut spread and not commercially boycotting brands using palm oil (Allard-Huver 2016). Crises and scandals are merely the symptom of a more complex violation of what food knowledge has taught us over generations: food is at the cornerstone of our culture and should not be trifled with for the sake of profit or convenience. As Freud once explained: 'the violated taboo itself took vengeance' (Freud 2012: 20); the last decade undoubtedly proved him right.

Notes

1. Europresse, from 1 April 2011 to 31 July 2011, keywords 'e-coli' and 'epidemic' (or *épidémie*): 316 (France), 230 (Europe without France).
2. Europresse, from 1 January 2013 to 1 March 2013, keyword 'horsemeat' (or *viande de cheval*): 103 (France) and 127 (Europe without France).
3. Europresse, from 1 January 2013 to 1 March 2013, keyword (head title) 'findus': 83 (France) and 26 (Europe without France).

This decade of food scandals and contamination has undermined the divide between

Part 2

Uses and appropriations of 'eating knowledge' in everyday practices

As we have seen in Part 1 of this book, an increasingly diverse array of messages and knowledge about food and eating are made available today. How are these messages perceived, interpreted and used? How do professional and non-professional knowledge mediators participate in the creative transfer of food knowledge? How are nutritional, medical and cultural norms and *doxa* reinforced, reworked or challenged?

Part 2 of the book explores the active appropriation of food knowledge by different actors in a range of contexts and spheres: education, advertising, medicine and health. As the authors show, knowledge appropriation is not a linear process of dissemination: individuals and institutions interpret, 'translate' and reorganize sources of information in a dynamic process.

In European countries such as France and Spain, new food knowledge mediators emerge as part of governmental health initiatives, publishing and advertising projects, changes in the medical profession as well as from bottom-up citizen-run educational and culinary activities. On the one hand, state-run or state-appointed information agencies and publishers are mandated to implement nutritional and education policy and curricular objectives through public service campaigns and teaching resources. Publishing and communication professionals as well as teachers work to make national health measures, educational programmes and their scientific underpinnings both understandable and acceptable to citizens. On the other hand, in the medical field, dieticians and other health educators now occupy an important position, recognized both academically and socially in Europe, from which to experiment new ways of informing and teaching patients about nutritional norms and practices. In addition, food advertising professionals use, reformulate and promote knowledge about new scientific and technological advances, thus playing a key role in the popularization of scientific discovery about food. Individuals create and reformulate specialized knowledge as well: patients and parents for example are keenly motivated to develop and share their own knowledge, be it theoretical or practical, through strategic information practices.

The transposing of scientific discourse for the general public or for one's peers, clients, patients or pupils is not merely a question of simplifying texts and rewriting difficult jargon using palatable words and attractive images. Food knowledge mediators select and weave together discourses, often creating a hybrid of old and new scientific messages and paradigms as well as popular wisdom. This process of appropriation inevitably introduces value systems and ideological biases. Translating health and education policy into practical guidelines, for example, is fraught with ambiguity: public nutritional guidelines tend to promote ideal standardized behaviours that can reinforce social inequalities. In addition, government information campaigns rely heavily on coercive communication strategies based on the notion of rational choice: individuals are expected to adhere to nutritional norms and are seen as both willing and able to modify their own eating practices to meet their needs. In Foucaultian terms, this rational choice approach to food knowledge transfer, characteristic of biopolitical modernity, is a way of responsibilizing citizens for their own well-being.

Dieticians and other medical professionals as well as teachers, patients, parents and pupils, increasingly call into question top-down transmissive and dogmatic approaches to learning and information about food and nutrition. For science teachers and other school education mediators, as well as for dieticians, this means recognizing the interpretive paradigms and cultural knowledge about food that pupils and patients bring with them, in order to avoid inculcative teaching methods while promoting reasoned co-creation of knowledge. Individuals are also increasingly involved in knowledge production allowing them to make decisions about their own food and health choices and medical diagnosis and treatment. New forms of social practice such as food blogging and community culinary activism attest to the emergence of alternative food pedagogies and renewed food information and communication strategies, conceived as countermeasures to governmental, medical and corporate prescribed eating behaviours. Differing discursive domains have also become increasingly porous due in part to new media and collaborative spaces of exchange which encourage hybridization and decompartmentalization of knowledge as well as new modes of socialization. These collaborative spaces for knowledge creation and sharing are designed to provide a sense of agency to individuals and families and to legitimize their experiences as sources of expertise.

These changes have consequences for the way that food cultures, traditions and beliefs are incorporated and lived out through social practice and shared commitments. Yet such creative bricolage and bottom up practices are not a guarantee of democratized access to, and use of, food information and knowledge. Challenging traditional forms of food information and knowledge production may offer possibilities for reform and renewal of food and media literacies and may also contribute to the ways that individuals perceive, construe and combine medical advice, corporate and media-based discourse and popular wisdom with regard to food. However, new food communication and information initiatives are also sources of tension and conflict which question individual and collective social, professional and political identities and alliances.

From disciplining bodies to patient education: Changing diabetics' eating habits in the nineteenth and twentieth centuries

Vincent Schlegel

Introduction

What should diabetics eat to keep their blood sugar at precise levels and how can caregivers foster compliance with nutritional guidance? Since researchers first established the link between food and diabetic symptoms two centuries ago, these questions have stimulated much debate within the medical field. Diabetes is a chronic condition characterized by consistently high blood sugar levels that can trigger many long-term complications such as retinopathy, neuropathy or cardiovascular disease. Nowadays, the management of diabetes consists mainly of insulin injections or oral anti-diabetics in conjunction with changes in lifestyle.[1] To ensure patient compliance, the current situation in France emphasizes the development of 'therapeutic patient education' (TPE) programmes. These programmes organize patients' training by providing them with complete knowledge and know-how about diabetes so that they can self-manage. In practice, people with diabetes can participate in individual or group workshops on various aspects of diabetes management, such as treatments, nutrition or physical activity.

One way to understand the development of diabetic patient education is to see it as a consequence of new medical knowledge, particularly the discovery of insulin at the beginning of the twentieth century. However, the history of dietary prescriptions for people with diabetes shows that educational practices existed long before the discovery of this treatment although such patient education remained largely informal until the 1970s. While various kinds of dietary practice have been promoted since the middle of the nineteenth century, both their content and the methods of ensuring that patients follow nutritional prescriptions have significantly evolved throughout the twentieth century. On the one hand, people with diabetes have been exposed to a wide range of dietary prescriptions, from a starvation diet to a balanced one. On the other hand, ideal methods of changing the eating habits of diabetic patients have taken various forms over the last two centuries, ranging from disciplinary methods to pedagogical approaches.

This chapter traces gradual transformations in dietary prescriptions from exterior constraints imposed by medical staff on diabetic patients to self-constraint through the development of patient training. The first section focuses on the long-standing controversies about diabetic diets. While patient education was discussed long before the discovery of insulin, physicians advocated for contrasting approaches to ensure patient compliance with prescribed diets. Nutritional norms became gradually more flexible. The second section offers an overview of the current French situation. We show that while nutritional self-control is now the norm, its underlying logic differs according to specific TPE programmes. While quantified restraint remains the preferred option, self-control based on bodily sensations sometimes presents itself as a 'natural' and more effective solution to controlling one's diet and body weight. Regardless of the type of self-control promoted, there are class-based discrepancies in the reception of nutritional recommendations.

Our study is based on two methodologies. The first section relies on existing work on the history of diabetes, with analysis of selected books, articles and lay literature related to diabetic care and education published in France between 1850 and 2015. The second section draws upon an ethnographic study of three different TPE programmes for diabetics in France, as well as interviews with medical staff (n = 33) and programme participants (n=21). The first programme takes place in a rehabilitation service of a public hospital where patients are admitted for four consecutive weeks; whereas in the second programme, participants are hospitalized for only one week and the programme is administered by a unit dedicated to educational activities in another care facility. Most people entering these two programmes belong to the working class or the lower middle class, and their diabetes is poorly controlled. An association led by healthcare providers supports the third programme. Participants are considered 'users' and not 'patients', meaning that they can attend workshops of their own volition. They usually belong to the upper middle class or upper class, and their diabetes is generally under control. In each programme, dieticians[2] direct most of the nutritional workshops.

From disciplining patients to patient self-control: The evolution of nutritional prescriptions for diabetics

Once the relationship between food consumption and sugar levels in the urine was established, this offered new therapeutic perspectives to physicians. At the beginning of the twentieth century, when various experiments revealed the diet's potential to keep patients alive, medical prescriptions to ensure patient compliance tended to become progressively more rigid. However, the discovery of insulin profoundly altered the landscape of diabetic care. Diabetes became a 'transmuted disease', as it was transformed from an acute to a chronic condition, reshaping the experience of diabetes for those who suffered with it (Feudtner 2003). Self-control was progressively promoted through systematic patient information and education. While physicians across the world debated the respective roles of insulin and diet in diabetes therapy, some began to think about the best way to educate patients within a broader context of promoting patient autonomy.

Body surveillance and coercion of patients before insulin

In the middle of the seventeenth century, Thomas Willis was the first to notice that the urine of diabetic patients contained an abnormal level of sugar (Presley 1991). Although his finding shed light on one of the main features of diabetes, it did not offer any clues as to how diabetics should be treated. A century later, the British surgeon John Rollo became the first medical professional to relate food intake and diabetes (Mauck 2010). Rollo concluded that diabetes resulted from an overworked stomach during digestion which led to increased blood sugar levels (Rollo 1798). Though he incriminated the wrong organ, he made a decisive step towards the care of people with diabetes by recommending a diet consisting of rancid meat rather than vegetables. He furthermore forbade carbohydrate and alcohol intake among patients. Thus, until the nineteenth century, little was known about diabetes, and no real treatment was available (Presley 1991). Therefore, a diabetes diagnosis was often fatal.

Though diabetes is often associated with the name of the French physiologist Claude Bernard – who is known for providing a quantitative definition of diabetes based on an excessive presence of sugar in the blood (Sinding 2005) – he did not make any relevant contribution to diabetic care. By contrast, his contemporary, the French pharmacist Apollinaire Bouchardat played a crucial role in the treatment of diabetes in the middle of the nineteenth century. His knowledge of chemistry combined with his strong beliefs in the principles of hygiene led him to refine Rollo's diet (Bouchardat 1875). Bouchardat focused on the daily consumption of carbohydrates which, he noticed, increased urinary sugar levels. In addition to a strict diet, he recommended that patients practice regular physical activity which fosters carbohydrate assimilation. Bouchardat also developed an easy way to test sugar in urine by mixing it with an alkaline solution and boiling it. The mixture would change its colour in the presence of sugar. For more than fifty years, a strict diet was the only way to extend a patient's life. Reducing quantities of carbohydrates soon became the cornerstone of such prescribed diets. Yet, physicians across the world debated the appropriate amount of carbohydrates, proteins and fat to prescribe to diabetic patients. In the United States, Frederik M. Allen and Eliott P. Joslin, two world-renowned diabetologists, popularized the use of a starvation diet (Feudtner 2003), which became widespread before the introduction of insulin. They prescribed a low-calorie diet, drastically reducing the volume of food to be consumed.

As diets were increasingly stringent, medical staff started looking for new ways to enhance patients' compliance. Managing diabetes was correlated to a moral lifestyle typical of some segments of the population, namely the white middle and upper class (Lecorché 1893). The fact that physicians mostly came from these social groups contributed to the dissemination of negative statements about obesity as a loss of self-control (O'Donnell 2015). A practising Protestant, Joslin published a book in 1913 that outlined recommendations imbued with religious principles (Feudtner 2003).

According to him, patients needed to possess moral qualities such as 'honesty', 'self-control' and 'courage', if they wished to manage the disease. In France, Ernest Monin similarly stated that the 'moral quality of patients' was more important than 'the scientific quality of the physician' (Monin 1896: 16). Among the leading physicians involved in diabetes care across the world, Allen (the United States), Cantani (Italy), and Naunyn (Germany) suggested confining people with diabetes to monitor their glycosuria, or urinary sugar, as well as their compliance to the prescribed diet (Mauck 2010; Presley 1991). In France, Guillaume Guelpa proposed that diabetes could be 'cured' if patients followed a strict diet, including long periods of fasting (Guelpa 1911). The efficacy of his regime was proven when he took a young patient into his own home; the patient's condition improved after a period of confinement. Although the dissemination of such methods of care during the pre-insulin era remained uncertain, the medical management of diabetes took on the characteristics of what Foucault would later call disciplinary practices. Close medical bodily surveillance, strict control of diet and punishment through food privation were all used to suppress glycosuria. Indeed, the absence of urinary sugar (aglycosuria) became the norm to reach (Sinding 2006). Glycosuria could easily be tested after Bouchardat's pioneering work, and any deviation could thus be objectified and punished accordingly. While coercion was by far the favoured option at that time, some physicians – including Bouchardat and Joslin – emphasized that medical professionals should educate diabetics about their disease. Nonetheless, they were more focused on the composition of the diet than on its implementation.

The discovery of insulin and the slow evolution of dietary prescriptions

The discovery of insulin in 1922 in Toronto was the result of decades of clinical and laboratory work (Bliss 1982). While most physicians considered the stomach (following Rollo) and the liver (following Bernard) to be the main organs responsible for diabetes, experiments conducted in France and Germany at the end of the nineteenth century shed light on a new organ that proved to be responsible for diabetes: the pancreas. Of interest were cells in the pancreas that secreted a hormone later called insulin, but whose precise role was somewhat uncertain at that time.[3] At the beginning of the twentieth century, Frederik Banting together with Charles Best, John James Rickard Macleod and Bertram Collip began to work on laboratory experiments to extract this hormone from dogs. After years of unsuccessful attempts to isolate insulin, they finally succeeded, and Leonard Thompson became the first patient to receive insulin successfully.

While some physicians were initially reluctant to leave patients to deal with insulin themselves, because of the medical skills required and the new risk of hypoglycaemia, they were forced to acknowledge the need for patients to manage treatment on their own. Although insulin is one of the major medical breakthroughs of the century, its worldwide availability did not mitigate the problems raised about its standardized production (Sinding 2002) or the transmutation of diabetes into a chronic ailment (Feudtner 2003). Maintaining the ultimate goal of an absence of glycosuria, physicians across the world promoted tailored diets based on close body monitoring. Physicians prescribed specific dosages of insulin while slowly increasing quantities of carbohydrates that could be consumed. Fat and proteins were progressively reintroduced into diets as they enabled adequate growth, especially among children.

Since diabetes was no longer a matter of life and death, physicians started paying attention to the social and psychological aspects of daily management of the disease, in line with their more frequent interactions with diabetic patients (Moore 2018). Most health care workers acknowledged that a significant element of daily diabetes management occurred far from their purview; this meant that patients were unable to visit a doctor or nurse several times a day at the hospital. Consequently, the use of disciplinary methods became more and more inappropriate. Still, physicians and nurses had to ensure that patients would be safe when injecting insulin by offering training during patient visits. The principle medical concern surrounding the nutritional aspects of the disorder was determining the best diet or the precise quantity of each food patients should eat. In other words, medical staff still imposed a specific diet.

Yet some initiatives resulted in the formalization of patient training. An example is the 'social service' initiated by Marcel Labbé at La Pitié-Salpêtrière Hospital (Paris) (Labbé 1933). In terms of organization, Labbé set up a 'therapeutic kitchen' aimed at developing the best diet for patients (Marchand 2014). Food was weighed and carefully prepared according to tailored medical prescriptions. Visiting nurses oversaw the 'anti-diabetic education' which mainly consisted of teaching patients how to control urine sugar levels and inject insulin, but also how to decide what they should eat, the exact composition of meals and how to compose their diet. Medical staff provided patients with a curriculum that served as a temporary substitute for what Bourdieu (1980) called the 'practical sense' for the period before they had fully incorporated medical advice.[4] Aside from patients' frequent visits, visiting nurses checked on them at their homes to make sure that they did not lack for anything (insulin, injecting devices, etc.).

However, this experimental therapy was rarely taken up in France for a period of almost fifty years – in contrast to Britain, where outpatient clinics were developed (Moore 2018). While there is evidence that the social service had some longevity at La Pitié-Salpêtrière (Uhry 1951), the institution's specific organization which combined social medicine, laboratory experiments and clinical wards within the same location was not easily reproducible in other French hospitals at the time. From 1939 onwards, the absence of visiting nurses in charge of most educational tasks also made it necessary to hand over patient education to other institutions.[5] While physicians specializing in the care of diabetics agreed that patients should be provided with knowledge regarding their disease (Chabanier and Lobo-Onell 1938; Mauriac 1941; Uhry 1951), they remained vague as to how to go about doing so.

Several reasons might explain the limited interest in formalizing patient training. On the one hand, there is evidence to suggest that patient education was more developed in outpatient clinics than in hospital settings. Primary care physicians could in fact consider 'education' as a medical act that could be charged for (Coussaert 1991). On the other hand, educational tasks were often implicitly delegated to newly created associations such as the Association Amicale des diabétiques (1938) or the Ligue des diabétiques de France (1939) founded by physicians.[6] Their goal was to disseminate medical knowledge through their patient-aimed journals, respectively *Le Journal des diabétiques* and *Diabète et nutrition*. In addition to nutritional guidelines, these journals included recipes as well as addresses where patients could receive appropriate food.

From patient education to therapeutic patient education programmes: The rationalization of patient training

In the years after the discovery of insulin, further research helped to purify insulin and increase the duration of its action. Long-term insulin came into use starting from 1936. By the end of the 1950s, insulin-dependent diabetes was distinguished from non-insulin-dependent diabetes, since newly available oral anti-diabetics were adequate only for the latter. If the survival rate of people with diabetes increased due to the development of effective treatment, the extended lifetime put people with diabetes at higher risk of long-term complications. This development ushered in a period of great controversy regarding the origins of such difficulties (Sinding 2000). While control has always been central to medical discourse about diabetes (Feudtner 2003), physicians began to focus on the degree of control to be achieved by patients. At that time, most physicians blamed consistent hyperglycaemia for diabetes-related problems. They promoted intensified insulin treatment associating multiple daily injections and a controlled diet to delay the appearance of complications. For instance, while Joslin acknowledged insulin as a decisive step towards the cure of diabetes, he maintained that a strict diet remained integral (Feudtner 2003). At the same time, some physicians – especially paediatricians in the United States and France –promoted a 'free diet' starting in the 1940s. They were more lax regarding patients' diet, considering that insulin helped them to maintain blood sugar levels within acceptable medical standards. Henri Lestradet, a paediatrician and one of the most preeminent advocates of the free diet in France (Sinding 2000), promoted 'a flexible adaptation of insulin therapy' made possible by patient training that would lead, he assumed, to 'strict control of diabetes' (Lestradet, Besse and Grenet 1968; Royer and Lestradet 1958). These competing visions were influenced by therapeutic innovations, but also by new standards of scientific research and different conceptions of doctors' professional role with regard to their patients (Mauck 2010).

At the beginning of the 1960s, however, the situation was about to change. In France, structural transformations within the medical field fostered the development of patient education. While hospitals had historically been dedicated to caring for the disadvantaged, they opened their doors to the middle and upper classes in 1941. This structural change led to the improvement of hospital premises, since prior dilapidated conditions were unacceptable to this new patient population (Chevandier 2009). From a medical perspective, informing and educating patients was a more natural undertaking with the often highly educated middle and upper classes, since these populations often shared common cultural and social knowledge (Pinell 1996). The

1958 reforms went even further by creating new kinds of hospitals in which clinical, research and teaching activities took place.[7] From that time onwards, doctors worked full time at the hospital. Taken together these factors created the conditions in which the treatment of chronic disease became a socially acceptable option for young physicians who sought a hospital career. Finally, public authorities paid increasing attention to budgetary issues. Training patients also aimed at reducing the numbers of acute episodes leading to expensive admissions. Developing care at home began to be considered as an essential way to reduce expenditures.

It was within this context that a new generation of physicians entered the hospital. Among them, George Tchobroutsky played a crucial role in the development of patient education in France, creating the first ward specializing in diabetes care. Convinced by the efficacy of intensive insulin treatment, Tchobroutsky and his colleagues carried out clinical and epidemiological research to prove that strict control is the best way to prevent long-term complications.[8] They promoted an intensive therapeutic protocol consisting of multiple daily injections and a strict diet. The implementation of such measures, however, remained dependent upon patients' compliance with prescribed treatments. As patients took on increasing disease management, new monitoring tools were developed in the 1970s and the 1980s. For patients, these tools included the availability of capillary blood glucose meters; for doctors, the determination of glycated haemoglobin enabled them to assess diabetes control for three months, and thus to evaluate compliance with treatment (Sinding 2004).

Building from these developments, it became clear that the best way to keep diabetes under control – that is, maintaining blood sugar levels (glycaemia) within medical standards – was to make patients responsible for their health by providing them with information about their disease. In other words, the predictability and preventability of long-term complications guided the development of patient education and the correlated promotion of self-control.[9] From a pedagogical perspective, medical staff mainly reproduced the conditions of their own professional socialization. This approach favoured the introduction of what French educational scholars refer to as the 'school form' (*forme scolaire*) into diabetology wards (Darmon 2020; Vincent 1980), breaking with the previously informal nature of the doctor–patient relationships and exchanges. In practice, patients were hospitalized to receive information about their disease and assembled in an education room. Medical staff, mainly interns, took on the role of teachers, providing top-down information to patients. Patients were often offered a weekly programmed schedule of training activities, including general information about diabetes, how to inject insulin or measure glycaemia and nutritional information.

By the early 1990s, as 'intensive therapy' was acknowledged as the best option to prevent long-term complications (Sinding 2004), European diabetologists had already begun developing new training practices. Most of the preeminent diabetology wards in Paris, such as Saint Louis, Saint Joseph or La Pitié-Salpêtrière hospitals, had developed training activities. The professional socialization of medical staff aimed henceforth to develop doctors' pedagogical skills, which would eventually lead to the radical transformation of diabetics' eating habits. The first medical professional to question this idea was the Swiss diabetologist Jean-Philippe Assal (Geneva). Together with Jean Canivet (Paris) and Michel Berger (Dusseldorf), Assal created the Diabetes Education

Study Group (DESG) in 1979 (Assal, Berger and Canivet 1982: 3–7).[10] Berger, it should be noted, was credited with the invention of 'functional insulin therapy'. Berger suggested that treatment should be adjusted to patients' eating habits instead of the opposite, meaning that patients could decide what dose of insulin should be injected to cover the amount of carbohydrates they planned to eat. In other words, Berger sought to ensure diabetes control and diet liberalization at the same time, which was made possible through rational patient training (Berger and Mülhausser 1995: 201–8; Chantelau et al. 1982: 612–16; Mülhausser et al., 1995: 591–7).

However, the recognition of patient education in France took a decisive step forward due to the work of actors outside of the medical field. The Bobigny School of Thought[11] led by Jean-François d'Ivernois and Rémi Gagnayre, both trained in therapeutic and educational sciences, had a major impact on the formalization of patient education. D'Ivernois and Gagnayre created a framework for implementing patient education (1995). They upheld the view that patient education would be more effective if it followed logical steps, including establishing patients' educative needs; setting up a contract with them; creating a tailored programme of training; evaluating behavioural changes. D'Ivernois and Gagnayre also suggested that patient training, inspired by current teaching methods, should be more efficient. This group joined together with the francophone section of the Diabetes Education Study Group (DESG-LF) and the French Health Education Committee (CFES)[12] which also showed a growing interest for this practice in the late 1990s. Lastly, they developed academic and professional training sessions to disseminate their model. Consequently, their ideas regarding patient education have gradually spread across France. The best practice guidelines published by the Haute Autorité de Santé (HAS, French Higher Authority for Health) and Institut National de Prévention et d'Éducation pour la Santé (INPES, French National Institute for Prevention and Health Education) in 2007 which define and frame patient education were primarily inspired by this model (HAS and INPES 2007).

The making of self-controlled patients: An ethnographic inquiry into Therapeutic Patient Education programmes

Training programmes promote the idea that patients should not consider themselves to be on a diet, but this approach raises a paradox. On the one hand, medical staff now agree after centuries of controversy that there is no specific medical or moral reason to prescribe food restrictions. On the other hand, providing participants with knowledge regarding food remains central in all programmes since certain eating practices are healthier than others in preventing disease recurrence. Indeed, awareness that long-term complications are predictable and preventable supports the very idea of participants' self-control. In other words, programmes aspire to produce patients who are responsible for their health and who exercise restraint. However, programmes differ in the way they seek to promote dispositions for self-control (see Table 7.1). While food quantification is the key in the plan managed by the association and the education units, an alternative based on listening to the body calls into question the real interest of a balanced diet.

Table 7.1 Description of observed programmes

	Association	Education unit in a public hospital	Rehabilitation service
Typology of participants	Upper-middle-class and upper-class 'users' with diabetes under control	Working-class and lower-middle-class 'patients' with poorly controlled diabetes	Working-class and lower-middle-class 'patients' with poorly controlled diabetes
Duration of the programme	Intermittent training and individual interviews for approximately six months	Weekly hospitalization	Four weeks hospitalization
Composition of the teaching staff	Nurses, dieticians, physical activity teacher	Physicians, nurses, dietician, physical activity teacher	Nurses, dieticians, psychologist, physical activity teachers, care assistant
Type of self-control promoted	Quantified self-control		Bodily sensations–based self-control

Eating like 'ordinary people': Lifting the nutritional ban

During educative programmes, dieticians often remind patients that they are not 'on a diet', and that 'nothing is forbidden', thus encouraging patients to behave like 'ordinary people'. Of interest is carbohydrates intake, which has long been banned from the diabetes diet. So-called 'slow sugars' are now presented as 'necessary fuel' to handle daily activities. Dieticians criticize certain diets as inadequate for producing long-term changes. Indeed, dieticians consider that diets based on the restriction of fast-release sugars could obstruct long-term behavioural change by creating frustration leading inevitably to relapse. This vision of nutrition contrasts with the way diabetic patients perceive food. During workshops, through questions presented to dieticians and judgements made regarding specific foods, participants draw up a 'space of eating possibility', structured around a set of oppositions (authorized/prohibited, necessary/unnecessary, good/bad, healthy/unhealthy): 'I eat everything that is *forbidden*'; 'Do I have the *right* to eat dessert'; 'But then what *can* we eat?'; 'So we shouldn't be *allowed* to eat it'; 'They'll tell you what you're *allowed* to eat, and what you're not *allowed* to eat!'; 'It is *good* to have honey once in a while, right?'. In participants' discourse, 'good for health' replaces 'tasty', underlining the effort that patients are willing to exert to comply with nutritional recommendations. This 'good dietary will' is particularly evident today among stable sections of the working or middle classes (Longchamp 2014) or certain intermediate levels (Régnier and Masullo 2009), which constitute the most substantial part of the hospitalized population. Most training sessions aim to provide patients with knowledge about the food they eat to enable informed choices. Such knowledge transmission during workshops seeks to attenuate the prescriptive dimension of dieticians' actions by encouraging self awareness among individuals.

Asserting that patients should eat like 'ordinary people' seems problematic since it hides the underlying nutritional norms that apply to all individuals regarding food. Most of these norms are drawn from the Programme national nutrition santé (or PNNS, the French national programme for nutrition and health). According to PNNS recommendations, food is presented as an essential means to improve and maintain health. Obesity is thus constructed in PNNS guidelines as an individual rather than a social problem, without regard to critical social discrepancies regarding the reception of nutritional recommendations. Nutritional prescriptions are modelled on the lifestyles of the middle and upper classes, and to a lesser extent on those of women. Therefore, middle- and upper-class dietary practices are already close to those promoted in educational programmes. A retired sales engineer expressed this idea during his visit to discuss his objectives within the programme: 'I was already doing quite a lot in terms of food … It makes me feel better about what I was already doing.' Aside from the fact that most middle- and upper-class participants are not overweight, their taste in food is primarily oriented towards what is considered healthy (Longchamp 2014). For instance, Audrey (26-year-old, engineer) stated that she has 'never been fond of sugar'. Likewise, Élodie (29-year-old, sales representative) considered herself 'lucky' because she never ate 'candies or cake'. Most already see food as a factor for maintaining good health, and they reject the idea of 'diet' in favour of the concept of food hygiene as an integral part of a lifestyle (Depecker 2010; Régnier and Masullo 2009).

Conversely, working-class individuals are often more critical of nutritional recommendations (Régnier and Masullo 2009). Observation of dietary workshops reveals a form of hostility on the part of working-class patients towards the norms conveyed in workshops. In the end, the permissive nature of nutritional prescriptions is likely to run up against individual representations, particularly those of participants from working-class backgrounds for whom weight control can only be achieved through a 'diet' (Lhuissier 2006). Although the idea of dieting has widely penetrated the working class, it remains short term and more curative than preventive (Régnier and Masullo 2009). Thus, the degree of transformation of dietary practices varies according to the social characteristics of participants.

The promotion of a balanced diet and quantified self-control

Persistent attempts by medical staff to emphasize that participants are not on a diet does not mean that participants can eat whatever or whenever they want. To meet its goals, the programmes managed by both the association and the education units promote a balanced diet, based on PNNS recommendations. Dieticians expect patients to exhibit self-control through two techniques of food quantification. The first technique consists of daily attention to the quantity of food to be eaten during a day. In the absence of measurement such as weighing, other tools are recommended to determine amounts.[13] In some cases, dieticians may refer to amounts predefined by the food industry, since many foods are presented in a standardized form. For example, dieticians may refer to a 'yoghurt' or a 'can', without explicitly referring to the quantity since the container itself determines this. Dieticians may also use standard markers – a spoon, ladle – or even the hand to define what a 'serving' is. These different strategies presented to patients also support visual learning of quantities. Food samples used in dietary workshops are thus generally given in the appropriate amount, thus materializing nutritional recommendations. Similarly, rations that are served daily to participants during their hospital stay are intended to enable them to hone their perception of the right quantity to be placed on a plate. The internalization of visual arrangements is achieved by linking the processes of measurement to the patient's practice of visually assessing quantity. Initially, the use of everyday objects provides a benchmark for judging the amount served. It is only in a second stage that the repetition of experiments over time shapes visual habits. However, the consistent attention to food quantity seems to be contrary to what Bourdieu (1979) used to call the *franc-manger populaire*, meaning the preference of working-class individuals for abundant meals. Consequently, lower-class participants must expend considerable efforts to comply with the nutritional prescriptions promoted during workshops. Furthermore, men and women from the working class do not behave the same way with regard to establishing a balanced diet. Working-class men focus almost exclusively on the overall quantity of food, considering that their problem is overeating. Women have proven to be more careful about balancing each meal – they are confronted with the standard of the thin desirable body more often than men.

Furthermore, dieticians establish the frequency with which certain food groups or products can or should be consumed during dietary workshops. As part of the promotion of a balanced diet, dieticians organize patients' food consumption by telling them what foods should be eaten at each meal or at specific meals, and what foods to avoid, preferably without completely eliminating them. Documents given to patients serve to remind them of directives which are presented orally. To take just one example, a summary sheet entitled 'Sugars: How to Consume Them' differentiates foods according to the frequency with which they should be consumed: 'Starchy foods/ bread and other flour-based foods' must be eaten 'at every meal'; vegetables should be eaten 'daily'; 'Fruit and derivatives about two to three times a day'; sweet products are 'to be avoided'. Thinking of diet as a 'balance' therefore implies anticipating different dietary intakes, taking into account both what has already been consumed and what will be consumed soon.

'Listen to your body': Bodily sensation-based self-control

Within the rehabilitation service in which we conducted our observations, patients' self-control relies on a completely different mechanism. The underlying method used comes from the Groupe de Réflexion sur l'Obésité et le Surpoids (GROS, French Research Group on Overweight and Obesity).[14] This group considers that nutritional advice, including PNNS guidelines, encourages individuals 'to eat with their heads rather than their sensations', as one GROS founder declared in an interview (quoted by Sanabria 2015). Thus, training aims above all to work on the recognition of 'hunger' and 'satiety'. The regulation of food practices presupposes the ability to finely discriminate between relevant body sensations and how to associate them with categories such as hunger and satiety. However, lower-class patients usually show more difficulty listening to their body, as their working and living conditions do not place them in favourable conditions to do so (Boltanski 1971). Defining hunger, therefore, requires a recognition of its bodily inscription. As per the principles of the GROS group, appetite appears as 'a set of physical sensations of variable intensity over time'. GROS assures participants that if they only eat when they are hungry, they will not put on weight. Just as it is necessary to know when to start eating, it is also necessary to learn when to stop. Here, the feeling of fullness is the criterion: 'Feeling full is that I'm no longer hungry, and I don't feel like eating more.' For patients, however, it is difficult to distinguish 'hunger' from other messages that would lead them to eat. Dieticians seek to overcome this obstacle by inviting patients to ask themselves about the origin of this desire to eat or to continue eating. Feelings of stress, sadness or anger are taken into account during workshops: such feelings lead naturally to eating comforting foods ('a soothing food, it is scientifically proven, is a fatty and sweet food').

However, it is not enough to present this 'natural' regulation as an alternative to rational constraint: participants need to be able to detect 'hunger', 'appetite for specific foods' or psychological situations that generate the desire to eat. Patients are thus invited to 'experience hunger' by practising a form of temporary and supervised fasting. This practice consists of suppressing breakfast or even lunch for four consecutive days while maintaining dinner and waiting for hunger signals. This duration is designed to 'push the intensity of hunger a little more each day', 'test its limits' or 'make it a known and easily suppressed sensation in order to fight the fear of hunger'. The experiment aims to develop the ability to identify 'good hunger', which is situated between 'small hunger' and 'big hunger', each of which produces specific bodily signs that the patient should be able to discern. 'Small hunger' produces a slight tightening of the throat, a small hollow in the stomach, while 'big hunger' produces more significant effects: headaches, feeling weak, difficulty concentrating and the like. As stated on a summary sheet describing the 'experience of hunger', 'the aim is not to resist the body's sensations for as long as possible, but on the contrary to be attentive to them, to start working with the body'.

Conclusion

The history of diabetes offers a new perspective on the dissemination of nutritional norms and on their reception. Patient education was promoted long before the discovery of insulin; however, the rigid diet imposed on patients favoured the use of disciplinary methods. It was only under the influence of educators and public health professionals that patient education took its current shape. The development of training practices contributed to the softening of nutritional prescriptions; this evolution led progressively to a therapeutic approach by which patients adjust their treatment according to their lifestyle rather than the contrary. Just as there are various ways to impose exterior constraints on the patient, there are also different logics which guide self-control. Our study shows that the incorporation of self-restraint practices with regard to eating depends on participants' social characteristics. Regardless of the kind of self-control promoted during programmes, participants' eating habits were initially more or less congruent with nutritional norms according to their social class. Lower-class patients' relation to food differs from the idea of food hygiene disseminated during programmes. Working-class obesity is interpreted as the manifestation of a departure from nutritional norms. Whether patient education programmes promote quantified self-control or self-control based on bodily sensations, working-class patients must make more significant efforts to comply with dietary prescriptions than other patients. The capacity of patient education programmes to transform eating habits thus depends not only on pedagogical frameworks and principles but also on the social discrepancies between participants before they enter a programme.

Notes

1. While patients suffering from type 1 diabetes must inject insulin several times a day, type 2 diabetic patients might only take pills at the onset of the disease. However, after several years, they will also eventually require insulin. In addition, lifestyle changes are considered more crucial for type 2 than type 1 diabetes patients since the latter have the possibility of adjusting their treatment to lifestyle with insulin injections.
2. While nutritionists are medical doctors, dieticians are not. In France, professional training of dieticians takes two years. Their work consists mainly in balancing the diet of both sick and well persons.
3. These cells were named 'islets of Langerhans' after Paul Langerhans, the German doctor who discovered them.
4. For a contemporary example, see Darmon (2012).
5. They were affiliated with the newly created professional group called 'social assistants', which changed both their training and their institutional assignment.
6. A third association was created in the late 1950s, named the Association des jeunes diabétiques (1956).
7. Ordonnance n°58-1198 du 11 décembre 1958 portant réforme de la législation hospitalière; ordonnance n°58-1199 du 30 décembre 1958 relative à la coordination des établissements de soins comportant hospitalisation; ordonnance n°58-1373 relative à la création des 'Centres hospitaliers et universitaires'.
8. The scope of the study went far beyond French borders (Job et al. 1976: 463–9; Tchobroutsky 1978). For a complete presentation of the demonstration and the consequences of research regarding the glucose hypothesis, see Sinding (2000).
9. Regarding the change of exterior constraint to self-control see the analysis of the civilizing process by Norbert Elias (1973, 1976).
10. French diabetologists later created a French branch in 1989, called Diabetic education study group langue française (DESG-LF).
11. Bobigny is a city in the northern Paris suburb in which a new university was founded in the 1970s.

12. CFES became the Institut national de prévention et d'éducation pour la santé (Inpes) in 2002.
13. This is particularly true in the case of functional insulin therapy. The carbohydrate intake should be as accurate as possible to calculate the correct dose of insulin, i.e. the treatment that will entirely cover the carbohydrate intake expected at a meal.
14. In French, the acronym used to name the group, i.e. GROS, means 'fat'.

The dietary consultation session as a place for mediating food knowledge

Viviane Clavier
Translated by Corinna Anderson

Introduction

This chapter explores the process of knowledge mediation during dietetic consultations. We present results of a questionnaire survey conducted in January and February 2020 (2020 Survey) involving 156 members of the French Nutritionist Dieticians Association (AFDN).[1] This study follows two previous questionnaire surveys. The most recent, carried out in 2018 among 44 nutritionist dieticians in the French Rhône-Alpes region (2018 Survey),[2] aimed to investigate the information practices of these professionals and their patients (Clavier 2019). A survey conducted in 2015 with Céline Paganelli (2015 Survey), targeting the patient population of a Grenoble-based nutritionist doctor, focused on information practices surrounding food and health.[3]

The results of these two previous surveys demonstrated an often sustained information-seeking activity on the part of both patients and dieticians. Given this result, we turn our attention to the 2020 study and to the following questions: Does the dietary consultation session foster exchange and transfer of information about food and eating? What forms does this knowledge take? Can we consider that dieticians as a professional body mediate public health policy? If so, does exchanged knowledge differ according to practice site or the dietician's specialty? In what follows, we present an overview of research in information and communication sciences (ICS) that has been conducted on the relationships between information practices and knowledge mediation. We then present the objectives and results of the 2020 Survey.

From information practices to knowledge mediation about food and diet

Information and communication sciences: Theoretical framework

This survey is a continuation of our previous research on health information practices (Clavier 2018). The study of information practices in the domain of health is central to Library and Information Science (LIS) (HjØrland 2018). In LIS, health information practice has been approached in the context of everyday life (Everyday Life Information Seeking). Finnish researcher Reijo Savolainen set out the scope of this perspective in a seminal article in 1995.[4] Studies following this approach explore information practices and the 'information behavior' of individuals as defined by Tom Wilson (2000).[5] This research focuses on information needs by taking into account the sociocultural, economic and linguistic context of populations under consideration. In health information research, particular importance is given to consideration of the relationships of exchange between practitioner and patient (McKenzie 2002) as well as to phenomena of information sharing (Savolainen 2011). Information practices are seen in this LIS research as the starting point of individuals' relationship to information. Such practices, importantly, also shed light on the ways in which knowledge is constructed and organized, and how it is transmitted and shared in the framework of social or professional activities and contexts (Clavier and Paganelli 2015).

ICS research on food and health in France has established that national nutritional policy (through the three national nutrition and health programmes, PNNS, 2001–5; 2006–10; 2011–15)[6] has 'imposed nutrition as a public health issue' (Romeyer 2015). One of the consequences of this public policy has been that new missions of information, education and prevention are assigned to institutional actors such as public schools (Berthoud 2018; De Iulio et al. 2018; Cardon and De Iulio 2021) and dieticians. Patient care provided by dieticians is part of a tendency towards the 'medicalization' of food issues, a phenomenon identified by the sociologist Jean-Pierre Poulain (2009), although dieticians are paramedical health professionals and not doctors.

Starting with France's first national nutrition and health programme (Programme National Nutrition Santé or PNNS) in 2001–5, dietetic professionals have been designated by public health policy as mediators on issues of food education and prevention. As far as we know, no ICS research has been carried out on dieticians, but we assume that this professional body shares many common features with other 'knowledge mediating professions', such as librarian-teachers, schoolteachers, so-called 'scientific intermediaries' and the like (Calenge 2015: 40). We approach the notion of knowledge mediation as an extension of research in information and documentation studies wherein information is characterized through both its material and signifying dimensions. As such, information is 'often fixed, conserved and transmitted' (Meyriat 1993); it is 'as fundamental a good as matter and energy' and, as Vincent Liquète points out, it 'contributes to the dynamics of knowledge construction and even constitutes its basis' (Liquète 2011: 157). In this perspective, the document is central: it is a 'knowledge mediation' object (Couzinet 2018). Indeed, the documents produced by a society reveal not only media choices specific to a given period but also, according to Jean Meyriat, content choices and communicational aims. For Meyriat, there are two types of documents (Meyriat 1978): documents 'by intention', produced for the express purpose of informing (e.g. a scientific article), and documents 'by attribution', whose primary purpose is not to inform, but which by their intrinsic properties also provide information (e.g. an archaeological object). Let us conclude this overview with a point of terminology in order to make a distinction between knowledge and information. It has already been established that not all information that is made available becomes knowledge (Miège 1997) and that a body of scientific knowledge does not result from the mere aggregation of individually held knowledge, but is subject to criteria of legitimacy, socialization and selection.[7] In addition, ideas and objects do not circulate without being transformed, or without producing something new (Jeanneret 2008). The aim of our study is to understand the role of dietetics professionals in the mediation of food-related scientific knowledge, and to explore the degree to which this mediation is a determining element of the process of socialization of food knowledge.

Dieticians as professional intermediaries

According to the Public Health Code, dieticians are health professionals who fall under the category of 'medical auxiliaries' and whose scope of intervention is defined by Article L4371-1 of Law No. 2007-127 ratified on 30 January 2007, a recent law which notes a lag in the level of training compared to other European countries:[8]

A person is considered to be practicing as a dietician if he or she habitually provides nutritional advice and, on medical prescription, participates in the nutritional education and rehabilitation of patients with metabolic or eating disorders, through the establishment of a personalized dietary assessment and appropriate dietetic education.

Dieticians contribute to defining, evaluating and monitoring the nutritional quality of food served in school cafeterias and other institutions, in addition to carrying out preventive public health activities in the field of nutrition.

Over the last ten years, the number of dieticians holding technical diplomas, technical university degrees or professional bachelor's degrees has steadily increased, almost doubling between 2010 (6,643) and 2018 (12,442).[9] This profession in search of recognition is 94 per cent female.[10] In a 2003 report on the evolution of the French dietetic profession, Michel Krempf, then professor and practitioner at the Nantes University Hospital, indicated that dietetic and nutrition professionals were the primary target for implementing the principles of the national PNNS campaigns in 'the social body'; to this effect, a mission letter was addressed to them (Krempf 2003). High expectations have been placed on these professionals as 'one of the essential cogs' in the system of nutritional education and in the prevention and treatment of diet-related diseases (type 2 diabetes, obesity, cardiovascular diseases). According to this report, other missions are entrusted to them in several areas of social, health-related and professional action, including intervening with underprivileged populations, organizing nutritional education and working in health care institutions, educational and childcare facilities and industry. Dieticians are also expected to develop the private and public health sectors, set up nutritional care networks with private medical practitioners and ensure a role of liaison among the various health professionals in the health care system. According to the 2017 White Paper on Dieticians (Livre Blanc 2017), members of the profession practice mainly under employee status within health or medical-social institutions. The fact that dietetic acts are not recognized in official health care system nomenclature or in social security insurance coverage remains an obstacle to establishing private practice or self-employment within the profession (2017: 10).

Our 2018 Survey showed that dieticians are becoming more specialized. Increasing specialization manifests itself in a variety of ways, including increased duration of academic studies by individuals, increased variety of continuing education formats and a wide-ranging offer of two-year technical degree programmes at the university level. The survey also showed that practitioners regularly consult specialized information sources, and that 61 per cent of professionals report having a specialty, compared to 39 per cent who do not. Increasing specialization is also seen in the diversity of organizational contexts in which these professionals practice, with a high proportion working in health care establishments, thus responding to the large number of diet-related pathologies which require knowledge of medicine. Finally, it should be noted that some dieticians consider themselves to be nutritionist-dieticians, a term that reflects their desire to specialize. Thus, as Michel Krempf mentioned almost twenty years ago, this profession seems to permeate and 'irrigate' society through the constantly growing number of professionals, the diversity of specialties, the multiplicity of host organizations and the increasingly important role of nutrition in therapeutic medical practice.

The role of information and communication in dietary consultations

The professional recommendations published by the French High Authority for Health (HAS) in 2006, outline the conditions for a successful dietary consultation:

> The aim of a dietary consultation is to advise a person and/or their family during a face-to-face meeting, helping them to solve, as far as possible, a problem related to their diet and health. It should enable them to choose the actions they can put into practice, if possible, or to direct them towards an action that will be favorable to their state of health (for example, elderly or disoriented people). Positive reception upon arrival at the appointment is an important part of the dietary consultation. It helps build a relationship of trust and a good listening attitude. (AFDN and HAS 2006: 50)

According to these recommendations, information and communication practices during dietetic consultation should serve to 'guide and advise', so that patients will 'appropriate dietetic (nutritional and dietary) knowledge for themselves', to 'give meaning to acquired dietetic knowledge', to make such knowledge 'acceptable in a perspective of better health and to choose adapted actions' (AFDN and HAS 2006: 62). Information and communication practices are therefore deemed essential to the missions of dietary education, advising and health prevention since they allow for appropriation of dietetic knowledge in line with public health policy (Hercberg 2014). We hypothesize that this approach to information and communication differs from the therapeutic consultation as carried out by doctors. In the latter case, informing patients is a legal obligation, and is intended to invest patients with decision-making power and with the ability to take charge of their health as an informed subject

(Cecchi 2008; Fainzang 2009). In dietary counselling on the other hand, information and communication seem more akin to a rhetoric of persuasion, with counselling and prevention aimed at convincing patients to change their eating behaviour while leaving particular methods of action to their discretion. As we will now see, the 2020 Survey allows for a clearer understanding of the role of information practices and processes during dietary consultations.

Results of our 2020 Survey of 156 dieticians

Main results of previous surveys and the new questionnaire

The 2018 Survey shows the information practices of dieticians to be quite divergent. Three-quarters of the respondents report taking an active approach to updating their own knowledge through public health information sources, professional journals, books and the specialized press, and through regular participation in day-long professional development and training sessions. A few professionals report practices similar to those of medical researchers, reading peer reviewed journals and participating in conferences and seminars as doctors do (Staii et al. 2006). On the other hand, a quarter of the respondents do not seek information or engage in training, possibly due to the absence of a legal obligation for continuing education among dieticians, unlike physicians who are subject to such requirements. The 2018 questionnaire also offers insight into patients' acquired knowledge as perceived by professionals during the dietary consultation. Three-quarters of dieticians say their patients are more informed than similar patients ten years previously. They report that the sources consulted by their patients are mostly the internet, television programmes, documentaries and finally their family and friends. Although their patients seem more informed than several years ago, professionals nevertheless point out that the information held by their patients remains 'approximate' and contains 'a lot of preconceived ideas'. This situation leads professionals to try to correct such lay scientific knowledge which, in their view, 'is not an easy task' and requires checking information sources consulted by their patients in order to 'take a stand on what they had heard or read'. These results confirm our 2015 Survey conducted among patients in a Grenoble nutritionist doctor's office; respondents express mistrust of contradictory information on nutrition and feel unsure about where to look for reliable information, despite the availability of a variety of information sources on nutrition.

For our 2020 Survey, we asked the AFDN to distribute our questionnaire on a national level. Between January and February 2020, 156 professionals responded to this new survey: 147 women and 9 men, ages twenty-two to sixty-two. Half of the respondents are in the age group thirty to forty-nine. Professionals with the equivalent of two years of higher education are in the majority: 119 respondents are technical degree holders in dietetics and 32 are technical university degree holders (Applied Biology with a specialization in dietetics). Six professionals report four years of higher education (Bachelor's or one-year Master's degree) and 14 completed five years of higher education (two-year Master's Degree, Master of Advanced Studies, Engineer,

Executive School). Fourteen respondents hold specialized intensive university diplomas (technical university degree or inter-university degree obtained through a several months-long programme).

The survey features thirty-two questions, almost all of which are open-ended; a total of 4,992 responses were collected and manually analysed. The survey begins with seven demographic questions (related to gender, age, seniority in the profession, geographic location) and then focuses on dieticians' specialties and location of practice (private practice, hospital, etc.). The next twelve questions deal more precisely with the dietetic consultation itself: its duration, the amount of time devoted to information practices, topics covered and the role of information sources in the exchange. The final thirteen questions address the materials used by professionals during the consultation.

Results

A diversity of specialties in dietetics

As with the 2018 Survey, results show that specialization is the rule among dieticians, with 138 professionals reporting a specialty in their field as opposed to 16 who do not. The specialties mentioned are varied and can be categorized according to the following: population treated (athletes, adolescents, the elderly, pregnant women); medical specialization (oncology, diabetology, digestive or bariatric surgery, gastro-enterology, geriatrics); pathology (obesity, eating disorders, undernutrition, metabolic disorders); or specific eating constraints (artificial nutrition). Specialties are also reported in reference to a care approach (holistic nutrition, micronutrition), a disciplinary perspective, a social issue (sociology of food, psycho-nutrition, sustainable food) or an education and prevention programme supervised by health authorities such as the HAS, as is the case for Therapeutic Patient Education (TPE). Finally, specialties are associated with place of practice (hospital or clinical specialty, university hospital). Of all categories, medical specializations are the most prevalent, representing almost half of the responses.

Thus, the professional field of dietetics involves a wide spectrum of specialties. The reasons behind the degree of specialization in any given professional domain are complex. For example, medicine is characterized by a high level of specialization:

> The number of specialties is steadily progressing and the older ones in turn tend to be divided into sub-specialties, covering an increasingly narrow range of objects while calling for increasingly specific skills. (Pinell 2005: 5)

For Patrice Pinell, this trend cannot be attributed solely to a logic of scientific progress which 'would appear to mechanically and inevitably command the a priori unlimited expansion of knowledge and techniques'. Socio-professional issues seem to be decisive in this context. In the case of dietetics, we can assume that the increase in the number of specialties is related to the position of nutrition in French university hospital academic disciplines. Ambroise Martin,[11] professor of nutrition and biochemistry at the University of Lyon, explains that nutrition is a 'recent, poorly developed and still fragile' university hospital discipline in spite of 'a consistent knowledge base' (Martin 2009: 7). Nutrition does not appear as a specialty in its own right in the official 2004 list of degrees granted for specialized studies in medicine but is presented, rather, as complementary training to other specialties (endocrinology, diabetology, paediatrics, gastroenterology). Could this lack of disciplinary autonomy influence the practice of the dietetic profession, which remains complementary to other medical or paramedical practices? The diversity of the therapeutic and public health domains in which nutrition is included, as well as the high level of required knowledge to be attained, indicate the need to adapt degree-granting programmes in nutrition to the French university system, based on a three-year undergraduate and five-year Master's degree structure. These demands are currently being put forth by the profession in order to align the degree structure with that of other health professions (Livre Blanc 2017: 15sqq).

The 'here-and-now' of dietary consultations: Location, duration and content

Our results show that 129 professionals practice in a single location, 17 dieticians practice in two locations and 1 professional works in 'several offices in different locations in the city made available by the municipality'. The 9 remaining respondents did not provide an answer or no longer have a place of employment (retired). Concerning work locations, certain patterns emerge through categorical analysis. Dieticians' principal work sites are as follows, in descending order: medical establishments (hospitals, university hospitals and clinics), 26 per cent; medical complexes 18 per cent; paramedical offices shared with midwives, nurses and physiotherapists, 12 per cent; and multi-professional spaces (health centres), 12 per cent. Taken together, these categories represent 70 per cent of respondents' places of work. Independent practices, which are sometimes located in professionals' homes, account for 19 per cent. As mentioned earlier, 56 per cent of dieticians work closely with medical professionals and 12 per cent with allied health professionals, a fact which probably favours increased specialization.

The duration of consultations varies and in general is relatively long: 60 professionals report one-hour appointments or even longer (27 report one and a half hour visits and 4 professionals report two hours). Many propose a one hour-long appointment for a first visit, followed by a shorter time for follow-up exchanges, with thirty minutes on average. The consultation itself is broken down into several phases or 'moments' dedicated to specific types of exchanges. Results show that 118 professionals distinguished several 'moments', compared to 35 without such 'moments', with remaining respondents not answering this question. According to the recommendations of the French Health Authority HAS (AFDN and HAS 2006), 'each dietary consultation should pursue a precise objective'.[12] Suggested communication techniques include active listening, reformulation and putting the patient in the role of decision maker. As indicated earlier, the last of these objectives is more characteristic of the medical interview. Several respondents characterize the different moments in the process of dietary diagnosis:

> Presentation, reason for the consultation, patient history, data collection, questions regarding the patient's knowledge, motivations, desires, what he or she

has understood, moment of therapeutic alliance, and negotiation of objectives and care strategy. (M, 33, Oncology, Gastro-enterology)[13]

The organization of the dietary consultation is often presented as a protocol to be followed:

> Listening, informing, explanations, practical exercises, education. (F, 39, General Dietician)

More rarely, sequenced steps are mentioned:

> Step 1: presentation + explanation of the consultation process; Step 2: data collection (history, weight measurement, dietary record, etc) only for assessment consultations; Step 3: information given to the patient and/or evaluation of the objectives set previously; Step 4: patient questions; +/- Step 5: 'free expression': sometimes the patient will 'open up' at the end of the consultation. (F, 26, No Specialty)

'Information' was cited twenty-seven times among the moments or steps cited, and responses show fairly consequential lengths of time (fifteen to thirty minutes) reserved for information practices. Some professionals feel that the entire consultation is, in fact, dedicated to the transmission of information; such responses suggest that information and communication practices are considered, if not indistinguishable, at least inseparable. One hospital dietician specialized in diabetes care asserts that information practices are linked to education: 'Information and therapeutic patient education are inseparable.' In the majority of cases (112 occurrences), information exchange between professionals and patients during consultations is reported. But more one-sided situations are also mentioned, where the patient asks for information – a situation expected by professionals (twenty-one occurrences) – or where the dietician initiates the communication of information (twenty-two occurrences).

The most important topics covered during consultations, from the professionals' point of view, fall into three broadly balanced categories:

1. The patient's knowledge regarding food and dietary balance, meal design and culinary practice, cooking methods, portion sizes, food quality, the role of fibre, vegetables and hydration. Some professionals refer to information on the nutritional composition of foods, food groups, how to read labels and the glycemic indexes of foods.
2. Knowledge about the patient and about his or her relationship to food: eating behaviour, food culture and food beliefs, eating sensations, guilt and self-image, the role of emotions and cognitive dietary restraint.[14] Knowledge about the pathology and about the patient's lifestyle, stress, sleep, perception of hunger and satiety.
3. Understanding the patient's motivations, needs or diagnosed needs. Here the professional seeks to understand how to accompany the patient, how to help him

or her feel less guilty, to determine whether or not the patient shows a sense of concern for his or her problem. Responses in this category also point to the need to be critical of information found in the media concerning food risks.

Care objectives differ for each patient, depending on the problems or requests expressed and on professionals' specific priorities. Thus, for TPE professionals, the aim is to foster patients' autonomy through education. But for the majority of respondents, the priority is to assess the patient's motivation to follow a prescribed diet; professionals specializing in eating disorders or behavioural nutrition give priority to the person's psychological well-being. Some professionals, regardless of their specialty, seek to 'help people understand' about 'food intake in order to manage it', about 'the assimilation of carbohydrates' or seek to 'make people aware of the relationship to the act of eating (hedonism, eating for comfort)'. Many take a pragmatic approach and teach patients to be better organized and to manage 'life's moments'. Often, several objectives are pursued together, closely combining information, communication, education and nutritional advice. It should be noted that risk prevention is rarely addressed, except in cases of undernutrition, nutritional deficiencies (by professionals specialized in gerontology and weight loss), cancer (oncology) or post-surgical complications (bariatric surgery or obesity).

Apart from questions related to specific pathologies or populations (such as athletes), professionals report the following subjects as those most often raised by patients:

1. Concerns about weight, eating behaviour and its psychological or physiological consequences including weight gain, loss of appetite, fatigue, social ties, sources of tension, fasting and other diets, food guilt, dissatisfaction with weight, managing emotions, food budgeting, motivation, diet-related failures, feeling 'fed up' with restrictions, sugar compulsions and the anxiety-provoking context of eating.
2. Knowledge about food: different kinds of fats, sugar addiction, dairy products, cheese, starchy foods, low-fat products, food supplements, good versus bad foods, forbidden versus authorized foods, frequency of consumption, brands and the role of food in health. Patients wonder if they should be gluten-free, lactose-free, starch-free or follow special diets because professionals in their entourage (such as osteopaths, naturopaths, sports instructors) recommend it.
3. Requests for advice on topics covered in the media, mobile applications, miracle methods, nutritional labels, food marketing messages, trendy diets, gluten-free or other diets, the abundance of nutritional messages and the Nutriscore (the nutritional value scoring label for packaged foods).

This last point calls into question the role of dieticians in media literacy and critical media analysis. Some professionals indicate that patients are looking for validation of the information they have encountered elsewhere, and expect professionals to take a clear position and to judge the accuracy of information about diets and about the link between certain foods and health. Our 2018 Survey showed in fact that professionals were under two kinds of pressure. On the one hand, they are expected to take in and evaluate information consulted by their patients and to 'untangle truths from falsehoods'; this entails verifying information on various controversial subjects, a task more related to mediation than to nutritional advice and support. On the other hand, they are often placed in a position of having to justify their expertise to patients who are inclined to believe self-proclaimed experts in nutrition (Hugol-Gential et al. 2018), or to give credibility and recognition to members of their circle of family and friends. The 2020 Survey thus confirms the expected role of dietetics professionals in terms of informational authority.

Dietary consultations and the role of information and communication

Our 2020 Survey also confirms the 2018 Survey results with regard to sources consulted by professionals. We asked professionals if they mentioned specific sources to their patients: 40 responded 'yes', 24 'sometimes' and 20 'no'. The remainder did not answer, with one person indicating that this was not always possible:

> Whenever possible, yes. But most of the time no, because one cannot quote bibliographies and other references off the top of one's head in the middle of a consultation. (F, 31, Therapeutic Education, Prevention, Positive Psychology combined with Dietetics)

When cited, sources mentioned to patients are those consulted by dieticians themselves. Sources cited are often officially validated by public health and nutrition policy guidelines and are accessible to the general public. These include: recommendations from the HAS, the PNNS, the World Health Organization (WHO), the French Agency for Food, Environmental and Occupational Health & Safety (ANSES) and the 'Eating and Moving' (Manger-Bouger) public health campaign (half of the cases); professional sources (AFDN Review); associative networks such as the Obesity and Overweight Research Group (GROS), the French Federation of Diabetics (AFD), the French Association of Gluten Intolerance (AFDIAG), the French National Cancer Institute (INCA); scientific journals available on Pubmed and Cochrane databases. Other sources are geared towards a popular audience (the websites drgood.fr and lanutrition. fr), and some respondents mentioned references to books (by Dr Chozen Bays), as well as television programmes.

Among the professionals who indicate their sources to patients, some take on a media literacy role by pointing out official nutrition and public health sources:

> Yes I can go on the internet with them to get information to show them which site is reliable: the CIQUAL food composition table online, open food fact, or the 'eating and moving' government website. (F, 44, Overweight, Obesity)

Some professionals position themselves in a teaching role and help patients interpret information on various media or applications:

> Yes, looking directly at products to teach them to read labels, and various nutrition applications. (F, 39, No Specialty)

Others use the authority of sources as a means of persuasion:

> [I do] not always [mention sources], and it's more to convince those who are in doubt. I often cite the PNNS and HAS Recommendations. (F, 45, Obesity)
>
>   Yes, if I'm challenged about the composition of food: I quote the CIQUAL source, or the composition on the packaging. (F, 55, Pediatrics)

Others refer to authoritative resources to legitimize their advice:

> Yes, I talk about the HAS, ANSES, and PNNS recommendations and it's essential for credibility. (F, 37, Eating Disorders)

Some also justify their expertise by mentioning their degree training or further education:

> I tell them that I have just obtained a D.U. degree [intensive degree program] in *Physionutrition* at the University of Grenoble with great recognized scientists such as Anne-Marie Roussel who is also at ANSES, and that my sources are extremely reliable and constantly updated thanks to lectures and other continuing education (F, 62, Bariatric Surgery)

Understanding the role of information practices and artefacts in patient–dietician exchanges remains difficult and complex. Various models of doctor–patient communication are described in the literature (Fournier and Kerzanet 2007). Among these we find the following:

1. Communication by stages or tasks
2. Communication encouraging patient participation (Fournier and Kerzanet 2007) including such variants as mutual participation, the deliberative model, the patient experience approach
3. So-called educational approaches found among TPE dieticians

The importance given to information practices and processes depends to a great extent on the communicational approach used.[15] For professionals who adopt an educational approach, for example, information practice is deemed essential in establishing patient autonomy and in monitoring health and diet: nutritional information helps to enlighten the patient, as in the medical context. For those who focus on the patient experience, however, acquiring and sharing information are not decisive aspects of the visit. Thus, when asked if there is a link between being well-informed and showing dietary compliance, 86 respondents answer 'yes' (all specialties combined), and 24 answer 'no' (with a majority of specialties related to obesity, eating disorders and diabetes) while 34 respondents answer 'yes and no', the others expressing no opinion. Some answers are categorical: 'Yes, it's obvious' or 'Absolutely not! Knowing and wanting to do something are not the same as being able to'. When professionals consider that information practices play a role in dietary counselling, it is linked to the patient's dietary compliance: 'Yes, it is easier to apply advice when one understands why and adheres to it'; 'Yes, understanding is part of the therapeutic alliance.' Some professionals suggest that information practice is crucial for analysis of current events, but that it is insufficient without the help of a practitioner:

> Information is essential, it allows for a critical approach, but knowing what one should do does not mean that one is able to modify behavior and food choices, hence the importance of personalized dietary care. (F, 44, Overweight and Obesity)

Professionals who believe that information processes and artefacts do have a role to play in consultations tend to consider other factors to be more conducive to dietary compliance, such as feelings, individual experience, motivation and willpower:

> No, learning to feel seems the most important thing to me. (F, 45, Heart Failure, Sports)
>
> Not necessarily, because we can see that even well-informed people have difficulty eating properly sometimes. I often find that this is a more personal problem that should be solved before we even bother about the contents of the plate. (F, 40, General Practitioner)
>
> No, compliance is linked to motivation and to adapting advice. (F, 40, Eating Behaviors)

These contrasting positions go very much to the heart of the classic debate between experiential and theoretical approaches to education; they show, as well, a keen awareness that a psychological problem may exist. Some dieticians express a cautious belief that there is sometimes a link between being informed and levels of compliance, for example, when the patient lacks knowledge of dietary principles:

> It depends on the patient. For some, it is a lack of information that leads to poor nutrition, but not always. (F, 43, General Practitioner)

A significant number of respondents share the opinion that personalized patient care is necessary, as is the need to adapt advice to the patient so that the information becomes useful:

> This is not enough, and the best compliance comes from trying it out and verifying the validity of the information in real-life situations, because for compliance to occur, information that is observed must make sense. One way to make sense of it is to verify in practice that the information is useful and helpful. (F, 52, Obesity and Eating Disorders)

Thus, the work of mediation appears to focus less on the content to be conveyed than on how and when to convey information. Respondents emphasize, as well, the need to react to the actual course of the session and to the patients' receptivity to advice; this idea is summarized by one respondent as follows:

Everything comes down to the method of informing. (F, 33, Excess Weight, Obesity and Cancer)

Half of the professionals indicate that during consultations they provide a lot of explanations (75 respondents), and that they try to 'make information accessible to the uninitiated'. Some qualify their explanations as popularization (34): 'I explain by popularizing and I suggest that they experiment and test for themselves.' Some seek to adapt their discourse as well as 'the level of detail of the explanations according to the patient's ability to comprehend and his level of curiosity' or 'according to the person (child, adult)', and by 'adapting the vocabulary' (12). The purpose of explanations is 'to enlighten but not to force, to negotiate', 'to make people understand', 'to interpret nutritional information'. Some respondents express their opposition to the idea of persuasion: 'I try to explain, I don't like to impose'; 'I try not to explain too much, but rather to make the person think.' For some professionals, on the contrary, such explanations are considered to be part of persuasive evidence:

I explain and present arguments so that they are convinced. (F, 43, Pathologies and Weight Loss)

I use a therapeutic patient education approach. A lot of listening, looking for ways to build on the patient's knowledge to take him/her to new knowledge. Presenting arguments to 'dismantle' preconceived ideas without negative judgment. (F, 40, General Practitioner)

For others, the therapeutic consultation does not aim to provide knowledge but is essentially a place to listen:

I try to let patients express themselves as much as possible through active listening and I respond by highlighting the objectives that are important to them and any ambivalence. (F, 31, Geriatrics, Eating Disorders)

In such cases, information exchange is present but is not necessarily part of a direct evidence-based argument:

I start from convictions and I bring in relevant information in order to increase the patient's awareness of the positive effects of modifying his or her behavior and to lead the patient to find a solution. (F, 47, Geriatrics)

The idea behind this form of knowledge transmission is that there is not a 'knower' who transmits knowledge, but a 'listener' who accompanies the patient to find his or her own way:

I don't judge. I'm helping. I position myself as a transmitter of knowledge and not as a judge – I let patients express themselves a lot so that they can build their own knowledge, rather than imposing it on them. (F, 33, Excess Weight, Childhood Obesity, TPE)

Finally, we wished to know whether professionals use any media, visuals or other material in addition to the classic tools of dieticians (height gauge, scales, etc.). Regarding tools used, 104 professionals answered 'yes', 7 answered 'no' and the others did not respond. For those who answered in the affirmative, a large majority said they create diagrams 'in the course of the consultation to tailor it to the patient'. These spontaneously drawn diagrams 'support technical explanations' such as 'metabolism or thought patterns in the case of eating disorders' or they 'illustrate' the point and are adapted to patients' particular cases: 'construction of the Fairburn circle with the patient, based on his or her own experience'. This propensity to use imagery during consultations is a major tendency which emerges from analysis of the questionnaire: 'when discussing balanced eating, I draw my hand or they draw theirs'. This tendency also extends to verbal interactions through use of metaphors and illustrations: 'lots of examples and recontextualization, otherwise the information is useless'. Some use tools that support interaction (Lilly conversation map); some professionals provide documents at the end of the consultation (recipes, menus, etc.) and patients take these with them in order to 'keep a record' and 'memorize' the information.

Apart from materials created by professionals, other documents produced 'by intention' are also presented, most of them in infographic form: the 'eating and moving' nutritional campaign materials, certain HAS diagrams on bariatric surgery, videos, food pyramids, brochures on calories and fat, comparative menus (provided by GROS), visuals representing photos of balanced meals with food portions (e.g. from Suvimax studies on vitamins and minerals), health-related graphs (evolution, body mass index, growth for paediatrics), photos of food packaging and photos of foods shown with carbohydrate and lipid equivalents.

Documents 'by attribution' are also used, such as play tea sets, dishes, play foods, games (for children) as well as food tins, food packaging and odour vials.

Discussion and conclusion

In this study, we considered dieticians as a professional body tasked by public health policy with informing, educating and promoting the nutritional model promoted by the PNNS public health campaign launched in 2001. Our objective was to explore the role that information practices and processes play in mediating dietary knowledge during counselling sessions. The lengthy questionnaire completed by a population of dieticians allows us to draw some conclusions.

For dieticians, 'information' refers to several realities, exposing the plasticity of the notion in its common-sense usage. Thus, in their answers, dieticians associate the notion of information with the media, with documents by intention and with documents by attribution: official sources (nutritional information), educational materials (objects, explanatory diagrams, nutritional pyramids), and written traces of consultations (such as notes). In addition, dieticians refer to information as the action of keeping oneself informed via oral sources, whether informal (word of mouth, social networks) or formal (television, radio), and via written sources (professional press, specialist journals and magazines). Finally, information is seen by dieticians as a practice promoting the construction of individual knowledge; such knowledge is influenced by current trends, by habits and by beliefs which professionals seek to deconstruct.

Due in part to the considerable length of sessions, the consultation is a rich and complex moment which allows for in-depth and wide-ranging exchange. The information practices of patients and professionals nourish these exchanges, while professionals are expected to provide authoritative opinions. Patients draw on media sources (internet and traditional media) as well as information passed on by word of mouth. Professionals are exposed to specialized information, including professional journals that relay public health and nutrition policy and scientific articles. Yet dieticians are also confronted with information meant for the general public in the same way as patients, due to the prevalence of food issues in society; this can be the source of tension.

If the consultation is a place for intense exchange, the main priority remains providing dietary support. To this end, professionals use various communicational approaches. For the majority of professionals, the information process helps to enlighten patients while contributing to their autonomy; this position is close to the communication model characteristic of the medical setting. In this sense, health information as it is practiced in the setting of dietary consultations contributes to increasing acknowledgement of patients' expertise, and to recognition of experiential knowledge. Informational asymmetry is thus attenuated in favour of patients, through a process seen by some as a form of 'empowerment' (Bourret 2011) or of individual capacity-building. Other professionals, however, feel that information exchanges are not sufficient for supporting patients' dietary compliance goals. For these dieticians, knowledge about the nutritional composition of foods or about dietary balance ultimately has little influence, as compared to patients' feelings, their eating behaviour and their relationship to food. This finding might explain why the last three French national PNNS health campaigns have not had the desired effect on the population; indeed statistics show an increase in the prevalence of obesity in France.[16] In this sense, information is not 'the raw material for decision-making' contrary to the role assigned to it by public health policy (Cecchi 2008).

Whatever their position on the role of information practices in dietary support, all professionals rely on expert knowledge to break down preconceived ideas, to explain, to illustrate, to help patients feel and understand, to quantify and to compare. Tools and media used during these sessions take varied forms including visual aids, lists and physical objects representing the culinary world. While some of these tools and media are made available by health institutions, others are created spontaneously by the professionals themselves to support verbal exchange and to adapt content to the patient. Thus, knowledge mediation does not occur as top-down dissemination of specialized information to patients. This approach, based on a relationship marked by listening and advice, differs from food pedagogy in the school setting, where prescriptive models of 'good nutrition' predominate (Berthoud 2018). The problem of how to promote critical approaches to information and media is mentioned by dieticians yet no definite solution emerges from their responses.

In conclusion, expert knowledge is mediated in the course of exchanges in ways which aim to support patient motivation and negotiated objectives. While professionals sometimes resort to persuasive arguments during consultations, their discourse departs from medical models of prescriptive discourse, with the exception of professionals specializing in treatment of a specific pathology. We can say that dieticians contribute to the advancement of national health and nutrition policy goals, but that as practitioners, their experience with the population has led some to personalize information in order to build meaning *with* patients, a posture that shows full engagement in the therapeutic alliance.

Notes

1. We would like to thank the French Nutritionnist Dieticians Association (AFDN) for distributing this questionnaire.
2. This questionnaire was distributed by the AFDN in the following departments: Savoie, Haute-Savoie, Drôme-Ardèche, Ain, Loire, Rhône. Forty-four people responded between June and October 2018 (40 women and 4 men), out of a total of 279 members.
3. One-day workshop on *Santé, information-communication et alimentation. Les alicaments* (Health, information-communication and diet: Functional foods), organized by Gresec and the LFBA at the Institute of Communication and Media, Echirolles, 6 June 2016.
4. 'Broadly defined, the concept of "Everyday Life Information Seeking (ELIS)" refers to the acquisition of various informational (both cognitive and expressive) elements, which people employ to orient themselves in daily life or to solve problems not directly connected with the performance of professional tasks. Such problems may be associated with various areas of everyday life, for example, consumption and health care' (Savolainen 1995: 266–7).
5. 'The totality of human behavior in relation to sources and channels of information, including both active and passive information seeking, and information use' (Wilson 2000: 49).
6. Available online: https://solidarites-sante.gouv.fr/prevention-en-sante/preser ver-sa-sante/le-programme-national-nutrition-sante/article/programme-national-nutrition-sante-pnns-professionnels (accessed 20 May 2020).
7. The notions of established (scientific) knowledge and acquired (individual) knowledge can be distinguished as follows: 'Knowledge for ICS is the sum of socially recognized acquired individual knowledge, and constitutes an objectified whole. While acquired individual knowledge has a personal and subjective character, established scientific knowledge is a set of constituent elements of a science. Once knowledge is rendered objective, it can in turn be partially transformed into exchangeable information. Thus, acquired knowledge is specific to the individual, built from and transmitted through information. This is called the process of signification. Signification is thus the result of a process of standardization, legitimization and provides objects of shareable meaning' (Gardiès et Fabre 2015: 5–6).
8. In contrast to other European countries, France is one of two countries, along with Germany, offering a short training course; all of the other countries offer traditional university degrees, i.e. Bachelor's, Master's and Doctorate (Livre Blanc 2017: 7).
9. The numbers stand at 6,643 professionals in 2010, 7,168 in 2011, 7,871 in 2012, 8,525 in 2013, 9,252 in 2014, 9,972 in 2015, 10,796 in 2016, 11,612 in 2017 and 12,442 in 2018, according to the following two complementary sources of information:

(1) 'Statistics on Health Professions. The Nutrition Professions', La Direction de la recherche, des études, de l'évaluation et des statistiques (Drees). Available online: http://drees.solidarites-sante.gouv.fr/etudes-et-statistiques/la-drees/qui-sommes-nous/6643 (accessed 20 May 2020); (2) 'Data', Drees Etudes et statistiques Available online: http://www.data.drees.sante.gouv.fr/TableViewer/tableView.aspx (accessed 20 May 2020).

10. These demands include the integration of primary professional training programme for dieticians into the university curriculum, as well as standard health care coverage for dietary consultations and acts, which are currently not included in France's social security and health insurance system. Cf. Livre Blanc (2017).

11. Ambroise Martin, nutrition expert, has been or still is a member of several bodies (National Food Council, PNNS Steering Committee, European Food Safety Authority).

12. Preparing a dietary diagnosis, preventive action, implementation of nutritional treatment, therapeutic education, monitoring of nutritional status, carrying out a global assessment.

13. After each verbatim quotation, we indicate in parentheses the following information about the dieticians who responded to our 2020 Survey: gender (H/F), age and one or more declared areas of specialization if pertinent; the self-reported terms indicating an absence of specialization vary: 'non-specialized', 'general', etc.

14. 'Dietary restraint refers to the attitude of individuals who deliberately limit their food intake in order to lose weight or to avoid gaining weight' (Le Barzic 2001: 512).

15. We do not know whether the communicational model is chosen deliberately or not, as the notion of 'active listening' is mentioned repeatedly in responses and is, moreover, recommended by the HAS.

16. 'Obésite: prévention et prise en charge. Ministère des Solidarités et de la Santé', Available online: https://solidarites-sante.gouv.fr/systeme-de-sante-et-medico-social/strategie-nationale-de-sante/priorite-prevention-rester-en-bonne-sante-tout-au-lon g-de-sa-vie-11031/priorite-prevention-les-mesures-phares-detaillees/article/obesite-prevention-et-prise-en-charge (accessed 20 May 2020).

Information practices and knowledge appropriation among gluten-sensitive individuals

Virginie Córdoba-Wolff

Introduction

In France and Germany, gluten-free food has been the focus of attention since its first important media coverage and the introduction of a range of gluten-free products in 2010.[1] Yet people have been following this regime since the 1950s.[2] Unknown or called into question by a large number of general practitioners or specialists trained in biomedicine, gluten sensitivities and intolerances have been poorly publicized by the medical sphere; we can therefore ask the following question: How do people who eat gluten-free gain access to information about this diet or about gluten-related disorders?

A survey conducted by CREDOC (Centre de Recherche pour l'Étude et l'Observation des Conditions de Vie)[3] and OCHA (Observatoire Cniel des Habitudes Alimentaires)[4] on food avoidance, revealed that 5.7 per cent of the French population avoided gluten consumption in 2018 (OCHA CREDOC 2018).[5] Among people who do not consume gluten, 43 per cent say they are 'allergic', 'intolerant', 'sensitive' or 'hypersensitive' to gluten, in other words, they make this choice for health reasons. According to this study, only one-third of people who do not consume gluten have received advice from a health professional (general practitioner, gastroenterologist, other specialist, homeopath, naturopath) not to eat gluten. Health professionals are far from being the only source of information for people who do not consume gluten. The objective of this chapter is to question the information practices and knowledge appropriation of people who do not eat gluten for health reasons. In order to understand the emergence of the gluten-free diet, the role of a multitude of new figures who contribute to the production and dissemination of imaginaries and practices must also be taken into account, such as the media, food brands and the people affected themselves, who share their own experience through different channels (people around them, associations, internet, etc.).

Health and nutrition information seeking:
From an attempt at reassurance to self-responsibilization

Research in the sociology of health and illness has reported the role of exchanges between patients (Gagnon 1999), through support groups and patient associations, as in the case of AIDS (Herzlich 1995, Barbot and Dodier 2000), cancer (Knobé 2009), rare diseases (Huyard 2011) or autism (Chamak 2008). These associations constitute groups where patients, relatives and professionals, that is, actors with different social positions, skills and interests meet up. Various sources of information circulate within these groups, including knowledge transmitted by professionals, but also knowledge derived from the experience of patients or parents of sick children. Several studies highlight the place of experience in the ways patients build up knowledge about health, particularly in the case of chronic diseases (Baszanger 1986). While patient associations are sometimes presented as real political and scientific actors (Rabeharisoa and Callon 2000), patient knowledge, sometimes described as 'lay' or 'experiential' knowledge, occupies an ambivalent place, as shown by Tijou-Traoré (2010) in her study on the role of experience in the production of knowledge on diabetes in Mali. While some studies are interested in the role of patient associations in the development of therapeutic education in health (Lecimbre, Gagnayre, Deccache and d'Ivernois 2002), very few go into detail about the types of advice given within patient groups, particularly with regard to nutritional advice.

Aside from associations, social media have become essential sources of information in the field of health: blogs or forums devoted to diseases or symptoms have developed widely in recent years. The first health-related sites were created in the mid-1990s (Romeyer 2012). 'Patient knowledge' is also transmitted through these new media (Akrich and Méadel 2009). Several studies show that information-seeking is a complementary practice to medical consultation (Fox and Fallows 2003): people are more likely to search on the internet for health information when they visit a doctor or a clinic, before and after the consultation. Adams and Blandford (2005) show the importance of temporal factors in understanding users' changing information needs over time, via an 'information journey' that involves the use of both online and offline resources. This raises the question of the kind of information required at particular moments and contexts. As Johnson (2003) explains, individuals are embedded in multi-contextual environments that must be taken into account in order to understand information-seeking, use and needs. The passage from one context to another during an information search can lead individuals to unexpected information and documentary resources that are sometimes conflicting. This approach seems to be of interest for understanding how people choose and appropriate some pieces of information and not others in a context where an abundance of information is accessible to the individual, in particular in terms of nutrition and health.

Before medical consultations, patients go online to prepare for the visit, to decide whom to see, to know what the doctor is going to talk about and to have relevant questions to ask. After the consultation they go on the internet for a better understanding of the diagnosis, to check the treatment and to look for an alternative (Attfield, Adams and Blandford 2006; McMullan 2006). Diet is often at the centre of alternative solutions, as with some cancer patients, who do not find enough counselling in official oncology institutions and who seek out 'alternative food movements' on the internet, in the press or in specialized books (Cohen and Legrand 2011). Similarly, in a context of uncertainty in the care of autism, parents of children with autism often consult online communities, which encourage gluten-free and casein-free diets to reduce the disorder (Rochedy 2019).

Hélène Romeyer's survey (2008), based on an analysis of the website Doctissimo, highlights the specific use of information found on discussion forums, namely health information. Users come to reassure themselves and exchange with the people who understand them best and who are experiencing the same situation. Internet users seem to differentiate between medical information and health information. According to Romeyer (2008: §33), what they are looking for on Doctissimo is practical information, given in a common language, while continuing to give a preponderant role to doctors and scientists. In other words, in addition to medical information, people are looking for practical information on the one hand and emotional support on the other. Fox and Fallows show that this is more often the case for women (2003).

Hence, information seeking does not necessarily have the objective of interfering with biomedical prescriptions, it can be very complementary and can help the patient be better informed, so that he/she can play an active role in his/her own health. As Lee, Gray and Lewis (2010) suggest, higher levels of internet use among cancer patients may lead patients to want to be more actively involved in medical decision making. Furthermore, the more frequently a person uses the internet as a source of health information, the more likely he/she is to change his/her health behaviour (Ayers and Kronenfeld 2007). In addition, health information seekers who live with a chronic illness or disability actively use the internet and are avid online communicators (Fox and Fallows 2003).

Acquiring knowledge about their illness is also described as a strategy to deal with uncertain illness trajectories or contested illnesses such as gluten sensitivity. For instance, Åsbring and Närvänen (2004) showed how the acquisition of knowledge enabled women with chronic fatigue syndrome and fibromyalgia to reduce anxiety and gain control over the situation and its effects. In the same way, Caiata-Zufferey et al. (2010) showed that the initial motivations for online health information seeking are found in the needs for acknowledgement, for reduction of uncertainty and for gaining new perspectives. Nevertheless, according to these authors, searching online for health information is also encouraged by personal and contextual factors including a person's sense of self-responsibility and the opportunity to use the internet. These phenomena reveal an ever-increasing dynamic of personal responsibilization, relating to both eating and health. Information and communication technologies (ICTs) seem to contribute to this (Lemire 2008). The patient or consumer is asked to be active in the management of his/her health, to inform himself/herself and to adopt 'good' practices. Lupton shows that health cannot be understood simply as the presence or absence of disease but represents a moral imperative that is embedded in social and cultural norms: people have to be capable to govern themselves and to adhere voluntarily, through procedures of knowledge, regulation and self-control, to the imperatives of their own government (Lupton 1995).

This process of responsibilization is particularly visible in the case of eating disorders. In the case of obesity in children, responsibility is often imputed to the mother (Maher, Fraser and Wright 2010). But more broadly, the general consumer is called upon to adopt a 'healthier' lifestyle. Discourses on what is supposed to be healthy are produced by public authorities or biomedical bodies yet 'health' discourse is also mixed with marketing discourse, as on Facebook, used for sharing health information and for the promotion of dietary products (Leis et al. 2013).

In the case of gluten-related disorders, diet plays a key role, since the only treatment available to date is the gluten-free diet. Furthermore, according to the OCHA-CREDOC study mentioned earlier, 92.9 per cent of people who do not consume gluten think that diet has an influence on health. According to the study, gluten-free people spend on average more time searching for information on healthy eating than the general population: they are significantly over-represented among those who spend more than thirty minutes a week searching for information, and even more so among those who spend more than two hours a week doing so. They are under-represented among those who do not seek any information. The process of media coverage of cooking – in the press, on television, on the radio or on the internet – and the development of culinary blogging have given people new resources with which to keep themselves informed. French culinary blogs first appeared around 2004, multiplying over the following decade (Naulin 2015), and the figure of the influencer, or 'prescriber', of consumer practices consequently emerged (Naulin 2014, 2017). The level of professionalism of these influencers varies from amateurs or hobbyists to professionals. In France, blogs offer mostly daily domestic culinary advice and are almost exclusively written by women. This finding can be related to gender inequalities in food and eating, but also to the distribution of domestic tasks (Fournier et al. 2015).

Methodology and framework of the survey

Based on data collected as part of a thesis in sociology on food avoidance carried out in France and Germany, this chapter focuses on how people search for, select, process and appropriate information and knowledge on food and health, particularly on gluten-free food and on gluten-related diseases. The questions we address are as follows: How do people who do not consume gluten find information? What resources do they have at their disposal? What information are they looking for? How much trust do they place in the information they receive and in the persons or authorities that pass it on to them?

The corpus under study is composed of fifty semi-directive interviews conducted with gluten-free people and twenty-four professionals concerned by this issue (including ten who do not eat gluten); participant observations (of meals, events or meetings attended by people who avoid gluten); a quantitative survey conducted in partnership with OCHA and CREDOC among the French population; and analysis of twenty-four French and German blogs and websites. My research proposes a *histoire croisée*[6] (Werner and Zimmermann 2003) of gluten-free eating and of the scientific and media controversies it has generated on both sides of the Rhine. It deals with finding points of intersection, which may be multiple, in the history of the emergence of the gluten-free diet as a social phenomenon. Germany and France are societies in contact, but also and above all, the people who live there may come into contact with the same objects and documents which circulate in the two countries. This is the case, for example, with scientific publications in gastroenterology, documents published by the Association Of European Coeliac Societies (AOECS), or books popularized for the lay public available in several languages. In my *histoire croisée*, attention is focused on the contexts of the emergence of the gluten-free diet. Different scales of observation are linked, in order to relate individual histories to one another and to reveal shared or connected histories on a transnational level. The experiences of the people concerned, in particular how easily or not they switch to the regime according to specific contexts (availability of products, access to information, support from health professionals and associations), are the entry point to this *histoire croisée*.

In order to collect general data on people's profiles and backgrounds, the interviews conducted with people who do not eat gluten covered several areas. These sometimes followed a slightly different order, depending on the thread of the discussion: how people came to the gluten-free diet, their social and professional life, food acquisition, daily diet, commensality, relation to medical knowledge, information searches, interactions with other people who avoid gluten. The questions related to information seeking were intended to allow people to answer accurately, give examples and relate anecdotes. Answers to the question 'How do you learn about gluten-free or possible gluten-related conditions?' were diverse for each individual. I wished to establish an inventory of the sources cited during the interviews and to specify in which contexts these sources, belonging to different registers, were used.

The results of my study show multiple and complementary practices, both online and offline. In particular, two types of information seeking appear: those oriented towards biomedical and/or non-biomedical information (theoretical knowledge) and those aimed at acquiring practical knowledge (know-how). In both cases, the sources may be varied: theoretical knowledge may include health information produced by biomedical specialists (general practitioners, gastroenterologists, paediatricians, etc.), non-biomedical specialists (naturopaths, acupuncturists, etc.) and information produced by people who have carried out research in a private or professional context (scientific journalists, people directly concerned with the issue). On the other hand, know-how is generally disseminated by private individuals (enthusiastic food bloggers, writers of recipe books), associations, private companies (selling gluten-free products) or by the press. Nevertheless, blogs which have as their primary objective the sharing of gluten-free know-how very often offer articles, or even entire sections, in which theoretical knowledge is popularized (albeit not necessarily scientific knowledge, which is sometimes highly contested). For example, bloggers present books that have helped them get a better understanding of their disease or that explain changes in cereal production.

There are several reasons why people avoid gluten consumption. I focus on people diagnosed with coeliac disease (an autoimmune disease, also called 'gluten intolerance') and those who define themselves as gluten sensitive or hypersensitive (when varying levels of pain and discomfort are relieved by the removal of gluten). This chapter is based on the information 'pathways' of people who avoid gluten consumption in France and Germany, and one of its objectives is to reveal the different uses and modes of appropriation of information resources in relation to their diet and/or conditions.

To further describe the resources used, I distinguish between searches oriented towards theoretical knowledge and information aimed at the acquisition of practical knowledge. Nevertheless, categorizing types of resources this way tends to mask what links or distinguishes how people use resources. For this reason, I focus on describing typical information-seeking experiences, while highlighting the disparities that may exist in the ways people get their information. I develop three categories of analysis that may offer clues to understanding differences in the information 'pathways' of the people I met. First, the way people access information has changed significantly with the emergence of blogs and internet forums. Second, the stabilization or non-stabilization of health status appears to affect both the amount and the type of information seeking conducted. Finally, differences in information-seeking practices appear to be gender-related.

Finding gluten-free information before and after the internet

The emergence of internet sites thematizing the topic of gluten-free eating seems to influence the periods of information seeking both before diagnosis and after diagnosis (if diagnosis has taken place). People who started the diet before the mid-2000s and parents of children diagnosed with coeliac disease before that date recount their difficult quest for information.

Towards the right track

Finding the doctor who knows about the disease

On the one hand, physicians' knowledge concerning coeliac disease or other conditions possibly related to gluten was minimal at that time, and yet physicians were one of the only sources available. Catherine (seventy-four years old, retired dietician, diagnosed coeliac in 1991, Alsace), mother of Carole (forty-five years old, diagnosed coeliac in 1977, pastor-theologian, Alsace) told me that her daughter's health was getting worse every day, that she did not eat anything and that she was constantly sick. The doctors she had seen in France either put her on the wrong track or had no answer:

> [My general practitioner in France] says to me: 'But your daughter has anorexia nervosa. We gotta get her into a day care centre.' We did that for two months, but then it didn't get any better. And then I saw a paediatrician. So, that was forty-two years ago. The paediatrician says: 'Well, I can't think what it can be.'

Only one interviewee who was diagnosed before the end of the 2000s was diagnosed coeliac directly after consulting their doctor.[7] The diagnosis sometimes occurred more than twenty years after the first consultation. For Catherine's daughter, it was a paediatrician, whom she consulted during a holiday in Switzerland, who hinted at the possibility of coeliac disease:

> We went to the mountains in Switzerland, with our little one who … who had bronchitis, or whatever. I saw the local paediatrician, who said to me, 'Haven't you ever thought of this disease?'

It was both the occasion of the trip to Switzerland (where the disease was better known)[8] and the need and the opportunity to consult a paediatrician during their stay which enabled Catherine to be given an idea of the diagnosis. Context, or the embeddedness of contexts, plays an important role here. Even though Catherine had trained as a dietician in the 1970s, she did not think her daughter's symptoms could be related to this disease.

> I had done dietetics, but I never thought about it … First of all, coeliac disease almost didn't exist … In France we talked very little about it. We were talking about … There was a name … For grown-ups … [She doesn't remember].

It was thus thanks to personal contacts from her family network that Catherine was able to have her daughter diagnosed in Switzerland:

> I had a cousin of my mother's who was a paediatrician, head of paediatrics in Lausanne. [My husband] says to me, 'Listen, go and see him.' And they did a biopsy right away. And they showed me the biopsy, they told me … It was incredible, that was it. It was coeliac disease, for them it was clear – gluten intolerance – within 24 hours.

With this first trajectory, it is possible to notice that before the internet, access to information seemed much more difficult, sometimes reserved for people who had contacts in the medical field and opportunities to travel to meet doctors competent in this field.

Adam (non-coeliac), the father of Tobias (twenty years old, diagnosed coeliac in 2002, Berlin), told me a similar story about his son's diagnosis. After the introduction of wheat into Tobias's diet, at about six months, his health gradually deteriorated – chronic diarrhoea, a lot of fatigue and withdrawal. His father confided to me that Tobias no longer dared to try new things (like walking or playing). He had become apathetic. He had the typical clinical signs of a young coeliac child, that is, those of an undernourished child (bloated abdomen and small limbs), but no paediatrician or even gastroenterologist was able to diagnose him. It was only during an emergency hospitalization for pneumonia that a gastroenterologist (affiliated with another clinic) came to his room, simply glanced at Tobias and concluded that he was coeliac. Tobias was cared for in the Charité University Hospital in Berlin, where it is possible to meet research doctors, who are more aware of the existence of certain emerging pathologies.

Informing yourself

Willingness to seek information

Before the internet, it seems that the only hope was to meet a knowledgeable doctor, or relatives who knew about coeliac disease, in order to have an idea of the diagnosis. The pre-internet era did not mean that the information was inaccessible, but that it was reserved for people who were able to invest a lot of time and willing to train themselves, like Heloise (seventy-seven years old, retired psychoanalyst, undiagnosed coeliac, hepatitis A and C, she has been avoiding gluten and lactose since 1993, Alsace). Her digestive problems began after contracting hepatitis C in 1967 (hepatitis was not diagnosed at the time).

Heloise:	But because I didn't know what I had ... I thought, Well, I've got to find a way to overcome this ... And I tried a lot of things. And it's true I had some ... I never had any medication, no.
Interviewer:	So, you didn't want to try drugs?
Heloise:	Medication was out of the question for me. First, the doctor told me: 'There's no medicine for it.' So there was nothing, there was nothing to look for. And ... Uh ... For hepatitis, there's no painkiller, there's nothing ... I stuck to homeopathy and I trained myself, I trained in nutrition a lot at that time.

Heloise turned to other health care practices because biomedicine offered no solution. This lack of response and treatment from her general practitioner encouraged her to find solutions on her own. As a result, she 'received a lot of training in nutrition' and even 'taught balanced nutrition in an adult education centre'. She says: 'I was very interested in it, first of all in relation to myself. The question was always, "What's wrong with me? Why do I have these digestive problems? I didn't know why."' She also trained in psychoanalysis and naturotherapy (among other areas). When she contracted hepatitis A in 1992, her digestive problems increased tenfold:

> After that, I came across Dr. Seignalet's work ... So obviously, I did some research ... And I found a doctor who was an acolyte of Dr. Seignalet, who also helped me a lot with regard to gluten-free, lactose-free information. He was in Brittany [She knew him] through friends, colleagues ... Yes, so I went there, we went there, twice a year.

Training, reading and travelling – access to information seemed to be conditioned partly by the possibilities in terms of organization, time, financial means, but also skills. Heloise was not diagnosed coeliac but found out for herself the foods that did not suit her. She says that a few years later, in 2005, she 'discovered allergy and intolerance tests, and Imupro. ... And that was when it was established – no lactose and no gluten.' This test is questioned by the biomedical community, as are homeopathy and the writings of Seignalet and Kousmine, which she cites during the interview. Since she did not get enough answers from biomedicine, she sought other approaches to health care.

The role played by individuals themselves in their diagnosis and treatment is a permanent feature, before and after the internet. There is a high degree of personal responsibilization, which essentially appears to be a personal initiative taken by the people I met. This was particularly the case when respondents felt that they were not getting adequate information from health professionals and when they thought their doctor was uninformed. In an attempt to seek out an answer or to avoid remaining passive, people gather information from different sources. Motivation to carry out further searches therefore also depends on the relationship with the referring physician or with the specialists that people have consulted. Many interviewees described their difficult medical encounters and the feeling that they were not listened to or taken seriously by the doctor when they talked about their symptoms. With the internet, a great amount of information is available quickly and free of charge, but differences persist between the practices of the various participants, particularly regarding their literacy and health literacy (Nutbeam 2008). People who have never dealt with the scientific or biomedical field in their professional career rarely come across information emanating directly from the biomedical sphere, such as scientific articles published in peer-reviewed journals.

Knowing how to select information

It is important to note that despite better access to information with the internet, disparities in information seeking are discernible according to patients' educational levels, areas of academic study, skills acquired elsewhere, and more generally, according to socialization. Maëlle (twenty-eight years old, biology teacher, diagnosed coeliac in December 2014, Alsace) explains, for example, that her doctor had no idea what coeliac disease was, and that she was the one who informed him. This case shows that a high level of education, in biology, led her to want to play a role in medical decision-making. Maëlle conducted her own research, both on the internet and in 'immunology books', which she had access to during her studies to become a biology teacher. She said:

I was lucky to arrive 'late'. Because there are people, I've talked to people who were diagnosed thirty years ago and it's much more complicated to ... It's much more complicated than that. So I went gluten-free in December 2014 and um ... It had been three years, actually, since I had been trying to find what the problem was ... I'd been practically on my own for three years, actually, looking for what was wrong. I was actually at university at the time and um ... So I was studying biology and uh ... And one day, in the third year of my bachelor's degree, we had an immunology class on autoimmune diseases. And someone mentioned coeliac disease. And, uh ... it was an unfamiliar word, actually, when the teacher said, 'Coeliac disease'. Well, everyone stayed in the lecture hall: 'What's that?' And then the teacher started explaining that it was, um … wheat intolerance. That's as far as he went. He didn't use the word 'gluten'. Because I didn't make the connection. And uh … It was on my mind for several weeks … And I started to do my research actually … Also in the immuno [immunology] books. 'Cause Doctissimo is not … that's not really my thing. Because I don't really like to search that kind of thing, because first, some things are wrong, and on top of that, it usually induces a lot of anxiety. I don't want to get lost on there. Because I know I'm the kind of person … [laughs] who is quick to worry. So I thought, 'Let's stick to science books.' And I stuck to immuno books to see how to diagnose this disease. And I found it was gluten-related. So I started looking into what it was.

Not all resources are used in the same way, depending on people's skills and expectations. Maëlle mentions her academic background, which led her to seek out a particular type of information. Access to resources, as well as the ability to understand scientific texts, also has an impact on searching and appropriation practices. Maëlle trusts immunology books: the fact that they are written and verified by biology experts makes them trustworthy for her. With regard to medical information, whether it is information on the diagnosis of coeliac disease or its etiopathology, she expresses her mistrust of forums and social networks. Scientific language is opposed to the emotional tone found on Doctissimo. To deal with uncertainty, she refuses to use the forums, which would cause her greater anxiety. Nonetheless, later in the interview she confided that she sometimes consults Doctissimo. Information needs are different in each context – for example, she uses Doctissimo to find the name of a 'good' doctor, and goes to blogs to find recipes.

After diagnosis, the quest for information continues

The exchange of 'tips and tricks' within organizations

The Association Française des Intolérants au Gluten (AFDIAG, created in 1978 and then refounded in 1989, with about 5,000 members) and the Deutsche Zöliakie Gesellschaft (DZG, created in 1974, with about 40,000 members) were among the few organizations where information on coeliac disease, its diagnosis and treatment was available. These two organizations made it possible to discuss with people who were going through similar situations and to exchange 'tips and tricks'. Carole's mother recounts her travels to Switzerland to meet other specialists, gather more information and get in touch with a coeliac patient organization. She wanted to acquire both medical and scientific knowledge, meet other people in the same situation, find moral comfort and take her daughter on a trip:

And so, once my daughter was diagnosed with coeliac disease, I tried to find a few other people … In Switzerland, there was an association that was already very good and so when it held general meetings, I took my eight- or ten-year-old daughter with me and we went to the meetings … in the French-speaking area, since that's where I come from … And my daughter was always delighted, she told me: 'Fancy that, tables with lots of cakes that I could eat!' For her it was nirvana, it was the only place where she'd ever seen that.

Before the 2010s, very few gluten-free foods were marketed. Gluten-free products were seen as a 'diet for the sick' and the food was only sold in pharmacies or health food stores (*Reformhaus* in Germany). My respondents often claim that these breads, pasta and cakes have a strange texture and taste, and that they took no pleasure in eating them. Since few gluten-free recipes were available, meetings with other parents of coeliac children, mainly through organizations, were also an opportunity to discover and share recipes that might appeal to them and be suitable for their children.

The abundance and diversity of practical advice on the internet

With the development of the internet, a multitude of recipes, developed and tested by parents or people who eat gluten-free, have been made available. The culinary advice offered by patient organizations has thus lost its appeal. Several people told me that they do not like the recipes presented during workshops or in documents provided by the organization, because they were often made with so-called 'industrial' flour blends offered by major brands. The dissemination of recipes on the internet has had the effect of making people more selective and eager to find diversified recipes. For example, Amélie (twenty-four years old, accounting employee, diagnosed coeliac in 2014, Alsace) explains how she finds ideas:

> I often look for several recipes and that's when I'll come across blogs. Sometimes they're not blogs … like 'Au Féminin' [the online version of a French magazine], they offer gluten-free recipes. Or … what was it the other day? Not Le Monde … but a newspaper like that.

In addition to specialized sections created by the general press, websites or magazines created by gluten-free brands are consulted. The brands offer both recipes and a variety of health information and are a source of inspiration for some of the respondents I met.

Adam (non-coeliac, computer scientist, Berlin), Tobias's father, tells how he set up a self-help forum on the internet because apart from a Wikipedia page, nothing could be found about practical matters in the early 2000s:

> Internet wasn't that great yet, so there was, there was Wikipedia, but otherwise not that much information … about gluten-free eating, what it means in practice, they [the doctors] don't know anything. When you say, 'Well, what can you do?' 'Well, I don't know …' And then we searched the internet and I also contacted the German Coeliac Society [DZG] and looked it up on Wikipedia.

What Adam points out is that doctors do not provide advice for everyday life: they simply prescribe treatment, that is, the gluten-free diet, without explaining how to go about it on a daily basis. Thus, in the forum he co-created, moderators answer questions about diagnosis and treatment, but also about daily life. This is the idea of a collaborative space in which non-professionals with knowledge, know-how and experience, pass on information that is not offered by doctors. After the creation of forums, blogs developed and disseminated the same types of information – recipes, product advice (e.g. which flour could replace wheat flour), ideas for restaurants offering gluten-free products. Such blogs almost always include a 'scientific information' section, covering gluten-related pathologies, diagnoses and the like. Most of my respondents have visited a few websites. The legitimacy given to bloggers is based on their experience and life trajectory. In other words, my interlocutors explained to me that they were interested in information provided by bloggers who had had similar experiences as they did, sometimes with complicated medical backgrounds, and who had had to change their daily lives and learn to manage their diet in different social contexts: at home, with their family, their friends or at work and outside the home.

In addition to practical information, bloggers slip in more theoretical and sometimes normative information. This can take the form of a sentence about the nutritional value or properties of a particular food. In other cases, readings about diet and health may be suggested. In the articles on recipes, bloggers encourage readers to consult the other sections, as in the post of a French blog, on 13 December 2019, devoted to making gluten-free *bredele* (Christmas cookies):

> Once the dough is ready, roll it into a ball and flatten it before putting it into the fridge for an hour, wrapped in plastic wrap. In the meantime, take the opportunity to read some articles [on the website] or ask us your questions on the forum!

The interviews with the people I met who conduct online searching also show that access to the internet contributes to a feeling of being able to act in the domain of food and health. Amélie (twenty-four years old, accounting employee, diagnosed coeliac in 2014, Alsace) feels she can rely on herself to find the resources that are useful to her in this context. She reveals that she feels 'autonomous' and that thanks to the tools at her disposal (internet), she is 'resourceful':

> I didn't feel the need [to go to more than one AFDIAG meeting]. Nah, because I think that in other days, it could have helped me. But today with the internet, you can find a lot of answers on your own. So, since I'm quite autonomous and resourceful, well, I got by, so I just didn't push any further.

The information available on blogs is perceived as understandable, but not all information is seen as directly usable. Preferred and selected recipes seem to be those with the least constraints (especially in terms of cost and time). Some recipes, which look appetizing but require too many ingredients (e.g. five different kinds of flour), are generally read 'for fun', but are not used.

Blogs offer recipes, moral support (as they show that other people are experiencing the same situation), but also deal with issues related to diagnostics, for example. The information provided sometimes overlaps with that offered by organizations. For people who do not wish to carry out further research, especially those in a stable state of health, this information seems sufficient.

Selecting sources for medical information

Nevertheless, with the emergence of gluten-free food blogs, the resources offered by organizations have played a major role in addressing other issues. First of all, patient organizations also play an important role as support groups. Second, for people who are at ease with the scientific and biomedical fields, such as Maëlle (twenty-eight years old, biology teacher, diagnosed coeliac in December 2014, Alsace), the information published by organizations, based on specialist knowledge and disseminated by doctors, is more reliable than content disseminated on forums or social networks, which are not moderated, or only lightly moderated:

> And fortunately, there was the AFDIAG. The organization … The organization actually saved me. Because … to feel part of a group. And their information allowed me to consolidate what I had found on my own. And actually, on the internet, you can see anything and everything, really. That's … crazy. I mean, if you google 'coeliac disease', the website that I found at the time was Passeport Santé, which said it was an allergy [laughs]. It was impossible actually to, to, to … to get clear and accurate information. And the only place I found it was the AFDIAG.

As explained by Barbot and Dodier (2000: 98), organizations are often perceived as relays for specialized authorities concerning medical information. This is also the case for the AFDIAG, which works with a medical committee (composed of gastroenterologists, paediatricians, nutritionists, dieticians). AFDIAG diffuses information from the medical profession, organizing several medical colloquia every year where doctors or researchers present their research. The proceedings of these symposia are then published and made available to members.

Differentiated practices according to health status and diagnosis

While information seeking can be seen as an initiative taken by people to obtain explanations and to control their bodies and their health on a daily basis, achieving a certain stability in their condition may lead them to reduce their information search efforts. For people whose disease is not stabilized or when there is no diagnosis, in other words, for people facing uncertainty, information seeking is generally a continuous process, and for them, sources are diversified.

As I mentioned earlier, the itinerary to becoming gluten-sensitive is seen as a dynamic process in three phases: the pre-diet phase, the beginning of the diet and the continuation of the diet. At each stage, there are different information needs. These phases are experienced differently depending on the stabilization of each person's health condition.

An intense, continuous quest in a context of uncertainty

When coeliac disease is not stabilized

At the beginning of the itinerary, before the diagnosis or when the diagnosis has just been made, but also when there is no diagnosis or when the condition is not stable, that is, when the body does not respond to the coeliac disease diet (if the antibodies do not diminish or there is no histological recovery), people tend to become more informed: they have many questions, which they try to answer by different means.

Observations made at medical symposia organized by the AFDIAG in Paris revealed that most of those present had been diagnosed recently, although a few had been coming for several years. In Berlin, I took part in several meetings organized by a small branch of the DZG. Appointments are more informal and intimate, in cafés or gluten-free restaurants. It is more a group meeting composed almost exclusively of coeliac women (usually about twenty). Most of them have complex health trajectories, their condition is not stabilized, or has stabilized recently. They continue to attend these groups, which could be described more as support groups — they know each other's health histories, and sometimes part of each other's private lives. They share cooking tips, health-related reading ideas and advice about how to carry on with the diagnosing process.

For people with coeliac disease who do not seem to respond to the gluten-free diet, that is, people for whom the only available treatment has no effect, it is the doctor who strongly urges them to review their practices, that is, their diet or even to consult a dietician. More information seeking will be directed towards practical advice on how to avoid mistakes, like detecting traces of gluten or possible contamination in a food or drug. The objective of the research is thus to learn how best to control one's environment. This was the case for Magda (seventy-two years old, diagnosed coeliac in 2013, housewife, Berlin), who followed the diet very strictly, but for whom the control biopsy performed one year after the beginning of the diet had not shown any improvement. Her husband confided to me that she came out crying after the appointments with her first gastroenterologist who pressed her, 'You must continue your diet or you will get cancer!' and referred her to dieticians to learn how to follow her diet better. Patient responsibility can thus also come directly from physicians. The help of dieticians was rarely mentioned among French interviewees. By contrast, most of the diagnosed coeliac patients I met in Germany received a prescription from their gastroenterologist, at least once after their diagnosis, to see a dietician who was familiar with coeliac disease, so that he or she could explain how to follow the diet, and especially how to 'avoid the traps', that is, how to detect foods containing gluten, sometimes a difficult task (especially with sauces, industrial preparations or even cheeses).

When there is no diagnosis

For people who do not have a clear diagnosis, knowing more seems to become an imperative. The search for information on healthy eating thus goes further, since it is not only gluten that is involved. The lack of answers from doctors pushes people to look elsewhere, towards other care practices, such as naturopathy or complementary practices. Information seeking thus also shifts towards more critical biomedical resources. The panel of sources often becomes larger, allowing for critical reappropriation of the discourses of doctors, but also of discourses found on the internet. This is notably the case for Léa (thirty-one years old, yoga teacher, undiagnosed, she has been avoiding gluten since 2015, Strasbourg). She is interested in non-biomedical care practices (acupuncture or other knowledge developed in Asia or Latin America), and is trained in the field of vegetal nutrition. Léa recounts how what she read got her worried about wheat:

> And therefore also the way in which the flour was processed, in addition to the ratio of these starches, the melopectine. Today's flours are filled with fungicide pesticides, and even nitrogen, which reinforces the gluten in the ear, and sometimes gluten is even added to this flour, which we are not aware of, we have no information about where it comes from. It's a little scary.

Some of the respondents, especially those who have not been diagnosed with coeliac disease, are critical of biomedicine and institutions, organizations in particular, but also of the agricultural system. Such respondents consider that biomedical research has not gone far enough and that these organizations merely relay the information, and thus do not inform them sufficiently. Moreover, the information provided by patient organizations is said to be too consensual, not calling current research into question, whether it be in biomedicine or in agriculture. These criticisms often come from people who also get their information through other channels, from the internet, magazines, books or after watching documentaries.

Those most willing to engage in in-depth information seeking also consult scientific publications and sometimes confront their gastroenterologist, like Alexandre who studied biology (forty years old, diagnosed coeliac in 2015, type 1 diabetic, Paris) and who sends emails to his doctor to ask him specific questions and to raise doubts about current research or ways of making diagnoses. It is precisely because he seeks answers to these types of questions that Alexandre wishes to be under the care of a university professor and hospital practitioner. Here again the role of respondents' level of education arises, as does the question of an individual's disposition to put questions to a specialist, out of a desire to participate actively in medical decision-making.

Standardization, adaptation and routine

Most of the time, it appears that more information seeking in health and science is carried out at the beginning of the itinerary. The progressive acquisition of knowledge, both scientific and practical, leads people to a stage where they feel they know 'enough'. They seem to reach a saturation level especially when the diagnosis is made or when the symptoms have disappeared or are under control. For example, Amélie (twenty-four years old, accounting employee, diagnosed coeliac in 2014) explains:

Maybe I don't learn enough either, not as much as I should. Because I feel good about my surroundings and I don't push any further, maybe ... At the beginning ... That's what I did in the beginning, I looked up a lot on the internet, to find out if it was really those symptoms.

When daily life with coeliac disease or with gluten sensitivity is in a phase of normalization (Kirchgässler et al. 1987), that is, when a new equilibrium is found and the condition is stable, the interviewees seem to be less interested in theoretical (medical/scientific) information, but often, they continue to search for gluten-free recipes or gluten-free restaurants. Here again, the situation in which the patient finds him/herself plays an important role. The temporality of the disease trajectory can be related to the temporality of the information journey – information needs are different according to the stages reached on the itinerary that leads one to become sensitive to gluten.

Gender differences in information practices?

While the gluten-free question is of greater concern and interest to women, men are not totally disinterested. Women are thought to be more frequently affected with coeliac disease than men, with a ratio ranging from 1 man to 3 women to 1 man to 1.5 women (Bai and Ciacci 2017). In the quantitative survey conducted with CREDOC and OCHA, out of 112 people who avoided gluten consumption, 40 were men (36 per cent) and 72 were women (64 per cent), while the total population surveyed was 1,052 women (52 per cent) and 977 men (48 per cent). According to the same study, among the gluten-free population, 24 per cent do not seek information on food and health, 60 per cent spend between a few minutes and an hour a week doing so, and 16 per cent spend more than an hour a week. Men are over-represented among the population not carrying out any information seeking, while women are vastly over-represented in the population that spends more than one hour a week doing so. Moreover, the interviews conducted reveal differences in the type of search carried out, that is, between research that is more theoretically oriented for men and more oriented towards the acquisition of practical skills for women.

Men are more interested in knowledge than in know-how...

For Marcelo (thirty-one years old, philosophy student and foreign language teacher, diagnosed coeliac in 2010, Paris), the topic of daily nutrition and particularly gluten-free food is not interesting. Although he did some research at first, reading scientific articles to learn more about gluten intolerance, he explains:

It's not something I consider as a news item or a small talk topic. I won't [see] people and say: 'By the way, did you see that there's a new gluten-free product?' 'Oh yeah, it's incredible ...' I don't find it to be a very interesting conversation ... No, I think food is very important in life, but you know, for me there are much more important things, like politics, equality … That's more important than eating gluten-free … Justice, or whatever.

Sebastian (thirty-three years old, diagnosed coeliac in 2014, Berlin), entrepreneur of a German artificial intelligence start-up, tells me during our interview that he has read many texts, on the internet and in books, related to food, nutrition and health. In particular, he tells me about a book summarizing scientific studies on the subject, which helped him to develop a more 'conscious' diet, to know 'good' and 'bad' foods. For some time, he was interested in the so-called 'Paleolithic' diet. Nowadays, he monitors his intake of animal proteins, sugar and salt more closely. On the other hand, he expresses 'horror' at being treated as a 'sick person' in books about coeliac disease. One can distinguish schematically those who consider the gluten-free diet as a treatment for a disease and those who approach the diet more broadly as one practice among others for a better life. Several coeliac patients do not consider themselves to be sick but see the onset of gluten intolerance as an opportunity to change their lifestyle (Wolff 2019).

…And leave recipe blogs to women

After explaining his interest in food, Sebastian indicates that he is not interested in cooking and that he does not look for recipes. When he prepares a meal, it is at most a mixed salad or ready-made foods that he puts together. His wife is not on a gluten-free diet, except when she eats with him. Yet she regularly explores gluten-free recipes on the internet or in books written by a friend who makes gluten-free recipes for the meals she prepares for herself and for her husband. The same goes for Marcelo (thirty-one years old, philosophy student and foreign language teacher, diagnosed coeliac in 2010, Paris), who is not very interested in cooking blogs: it is his wife who looks for recipes or restaurants specializing in gluten-free food.

On the one hand, women are often the primary seekers of health care (and therefore health information), not only for themselves but also for their children and other family members (Fox and Fallows 2003). On the other hand, women and mothers seem to put more effort into finding practical information. They are more likely to report consulting food blogs to look for recipes for themselves, their children or their husband if he is on a gluten-free diet. During the interviews, many women recounted the routine of looking for recipes or advice on healthy eating, making it an almost daily activity, even if it is sometimes just to look for ideas.

Several studies highlight the differential and unequal dimension of consumption between women and men (Fournier et al. 2015). Gender differentiation occurs at two levels: first, from the point of view of eating behaviour, in terms of representations and practices. In particular, there seems to be an increased reflexivity and greater permeability to nutrition among women (Beardsworth et al. 2002; Counihan and Kaplan 1998). Second, the gendered distribution of roles can be observed at the level of household food management, that is, buying provisions and cooking, which is thought to be the responsibility of women. In France, 80 per cent of domestic production is carried out by women (Nabli and Ricroch 2012), and daily food is one of the tasks.

Whether it be for preparation or procurement, food management is an activity that occupies more of women's time than mens' (Warde et al. 2007), not to mention the 'mental load' (Haicault 1984) of anticipating culinary preparation to ensure meals are suitable for the whole family, 'balanced' and adapted to each person's health, since the assignment of women to the task of preparing 'healthy meals' for their 'sick' spouses is considered to be normal (Beverly, Miller and Wray 2008; Fournier 2012).

At organization meetings, too, there are very few men, both in France and Germany. Adam, Tobias's father, says he is 'an exception'. He became involved in his son's treatment because he studied computer science and he and his wife had the idea to create the forum mentioned earlier. It was because he had taken on a 'technical' responsibility that he took part in the meetings organized by the support group. Women are more involved in daily care activities, including information seeking on healthy eating, and this is not so different among people who eat gluten-free. Studies on health and domestic care work have also shown that this work is devalued, ignored and trivialized, especially in its daily dimension (Cresson 1998) and I have observed in my survey how some men talk about it, saying they prefer 'scientific' readings. This behaviour tends to reinforce the process of differentiation between men and women in the relationship to knowledge and to food.

However, as I have shown in a previous paper (Wolff 2020), many specialized gluten-free blogs add theoretical information to the recipes, with specific sections entitled 'scientific news' or 'personal development'. The information is thus very diverse: there are articles presenting the nutritional properties of foods, others presenting research in progress in the field of biology or gastroenterology through book reviews or interviews, and also presentation of non-scientific or biomedical approaches, care practices or books to help the sick, which are questioned by scientists. Gluten-free blogs present a multitude of information from very different spheres. People who consult blogs in order to find recipes read these articles, often out of curiosity or for entertainment, without doing further research. This practice of 'scanning' (going over everything that is said on the subject without analysing each study in depth), carried out on a regular basis, can be contrasted with a more careful reading of previously selected sources carried out over a short period of time. According to my observations, the first practice seems to be carried out more often by women, while the second is more likely to be carried out by men, but also by women whose state of health has not stabilized.

Conclusion

An important element that emerges from this chapter is the articulation between the health itinerary and the information-seeking pathway. On the one hand, the type of information seeking carried out may vary over time: research is not the same before diagnosis, at the beginning of the gluten-free diet and when people are already on the diet. To this variation over time is added variation depending on the stabilization of the health condition, and therefore the degree of uncertainty associated with it. The main reason people seek information is because they want to know what they can do, or what they should do, to feel better. There is a tension between the reassuring function of information seeking (knowing that they are not the only person in this situation and that there are solutions to get better) and encouragement to assume self-responsibility for one's own health.

Information seeking is first of all about finding at least some information. In this respect, the emergence of the internet and blogs has changed search patterns – the objective is no longer the search for any information but the selection of information from among all the results found. Selection is made according to external resources (access to scientific publications, books, internet) and internal resources (skills necessary to read and understand these publications).

Above all, the emergence of the internet has led to the expansion of information provided by people who themselves are concerned with the disease and who are experiencing the same situation. The internet has enabled circulation of know-how disseminated by professionals and non-professionals – often women, wives or mothers, who share their tips and tricks, but also by start-up companies and brands of gluten-free products. In terms of selecting sources of information, what seems to interest people is the fact that the person who talks or writes is himself/herself concerned with the issue. Only someone who has been through the same situation is likely to be considered as someone who can understand and help. On a practical level, people seek advice based on other people's know-how (e.g. recipes). Aside from sections devoted to recipes, these mediators publish articles presenting books, articles, documentaries, which have helped them to know more about their own symptoms and their illness, and which have also led them to question the food system and sometimes the biomedical system. The characteristics of the various sources available on the internet lead internet users to 'stumble upon popularized knowledge'. The emergence of social networks and blogs has decompartmentalized health information: by enabling the acquisition of knowledge from different registers (theoretical information and practical advice), it has also changed the criteria for selecting and validating information. Disseminated information is not regulated by the biomedical or scientific sphere and some of it is reused by market actors (brands used in recipes, promoted restaurants, etc.). The reduced influence of the biomedical field in the circulation of information on health and nutrition is coupled with increased influence of people putting forward their personal experience.

Notes

1. In 2009–10, distributors such as Auchan and Casino launched a range of gluten-free products. Other distributors followed in subsequent years. In addition, the number of articles published in the French press dealing with the gluten-free diet has gradually increased from 2010 onwards.
2. In 1950, the Dutch paediatrician W. Dicke established the link between the ingestion of cereal products and the manifestations of coeliac disease, while identifying the triggering role of gluten. A wheat-free diet was recommended at that time for young children with coeliac disease. Until the 1990s, the scientific community accepted that only children were affected by this pathology. Moreover, in the 1970s, initial studies

suggested the existence of a sensitivity to non-coeliac gluten, but it was only in the 2000s that research on this sensitivity was taken up again (Sapone et al. 2012) and that other investigations into possible gluten-related conditions were conducted (e.g. link with autism; Knivsberg et al. 2002).

3. A research centre that conducts surveys on the lifestyles, opinions and aspirations of French people.

4. A research and resource centre serving the dairy interprofession. OCHA explores the relationship that eaters have with their food as part of a multidisciplinary approach emphasizing the humanities and social sciences.

5. The prevalence of coeliac disease is estimated at 1 per cent of the population in Europe. Very few people are diagnosed (Bai and Ciacci 2017).

6. This specific concept shares common concerns with those of 'connected', 'shared' or 'entangled' histories.

7. Out of the twenty-two coeliac people I met, eight were diagnosed before 2009. The only person who was identified early was Catherine, the mother of a coeliac who had already been diagnosed.

8. Coeliac disease and other gluten-related conditions are not considered or problematized in the same way in different countries, whether scientifically, medically, politically or socially. In the case of coeliac disease, the ratio of diagnosed to undiagnosed cases varies widely among countries (1:2 in Finland, 1:10 in Argentina, Germany and the United States) (World Gastroenterology Organization in Bai and Ciacci 2017). The organization explains that in some regions, there is a lack of awareness of the disease on the part of physicians and patients, a lack of diagnosis, but also myths 'such as the idea that celiac disease is rare, limited to whites living in Europe and the United States, that it is a childhood disease that can be outgrown after a period of diet, and that it is a mild disorder' (Bai and Ciacci 2017).

Vitamins in school resources and food advertising, 1950 to the present:
Between prevention and health capital approaches

Simona De Iulio, Laurence Depezay, Susan Kovacs,
Denise Orange-Ravachol and Christian Orange

Over the course of the twentieth century, new insights in nutritional science research increasingly find their way into ordinary knowledge about food. In particular, the discovery of vitamins in the 1910s puts an end in the United States to the so-called 'new nutrition' paradigm which emerged in the 1880s, replacing it with 'newer nutritional knowledge' (Levenstein 1988). The 'new nutrition' paradigm regards the human body as analogous to a steam engine with food as its carbohydrate- and fat-based fuel. From the late 1910s onwards, however, as discoveries made by nutritionists are widely disseminated in the national press, the American middle classes begin to become familiar with the idea that food contains substances that are essential to sustain life and yet which can only be detected in laboratories by scientists. The discovery of vitamins contributes to this 'newer nutritional knowledge' paradigm (McCollum 1918) and to the increased interlinking of nutritional science and food consumption recommendations.

The mediatization of vitamins as of the 1910s can thus be seen as a major factor in developing the general public's relation to nutritional knowledge. The details of this mediatization process deserve particular attention and raise a number of questions: through which media did the general public gain access to knowledge about these new mysterious substances? What does knowledge dissemination regarding vitamins reveal about public understanding of, and engagement with, nutritional science and nutritional advice?

This chapter focuses on the reception and rewriting of nutritional science in France in the second half of the twentieth century. We examine the mediatization of discoveries related to vitamins and the ways in which principles of nutrition become part of general knowledge used to promote eating choices. Our focus here is on children's nutrition: we highlight the ways in which the properties of vitamins were explained and extolled in two specific communicational contexts: school textbooks and advertising campaigns. We first consider the ways in which French biology textbook publishers present knowledge about vitamins in accordance with school curricula and second, we analyse the ways in which advertisers and advertising agencies in France offer information about vitamins as part of promotional discourse about food and food products for children. Our focus is on the post-war period when vitamins, while no longer a scientific or nutritional novelty, find their way into both pedagogical and commercial discourse. How does the process of nutritional vernacularization, by which vitamins become a standard feature of both the school biology curriculum and food advertising, contribute to transforming the vitamin into an object of everyday discourse?

The popularization of so-called 'newer' nutritional knowledge through different media is the subject of significant research among scholars who have considered this phenomenon in the American context (Biltekoff 2013; Levenstein 1988; Levenstein 2013; Nestlé 2003). Recent research on the mediatization of vitamins emphasizes the importance of the historical period of the 1920s and 1930s when information about the virtues of the vitamin, a recent discovery, became part of a variety of communicational artefacts and events (Lutz 2016). With the exception of a doctoral thesis in sociology on the history of nutritional labelling in France (Séguy 2014), however, the dissemination of nutritional knowledge in France remains largely unexplored.

Considering all forms of science writing as part of knowledge production (Babou and Le Marec 2003; Jeanneret 2008), we examine how scientific knowledge about vitamins was rewritten and recast in two very different kinds of documentary forms – French school textbooks and advertisements published in the French illustrated press. These two document types contributed to increasing public awareness of nutritional discoveries, including the issue which concerns us here, the existence and role of vitamins. How was the concept of the vitamin defined, described and used outside of academic circles by textbook editors and French advertising professionals? How do school resources and commercial advertisements appropriate the concept of the vitamin? What do these sources say about vitamins and why?

Circulation of nutritional knowledge in school resources and advertising

Textbook production and the changing biology curriculum in France

In the French secondary school teaching curriculum, topics relating to food, including the questions of eating and nutrition, fall primarily within the purview of the school subject of biology, also known as natural sciences or life and earth sciences. The French biology curriculum varies over time; curricular changes reflect both scientific paradigm shifts and evolving societal preoccupations (Kovacs and Orange Ravachol 2019). Thus while certain key topics relating to food are consistently present in the twentieth and twenty-first century French biology curriculum (types of foods and nutrients, digestion, eating as a key to well-being, nutritional balance), explanatory models and specific details slowly undergo change, taking into account new scientific discoveries and technical advances, as well as dominant scientific discursive models, health policy measures and concerns, and socio-economic and epidemiological trends. It is not surprising, for example, that in post-war France, the school biology curriculum emphasizes the need to teach children to 'eat enough' and to 'eat a varied diet' at a time when the population is slowly recovering from the effects of food rationing and shortages. More recently, the global obesity pandemic has been taken on by biology curricula in an effort to instil good eating habits in children at an early age and thereby reduce the risk of overweight and obesity among children.

Summarizing these curricular trends, we can say that the school biology programmes undergo a significant first shift, culminating in the 1980s, from concerns with social and personal food hygiene (dictating how to eat correctly and to avoid contamination and infection), to explanations of the proper functioning of the bodily 'machine' from a biomedical perspective. Starting in the 2000s, a second shift occurs towards a health literacy perspective highlighting individuals' control over their eating routines and habits. These changes are directly reflected in biology textbooks which are written by respected authors from the educational milieu (generally highly qualified secondary school science teachers in collaboration with regional educational inspectors) and edited by publishing houses such as Hatier and Hachette, known for their long history of relations with the national education ministry. Thus, while school textbooks are written and prepared to provide reliable and up to date sources of information to pupils on scientific phenomena, they are very much the product of political, social and economic positioning and repositioning. Education scholars and historians have shown that scientific knowledge is transposed and didacticized within textbooks as a function of societal pressures, norms and cultural values (Apple and Christian-Smith 1991; Clément 2004; Perrier 2002). Careful analysis of biology textbooks can thus help us understand the ideologies and biases that underlie the rewriting of science for different audiences.

Nutritional science and children's food advertising

In recent decades, the links between scientific knowledge and commercial advertising have attracted the attention of researchers in the humanities and social sciences (Cooter and Pumfrey 1994; Dodds et al. 2008; Wigelsworth 2010). According to communication science scholars Nico Pitrelli, Federica Manzoli and Barbara Montolli, 'given the discursive nature of advertising and its ability to introduce scientific concepts and share them with the general public, advertisements constitute an important opportunity for research into how science is experienced in the public sphere or, in other words, a relevant indicator of the non-specialist public's image of science and technology' (Pitrelli et al. 2006: 208). Historians of medicine and pharmacy have recently begun to consider advertising as a documentary source in their research on the history of the commercialization of medicines (cf. among others Bonnemain 2007). Historians of science have highlighted the relationship between the widespread awareness of scientific achievements and food advertisements in the press and on radio and television. In particular, the role of food advertising in popularizing knowledge about vitamins during the 1930s and 1940s in the United States and the

United Kingdom has been extensively studied (Apple 1988, 1996; Horrocks 1995; Kamminga 2000).

The inclusion of scientific knowledge in advertising discourse goes hand in hand with the promotion of use values of food. According to the categories of consumer value identified by Jean-Marie Floch (1990), one of the ways in which French advertising enhances the value of food is by highlighting the functional and utilitarian qualities of products. To this end, food advertising emphasizes a product's characteristics, such as its nutritional properties or the qualities of the ingredients. Functional enhancement claims associate properties of foods with positive physiological effects for health. In advertising, as Roland Barthes remarked, 'health is indeed, mythically, a simple relay between body and mind, the alibi that food gives itself to signify materially an order of immaterial realities; health is therefore experienced through food only in the form of dispositions, implying the body's ability to cope with a certain number of mundane situations' (Barthes 1961: 984). In this mode of valorization, food remains linked to its physiological function: it provides the human body with benefits that are immediately put into effect. It offers 'dispositions' – to use Barthes's expression – that start from the body, but go beyond it: energy, vitality, relaxation, enabling individuals to adapt effectively to the situations in their lives.

Other scholars have observed that in food advertising different categories of values can exist simultaneously. As Nathalie Heinich (2017) notes, a food can be presented and valued as 'good', 'beautiful', 'healthy' and 'cheap' at the same time, or 'beautiful but not very good', 'excellent but too fatty', 'good and beautiful but too expensive'.

Methodology

How are vitamins presented and explained in school resources and advertising for food aimed at children, in light of these general trends? How does the 'miraculous' discovery of vitamins and of their role in nutritional function and disease prevention find its way into school textbooks and food advertisements in the second half of the twentieth century? How does this knowledge translate into explanatory and descriptive discourse on food and eating aimed at French pupils and readers of monthly magazines?

Our study seeks to answer these questions through analysis of two corpora: one composed of fifteen school biology textbooks, and the other of sixty-eight advertisements published in the two weekly magazines *Paris Match* and *Elle*.

We selected a small representative corpus of secondary school-level biology textbooks published between 1955 and 2008. These general biology textbooks were produced for pupils aged fourteen to fifteen enrolled in the final year of obligatory schooling (the fourth and final year of the French *collège*). This is traditionally the grade level at which teaching about human nutritional processes (digestion, intestinal absorption, assimilation) is developed in some depth. The content of these textbooks represents knowledge which the majority of secondary school pupils are exposed to; the goal of our analysis is thus to identify what understanding of the vitamin is to be reached at this point in the general curriculum, that is to say, before students either leave school or engage in specialized tracks typical of the later years of secondary school, in the French *lycée*.

Our choice of advertisements on the other hand is a subset of a pre-existing corpus of 634 ads on children's food products placed in the general-interest weekly *Paris Match* between 1949 and 1973 and in the lifestyle magazine *Elle* between 1973 and 2001.[1] From this corpus, we selected all ads which mention vitamins, thus obtaining a total of sixty-eight advertisements, forty-eight appearing in *Paris Match* and twenty published in *Elle*. Through these weekly French magazines, food advertisers targeted female readers who could afford their products. Founded in 1949, the weekly *Paris Match* covers major national and international news with celebrity lifestyle features. In 1958 *Paris Match* had a circulation of 1.8 million copies and at the beginning of the 1970s it was still the bestselling news weekly in France. The weekly magazine *Elle*, founded in 1945 just after the war, focuses on fashion, beauty, health and entertainment. The target readership is upper-middle-class, urban-educated and working women and it had a circulation of about 400,000 copies in 1950. By the 1960s, *Elle* had a readership of 800,000 across the country. After 1970 *Paris Match* changed its editorial policy and no longer included advertising for children's food products; this explains our use of two sources of ads, since *Elle* magazine allowed us to create a complete diachronic account of advertising on children's food products for the period under consideration.

Vitamins in school resources

In our study of the corpus of biology textbooks we focused on two primary issues:

1. How are vitamins presented in these biology textbooks? Is the role of vitamins in nutritional and metabolic functioning explained? If so in what way?
2. What seems to be the underlying rationale behind discussion of vitamins in these textbooks?

Our results show that biology textbooks devote considerable attention to vitamins up until the 1990s. Textbooks in our corpus present vitamins as essential nutrients required in 'small' amounts to ensure proper bodily functioning and to prevent nutritional diseases. Textbooks published during the period 1955–90 give particular emphasis to the serious health consequences of vitamin deficiencies (lack of vitamin A and growth disorders, vitamin D deficiency and rickets, lack of vitamin B1 and the fatal disease beriberi, vitamin C deficiency and scurvy, etc.). Such deficiencies are in fact the most common entry point into the discussion of vitamins. Textbook authors of this period delve as well into the scientific discovery of vitamins, detailing the experiments leading up to the identification of vitamins A, B and D. In a 1980 textbook, for example, experiments conducted in 1912 are explained, showing that when rats are fed with powdered milk, fat and starch, they experience normal growth, whereas rats fed with mineral salts and casein (a milk protein) waste away (Brun-Cottan, Debrune, Debrune 1980: 24). As explained in the textbooks, this experiment led researchers to discover the fundamental role of vitamin A, a substance contained in milk, butter, eggs and other foods. Similarly, Eijkman's landmark 1890 experiments on chickens, which identified beriberi as a deficiency ailment, are mentioned in a 1972 textbook (Orieux and Everaere 1972: 158). In textbooks published from the 1950s to the 1970s, deficiencies such as scurvy, rickets and vitamin A deficiency are described or are depicted visually through often jarring medical photographs of symptomatic (especially young) patients.

In the 1980s and 1990s, such deficiencies are still addressed in textbooks, but their presentation is usually limited to a summary table. Lists or tables presenting the principal vitamins (A, D, B1, B2, C, PP) and their food sources and recommended daily requirements are sometimes provided, with brief indications of the disorders connected to each type of vitamin deficiency. However, in these tables no real distinction is made between vitamins in terms of their role and action in the functioning of the healthy body. Textbooks emphasize the essential need for vitamins, linked to certain foods such as fresh fruits, vegetables, dairy products and fish. Little or no mention is made of red meat as a source of vitamins during this period. Thus a 1989 Nathan textbook (Périlleux et al. 1989: 143) provides the following list of foods containing vitamin D: 'Eggs. Fish. Fish liver oil (very rich)'; by contrast, in textbooks from the 1960s and 1970s beef, fat and lard are mentioned (Oria and Raffin 1966: 221–2). Photographic depictions of young patients suffering from vitamin deficiencies remain a feature of textbooks of this period, with, for example, images of X-rays showing bone deformities in a young subject caused by a vitamin D deficiency (Périlleux et al. 1989: 143). The issue of malnutrition in poor countries is, however, less present than in earlier textbooks, and is relegated to supplemental chapter sections and exercises 'for further reading' ('Pour aller plus loin', in the section 'World hunger' in the 1989 Nathan biology manual, Périlleux et al. 1989: 154). In addition, vitamins are also presented as fragile substances, 'easily destroyed under certain conditions' (Brun-Cottan, Debrune, Debrune 1980: 24) such as during the process of cooking (Bergeron et al. 1980: 73).

In a general sense, knowledge about vitamins in biology textbooks is expressed through dramatic accounts of the pathologies which they prevent. Discussion of vitamins thus serves primarily to highlight the importance of nutritional variety while promoting certain foods (such as milk, eggs and fruits) as sources of several different vitamins.

In all of the textbooks analysed, the actual physiological or metabolic action of vitamins is rarely explained through anything other than vague or peremptory assertions. A 1980 Belin textbook mentions, simply, that humans are not able to produce vitamins (Brun-Cottan, Debrune, Debrune 1980: 24). In a 1959 Hachette textbook, the reader is told, briefly, that vitamin B2 helps in glucid absorption (Paniel 1959: 112). More commonly, yet just as succinctly, vitamins are described as having a positive effect on growth, bone formation or the proper functioning of different organs. The same 1959 Hachette textbook mentions that vitamin PP is essential for the proper functioning of the nervous system (Paniel 1959: 113), and in a 1966 Hatier textbook, vitamin A is said to promote 'normal tissue growth thus allowing the body to reach a normal height' and that vitamin D 'ensures good skeletal and tooth mineralization' (Oria and Raffin 1966: 220). A 2003 Nathan textbook offers the most complete account, among the textbooks considered, of the action of different vitamins (Bal et al. 2003: 233). In this textbook, a synthetic table presents the scientific names of ten vitamins, the food sources for each, the disorders which they prevent, daily recommended quantities of each and their action in cellular respiration and formation, antibody formation, mineral absorption, blood coagulation. This informative multiple-entry table is, however, located at the back of the textbook as a supplemental reference tool rather than as core learning material.

The central pedagogical argument attached to the vitamin in French biology textbooks is one of prevention. A Hachette textbook published in 1980 notes that vitamins play an important role in bodily functions despite the fact that they provide 'neither matter nor energy' (Larue et al. 1980: 18). This is a revealing statement: the dominant explanatory model relating to nutrition evident in all biology textbooks in the corpus is that of food's role in energy production to support physical activity. Vitamins are thus key but marginal players offering a competing discourse to the all-important 'accounting' model of eating based on caloric 'input' and 'output'. This robust explanatory model, a heritage of the 'new nutrition' age, is incompatible with 'newer nutrition' conceptualizations of eating heralded by the discovery of vitamins. Biology textbook authors seem at pains to associate vitamins with anything other than a preventive message materialized through often sensationalized depictions of vitamin deficiencies.

In the textbooks for the period under study, the overriding trend is in fact that of a progressive waning of interest in vitamins, especially after 2000. This is evident in the number of paragraphs or pages devoted to vitamins in individual textbooks, which gradually decrease; historical references to the discovery of vitamins are phased out or noted only in end-of-chapter exercise sections. As mentioned, tables and lists presenting vitamins and their food sources and pathologies are still present in textbooks in the 2000s but this information is annexed as additional end of volume material. A 2008 textbook contains no reference at all to vitamins (Rojat, Pérol and Salviat 2008). How can we explain this trend? Simply put, vitamins lose their relevance as a teaching tool for nutritional topics, as other pressing health concerns come to dominate the curriculum such as the prevention of obesity and cancer.

Vitamins in advertisements for children's food

In the analysis of the corpus of advertisements, we focus on the following questions: What vitamins are mentioned and explained, why and in what way? What specific discourse emerges around a particular vitamin? What types of foods, brands, products or ingredients are associated with vitamins?

Advertisements promoting food products for children since the post-war years are filled with various scientific and scientific-sounding claims, vocabulary and imagery referring to nutrients in general and to vitamins in particular. Advertisements published in *Paris Match* from 1950 to 1972 and *Elle* from 1973 to 2001 link vitamins with a wide range of foods: mostly dairy products (condensed milk, ultra-pasteurized milk, yogurt, cheese), fruit (oranges, dates, apples) and fruit juices (orange and apple juice), but also canned baby food, pasta, margarine, chocolate bars, chocolate powder, corn flakes, soft bread, dehydrated soups, biscuits and chestnut cream.

Invisible and tasteless, vitamins, like other nutrients, are never shown in the visual elements of the ads. While no attempt is made to visualize them, vitamins are always named and qualified verbally in more or less detail. The word 'vitamin' generally appears in the main body of the copy text, very seldom in the headline of the advertisements. Presented as a category of nutrients, during the 1950s vitamins are often mentioned vaguely and in the plural ('vitamins', 'full of vitamins'), very rarely in the singular as in the case of an advertisement for oranges from North Africa claiming to contain 'vitamin C, the key vitamin for your health'.[2]

Over time, vitamins make their way into the body copies of advertisements and are generally presented in list form. For example, in mid-1960s advertisements, Nestlé brand chocolate is said to provide 'a wealth of vitamins: A, the growth vitamin, B, C, D, etc.'.[3] Vitamins are often mentioned in combination with other nutrients considered as essential: minerals and macronutrients (proteins, fats, carbohydrates). An advertisement published in *Elle* in 1975 states, for example, that 'dates contain phosphorus, magnesium, calcium, protein and lots of vitamins A and B',[4] and in the LU brand Ourson biscuit 'there are fast carbohydrates, vitamin B2 and vitamin E, very few fats and only good ingredients'[5] as claimed in an advertisement published in *Elle* in 1998.

Some vitamins are presented as being inherent to certain kinds of foods: post-war advertising refers, for example, to the 'good vitamins of milk'[6] as well as to 'the vitamins of vegetables, fruit and meat',[7] and to 'all the vitamins of apples'.[8] Some advertisements state that vitamins are found in one specific ingredient of the product: for example, readers are told that there are vitamins in the milk contained in chocolate bars, cheese or cakes, and that there are vitamins in the eggs contained in pasta.[9] An advertisement for Kellogg's corn flakes states that 'eaten with milk and sugar, this cereal provides vitamins'.[10]

Despite the importance given to vitamins to persuade readers of the benefits of advertised products, food advertisements do not explain what these nutrients are and how they work. As early as the 1950s, advertising discourse focuses instead on the quantity of vitamins contained in foods. The readers of *Paris Match* and *Elle* learn that a food product for children is 'full of vitamins',[11] 'rich in vitamins',[12] 'have a wealth of vitamins',[13] and that it has 'twice as many vitamins',[14] 'five vitamins',[15] 'seven vitamins',[16] 'eight vitamins',[17] a 'high vitamin content'[18] or 'vitamins in abundance'.[19] In some cases the quantity of vitamins contained in a product is specified (e.g. the chestnut cream Faugier is said to contain '11 mg of vitamin C and 0 mg 6 of vitamin B1 in 100 gr')[20] as is the amount of vitamins and nutrients that children's bodies need: 'Breakfast should provide one-quarter of the caloric requirements but also essential elements: protein, vitamins and minerals.'[21]

Some advertisements suggest that vitamins are fragile nutrients which can be lost. Modern industrial processing, generally assumed to 'rob' foods of their vitamins, is presented in some advertisements as a guarantee of the product's freshness and of the preservation of its vitamins. In an advertisement published in 1969[22] for example, the reader is told that *Ninello* brand fruit juice is produced through the 'ultra-modern freeze-drying process': 'From -40° under vacuum, their water is literally evaporated. The pulp and fruit juice crystals formed in this way retain their juice, vitamins, fragrance and flavour.' An advertisement for fresh cheese *Gervais* stresses that 'the pipes, all in stainless steel, are sanitized after each use!'[23]

Analysis shows a marked tendency to 'scientize' discourse on food through the frequent use of scientific terms ('calcium pantothenate', 'phytosterols', 'essential fatty acids') as well as through medical vocabulary, scientific jargon and scientific-sounding language. The body copy of an advertisement for margarine published in *Paris Match* in 1960 claims, for example: 'For children: vigorous growth thanks to its pro-vitamins A; young arteries and a strong heart thanks to its phytosterols and essential fatty acids; an effective protection against the rapid destruction of vitamins thanks to its vitamin E.'[24]

The visual elements in the advertisements often seek to illustrate the validity of the scientific claims made in the copy. They show the positive benefits of the product containing vitamins through drawings or photos of smiling and healthy children, eating with appetite (a slice of bread, a slice of orange, a bowl of chocolate) or playing (jumping, playing table tennis, going down slides, using swings, throwing a Frisbee), or doing sports (sailing, football, fishing, gymnastics). The visual imaginary of vitamins and especially of vitamin C is often associated with healthy activities, environments and situations – outdoor scenes, sunny landscapes, holidays – and with the colours orange, yellow, and red. A recurring image is that of sunshine projected onto a winter landscape thanks to a product containing vitamins.

Vitamins are mentioned in order to convince the reader of the product's quality and beneficial effects. They are presented as the reason why the consumption of the advertised food can improve the development of children's bodies. Various ads point out that vitamins promote children's growth: vitamins are needed 'to grow',[25] they 'are essential for the formation of bones and teeth',[26] for 'vigorous growth',[27] for 'steady growth',[28] for 'building muscles'.[29] Advertisements not only establish a connection between vitamins and children's good health but also assert that the presence of vitamins in processed foods guarantees children's fitness and good school performance.[30] Various food advertisements stress the need for vitamins in the daily diet because they give energy to body and mind, providing strength, cheerfulness, liveliness, vitality.

Using the distinction proposed by Appadurai (1986) concerning knowledge about commodities, we can identify two different types of knowledge mentioned in food advertisements: on the one hand, technical and scientific knowledge or know-how relating to the production of food and on the other, knowledge related to food consumption.

In some cases, the advertiser pretends to assume the role of the expert. The acquired knowledge applied to the production of food is said to guarantee the quality of the product or of the brand: for example, Danone claims to be 'the world's leading specialist in real yoghurt, with 40 years of experience, guarantees consistent quality and unequalled freshness',[31] and Nestlé states it should be trusted because it 'has been feeding millions of children around the world for a hundred years'.[32] In some cases, the product or the brand itself claims to hold authority: 'The Charles Gervais brand is your guarantee! It should appear on all your Fresh Cheeses'.[33]

In other cases, advertisements emphasize the believability of scientific or medical expertise, with reference to the scientific knowledge of dieticians and nutritionists. Heudebert brand toasts and LU chocolate cake claim to be developed with the help of nutritionists. Food products like Kellogg's breakfast cereals or Lustucru noodles are advertised as being recommended by nutritionists or dieticians. An ad for milk chocolate bars claims that 'it is milk, dieticians have proven it, which makes milk chocolate the most digestible of chocolates'.[34] Names of scientific experts are never mentioned, nor is the source of the information they provide. The only exception is the reference to a Professor Mazé in advertisements for Gervais products. His expertise, of a technological nature, is highlighted as beneficial to the nutritional properties of products. Several other technical experts are also put forward during the fifty-year span of advertisements in our corpus, seemingly in a bid to reassure the public as to the steady progress of new technologies in the food industry.

Finally, by virtue of their knowledge as consumers, mothers and children themselves are depicted as authorities. Their expertise comes from their experience and from knowing how to evaluate the product and estimate its nutritional value. Food advertising suggests that greater understanding of science leads to improved decision-making. Informed mothers know what to choose ('His mother chose margarine: she knows that to ensure her son's vigorous growth, to make him a strong and perfectly balanced man, he needs a complete and balanced diet, too')[35] and children testify, directly or indirectly, to the beneficial effects of the product ('Orange juice is good for me').[36]

Discussion and conclusion

As we have seen, in school textbooks, vitamins are gradually marginalized as an object of study. This evolution suggests that vitamins interest pedagogical actors not so much as substances to learn about, but rather as arguments to promote healthy eating and nutritional variety. From this brief analysis we can conclude that vitamins play an important role in school textbooks between the 1950s through to the 1990s in establishing links between eating and health, and in the increasing medicalization of food and eating, through dramatized depictions of vitamin deficiencies. The discovery of vitamins in the early twentieth century challenged previous assumptions and beliefs on both the importance of 'eating enough' and on the role of food's caloric content (Biltekoff 2013). The early textbooks in our corpus suggest that learning about vitamins is used as a means to promote eating not only as a question of caloric intake and expenditure but as a matter of general health. Once eating and health became inextricably linked in school discourse, vitamins had, seemingly, served their purpose and appeared less often and in a less prominent position in biology textbooks.

Depiction and discussion of vitamins in French biology textbooks highlight the links between vitamins and pathology avoidance rather than the contribution of vitamins to the normal functioning of the body. The approach is more descriptive than explanatory; textbooks tend to enumerate or catalogue, without clarification, the dangers that vitamin deficiencies pose and the foods in which certain vitamins are to be found. This descriptive approach also characterizes today's popular science resources for children such as those available online through YouTube videos or science documentaries on television. Pedagogical discourse about vitamins found in schoolbooks thus closely resembles vernacular descriptions of vitamins in popularizing media. Yet popular depictions of vitamins, such as those to be found in advertising, unlike school textbooks, remain resolutely positive and euphoric.

Advertisements for children's foods published in the French press in the post-war period contribute to constructing and reinforcing a connection between food and science. As is the case in the United States, starting from the mid-1920s (Apple 1996), in advertisement after advertisement, scientific discourse is exploited to lend legitimacy and to promote products of the food industry in France. By integrating science into commercial discourse, food advertisements reinforce French readers' awareness of the existence of vitamins and their importance for good nutrition and health. Scientific half-truths are rewritten and combined with advertising techniques based on emotional appeal in order to reassure mothers through promises of health and growth for their children. In this sense, the popularization of scientific knowledge about vitamins through advertising participates in the shift from the task of feeding children to that of correctly nourishing them, or, in other words, ensuring that their daily diet contains all the nutritional components necessary for a healthy life and regular growth.

Advertisements for children's foods published in the French press during the post-war period also contribute to transforming the way food – and in particular processed food – is judged. In the French national context, where food is traditionally appreciated on the basis of quantity or of gastronomic quality, advertising places emphasis on other, inherent, properties of food products. Advertising discourse not only highlights invisible nutritional components by naming them but also uses them as a selling argument. Advertisements in *Paris Match* and *Elle* have in this sense contributed to transforming vitamins and nutrients into commodities.

The attributes used to qualify vitamins and other nutrients such as minerals and proteins often employ language derived from the semantic domain of wealth, money and calculation: valuable foods are foods which are 'rich in vitamins' and are 'precious' components essential to 'protect the Vitamin Capital'[37] of children's bodies or to ensure their 'health wealth'.[38] In the promotion of food products containing vitamins, nutritional knowledge is blended with knowledge related to economic theories of health. Rhetoric about vitamins in advertisements for children's food products echoes Michael Grossman's economic theory of health capital. Extending Gary Backer's theory of human capital, Grossman assumes that at the beginning of life, everyone is equipped with an inherited stock of health. This stock depreciates with increasing age but can be expanded by investing in it. Grossman's model further assumes that each person produces his/her 'healthy time' by investing in actions that can slow the decrease of health caused by ageing. With the right food choices, among other choices such as exercise, medical care, housing, one can produce 'good health', and increase 'healthy time' (Grossman 2008).

The main assumption underlying Grossman's theory is that an individual requires certain foods because they can increase health capital. Foods, and especially processed foods, are depicted in the advertisements that we analysed as desirable because they provide valuable components and are good investments for children's well-being, growth, bodily health and physical and intellectual performance. Through this link between nutritional value, economic value and moral value, advertising discourse contributes to new forms of commoditization of foods.

Didactic discourse on the vitamin in school textbooks and commercial advertising about vitamins in food occupy two different axiological registers with regard to health, the preventive and the positive. Both however institute a metonymic relationship between foods and the vitamins they contain. Represented as properties of foods rather than as chemical agents in nutritional or metabolic processes, vitamins come to mediate representations of food and eating in the social imaginary.

Notes

1. This corpus was created by Simona De Iulio for the research project 'Children's Consumption of Fun Food between Risk, Pleasure, and Education' with the support of the French National Research Agency (2007–10).
2. Advertisement for oranges from North Africa in 'Oranges d'Afrique' (1957), *Paris Match*, 407, 26 January.
3. Advertisements for milk chocolate, 'Chocolat au lait Nestlé' in 1965: *Paris Match*, 824, 23 January; *Paris Match*, 830, 6 January; *Paris Match*, 831, 14 March.
4. Advertisement for dates, 'Dattes' (1975), *Elle*, 1521, 3 March.
5. Advertisement for cake, 'Ourson LU' (1998), *Elle*, 2728, 12 April.
6. Advertisement for cheese, 'Carré Gervais' (1960), *Paris Match*, 570, 10 March.
7. Advertisement for canned baby food, 'Jacquemaire' (1957), *Paris Match*, 444, 12 October.
8. Advertisement for concentrated apple juice, 'Jus de pommes' (1960), *Paris Match*, 588, 16 July.
9. 'Fresh eggs contain this vitamin in abundance', advertisement for noodles, 'Lustucru' (1959), *Paris Match*, 559, 26 December; 'especially the egg yolk contains vitamin A', advertisement for noodles, 'Lustucru' (1960), *Paris Match*, 563, 23 October.
10. Advertisement for breakfast cereals, 'Corn Flakes Kellogg's' (1988), *Elle*, 2229, 26 September.
11. Advertisement for canned fruit juice, 'Pam Pam' (1961), *Paris Match*, 635, 10 June.
12. Advertisement for oranges, 'Oranges Outspan' (1962), *Paris Match*, 702, 22 September.
13. Advertisement for cake, 'Ourson LU' (1998), *Elle*, 2728, 12 April.
14. Advertisements for soft bread, 'Pain de mie Jacquet' (1989), *Elle*, 2262, 15 May and (1990), *Elle*, 2313, 7 September.
15. Advertisement for toasts, 'Biscoto Heudebert' (1990), *Elle*, 2773, 22 February.
16. Advertisement for chocolate drink, 'Nesquik' (1969), *Paris Match*, 1029, 25 January.
17. Advertisement for breakfast cereals, 'Corn Flakes Kellogg's' (1988), *Elle*, 2229, 26 September.
18. Advertisement for noodles, 'Lustucru' (1961), *Paris Match*, 625, 1 April.
19. Advertisement for noodles, 'Lustucru' (1959), *Paris Match*, 559, 26 December.
20. Advertisement for chestnut cream, 'Faugier' (1955), *Paris Match*, 343, 5 November.
21. Advertisement for breakfast cereals, 'Corn Flakes Kellogg's' (1988), *Elle*, 2229, 26 September.

22. Advertisement for fruit juice, 'Ninello' (1969), 1046, 24 May.
23. Advertisement for cheese, 'Carré Gervais' (1960), *Paris Match*, 570, 10 March.
24. Advertisement for margarine, 'Margarine' (1960), *Paris Match*, 578, 7 May.
25. Advertisement for oranges from North Africa, 'Oranges d'Afrique' (1957), *Paris Match*, 407, 26 January.
26. Advertisement for oranges, 'Oranges' (1951), *Paris Match*, 100, 17 February.
27. Advertisement for margarine, 'Margarine' (1960), *Paris Match*, 578, 7 May.
28. Advertisement for canned baby food, 'Jacquemaire' (1957), *Paris Match*, 418, 13 April.
29. Advertisement for dairy products, 'Produits laitiers' (1979), *Elle*, 1758, 3 September.
30. A child drinking orange juice claims, 'I work better at school' in an advertisement for oranges (1951), *Paris Match*, 98, 3 February.
31. Advertisement for yogurt, 'Yaourt Danone' (1962), *Paris Match*, 684, 19 May.
32. Advertisement for condensed milk, 'Lait concentré Nestlé' (1968), *Paris Match*, 993, 20 April.
33. Advertisement for cheese, 'Carré Gervais' (1960), *Paris Match*, 605, 12 November.
34. Advertisement for milk chocolate, 'Chocolat au lait Nestlé' (1965), *Paris Match*, 824, 23 January.
35. Advertisement for margarine, 'Margarine' (1960), *Paris Match*, 578, 7 May.
36. Advertisement for oranges, 'Oranges' (1951), *Paris Match*, 100, 17 February.
37. Advertisement for margarine, 'Margarine' (1960), *Paris Match*, 578, 7 May.
38. Advertisement for apple juice, 'Jus de pomme' (1965), *Paris Match*, 841, 22 May.

The circulation of knowledge about food in schools

Marie Berthoud

In this chapter, we question how knowledge about food circulates in primary schools in France and how teaching and support staff appropriate such knowledge. Over the past twenty years, French health authorities have increasingly focused on food and nutrition as an area of public policy intervention. Food behaviour, associated with health risks such as obesity, diabetes or malnutrition in developed countries like France, has become an educational issue for authorities. The objective of health authorities is to teach people to 'eat well' starting from an early age. Children are therefore the primary targets for educational programmes in food and nutrition; public schools, which come under the responsibility of the government, have been designated as the best site for implementing food education. To fulfil this objective state and public health authorities have developed ambitious education campaigns in order to teach children to 'eat well'.

Recent studies in sociology and information and communication sciences concerned with public information and education campaigns have shown that food and eating practices are informed by social norms about what is 'good' to eat and what one must do to 'eat well' (Berthoud 2019; Boubal 2019; De Iulio and Kovacs 2014; Romeyer 2015; Tichit 2015). Other studies in sociology (Rayou 2002; Denis 2007) and information and communication sciences (Darbellay 2012; Delamotte 2004) on processes of knowledge circulation in the field of health and education have also led to a reconsideration of the opposition between 'expert knowledge' and 'lay knowledge' by showing that complex types of hybrid knowledge emerge in social situations.

Despite these important recent contributions, the circulation of food knowledge in schools remains a little-explored field of study. Yet detailed examination of the ways in which knowledge about food is received and appropriated by school actors can enrich our understanding of key issues regarding the expanding role of public policy in knowledge circulation. On the one hand, food education in schools shows the willingness of public authorities to intervene in the daily and universal act of eating. On the other hand, educating children about food and nutrition requires both tools and mediators to disseminate this knowledge. Finally, food education in schools contextualizes a universal and ordinary practice, that of eating, within the institutional framework of the school. Given these characteristics of food education, it seems relevant to question the nature of the knowledge disseminated in schools; the types of mediators and mediating objects used in the school context; as well as how institutional food education can run counter to the experience of individuals.

Addressing these issues in 2014, Mathieu Quet explains that the notion of 'knowledge circulation' implies three sets of questions: 'What circulates?' (2014: 221), that is to say, what and who are the knowledge mediators? How is knowledge introduced and used in the school setting? Finally, what is the nature of this knowledge? In this chapter, we seek to answer the following questions: What knowledge is produced in the context of food education programmes? How is this knowledge relayed in schools? How do those involved in information production and dissemination appropriate such knowledge themselves? My intent is to explore the process of knowledge circulation on food and nutrition in schools, and in so doing to question the very notion of 'circulation'.

The corpus under consideration here, constituted in 2017 for a previous study, includes educational tools and pedagogical resources produced by public health authorities since 2001 to support food and nutrition education in schools. The year 2001 marks the creation of the first of a series of French public health programmes in nutrition and health, the so-called 'PNNS 1'. This national programme set out nutritional goals and guidelines in France for the general population. As of 2001, public schools were favoured by health authorities as places for regulating nutritional behaviours, and many educational resources were produced for this purpose. In the course of our research, these resources were collected from official websites of the Ministries of Food and Education and the National Institute for Prevention and Health Education (INPES). These teaching tools were expressly conceived for school professionals dealing with food and nutritional education as a primary or secondary objective. We created a corpus of over one hundred textual, iconographic or video documents which are offered to teaching staff as 'educational kits' in paper or digital format; these documents are varied in nature and include lessons, exercises, games and illustrations. Our objective was to study the types of knowledge presented in this corpus of resources and also to gain insight into the practices of knowledge appropriation within schools. To this end, we conducted participant observations over several months in 2013 and 2014 in five primary schools in Lille, in the north of France. The choice of the primary school level was made in light of the fact that the national programmes mainly target children aged six to twelve, considered to be at the appropriate age for learning 'good' eating practices. We use a semiotic-pragmatic approach (Odin 2011) linking discourse analysis to the processes of production, dissemination and reception of resources. By linking discourse analysis to consideration of the 'communication spaces' in which documents are situated and used, we seek to understand how knowledge related to food is constructed by public authorities and the way such discourse circulates and is appropriated within the school context.

Through our choice of research object and methodology, following work initiated by Yves Jeanneret, we study communication as a process of creative circulation. From this perspective, knowledge 'does not remain locked in on itself, but circulates and passes between the hands and the minds of men ... and is enriched and transformed as it crosses social spaces' (2008: 14). We consider communication to be a 'creative practice' (2008: 13) by which knowledge and norms are continually transformed and appropriated by social actors.

Practical knowledge related to nutrition

As mentioned, analysis of the documents in our corpus is based on a mixed methodological approach. We first conducted discourse analysis, identifying arguments and discursive strategies. Second, we studied educational tools quantitatively using the software Tropes, a lexical-semantic analysis tool which allowed us to create a lexicon which we then applied to analysis of the entire corpus.

Our results show that eating is principally defined in these documents in nutritional terms, as a guarantee of good health. Resources show a similar lexical pattern: one's diet is described as a set of foods identified by nutritional components such as vitamins. The concept of eating is itself entirely subsumed by that of nutrition. The chapters, educational lessons, stories, games or exercises on the subject of eating focus on the 'energy needs of the body', 'the nutritional value of each food', 'the nutritional quality of the products'. They present the links between energy and food, food and nutrition, nutrition and health, often representing eating as an absorption process in which food is a 'battery' that fuels the body. While the sensory dimension of eating is also present in these resources, this aspect is often limited to the advice that one 'taste' different kinds of foods in order to ensure a 'healthy' and varied diet. Likewise, the notion of eating for pleasure often appears in lessons and exercises devoted to fruits and vegetables, which are promoted for their nutritional benefits. A functionalist aim thus prevails in these documents; eating appears as a means by which the child can, in accordance with the three principles of nutrition education discourse targeting children, 'grow well', 'be strong' and maintain 'good health'. Illness, fatigue or even obesity are occasionally mentioned in the corpus as the consequences of poor eating habits including snacking or eating sweets and fatty foods such as French fries.

All of the documents studied make explicit reference to food groups and to the nutritional pyramid presenting the 'families' of foods. Children are invited to learn these food classifications through lessons, stories or exercises. In these resources, the activities of classifying, sorting and categorizing foods into groups are shown to be a fundamental skill to be acquired in nutritional instruction. Food groups are mainly organized according to their 'nutritional value'. Foods are thus differentiated using nutritional standards, according to their health benefits or risks: cereals and carbohydrates are to be 'consumed with each meal and according to one's appetite', while sweets are to be 'limited'.

Another example from our corpus which is of particular relevance to our inquiry into the social dimension of knowledge circulation illustrates food education as the transmission of a set of behavioural models. The *Vinz and Lou* kits are short videos funded by the ministries of education and food and branded by the PNNS, an official partner. These 'educational' videos, as they are defined, cover various themes. In an episode entitled 'On a Tray', Vinz, a teenager, and Lou, his younger sister, are in the school canteen at the self-service counter selecting their lunch. The video shows them serving themselves and deciding on their own what they will eat. Lou fills her tray in a methodical way. She chooses a salad, a plate of fish, fries, a slice of bread, a glass of water and fruit yoghurt. Her tray is organized and clean; containers separate food, and cutlery is positioned to the left of the tray. Her brother Vinz has chosen a single plate piled up with French fries covered with sauce, four slices of bread and a soda, without cutlery or a glass. The tray is overflowing and disorganized and shows a large serving of mayonnaise. Each character comments on his food choices. Lou states, 'a little of this … goes well with the fish … a little bread and also water'. Measured and thoughtful, seeking to combine a variety of foods, Lou carefully calculates and plans her meal.

On the other hand, as Vinz fills his plate, he sings 'french fries, and then more fries, fries, fries … I'm too hungry'. Poorly balanced and lacking variety, his lunch is reduced to a catchphrase and a game. Lou then decides to use a computing device to measure the nutritional balance of her chosen meal. Lou's tray is evaluated by the computer and declared 'perfectly balanced'. The computer rewards the little girl by praising her choices as 'Perfect … Bravo'. Vinz's tray causes an alarm signal to sound, with the computer announcing: 'Alert! Too much sugar, too much fat! Alert.' Finally, the machine blows up, ejecting Vinz. This episode provides an obvious and caricature-like account of ideal nutritional balance. The characters are stereotypical: Lou is the 'perfect' little girl and embodies the ideal of a balanced diet. However, no clear explanation is provided as to why her meal is 'perfect' or what the consequences of these choices might be. Vinz' platter is also a caricature of 'bad' food (French fries, sauces, sodas, no vegetables) yet no explanations are given other than 'too much sugar, too much fat'.

As these examples show, nutritional knowledge is presented and disseminated in general, obscure, or even caricatured terms, promoting a value scale in which 'good' eating is often characterized, but rarely explained. Camille Boubal explains this phenomenon by positing a dual tendency in public health discourse. First, authorities seek to disseminate a positive image of eating, with little or no mention of health risks, in order to model, as efficiently as possible, the 'right' behaviours to follow for good health (2019: 467). Consequently, nutritional messages carry a consensual dimension, by which any possible 'cacophony' of information is seemingly erased (Fishler in Boubal 2019). The resources we have studied respond to this dual tendency to produce consensual nutritional knowledge by which 'good eating' appears to be accepted, unquestioned and obvious to all.

Our research also shows that nutritional knowledge is almost systematically formulated as practical knowledge to be assimilated by children; the scientific basis of this knowledge is rarely exposed. Indeed, in our corpus, food education is less a question of knowledge transmission than of disseminating behaviour patterns and norms. Public health authorities themselves acknowledge this objective of modelling eating practices, stating that 'in order to reinforce nutritional education in schools, the aim is to use entertaining tools, to inform, educate and guide young consumers towards nutritionally appropriate food choices' (PNNS 2011). The challenge is thus to transmit knowledge about nutrition, but also to ensure that children adopt nutritional guidelines from an early age through the educational institution. The PNNS campaign defines the aim of nutritional education as 'promoting the passage from knowledge to application' of nutrition (2011: 22). To this end, nutritional knowledge is translated into practical knowledge and most often appears in the form of catchphrases encouraging children to adopt one behaviour rather than another: 'for your health, eat five fruits and vegetables per day', 'for your health, avoid fatty, salty and sweet foods', 'for your health, at least one dairy product per day'.

The stories, exercises or games in the teaching kits are also constructed to inculcate models of action. This aim is particularly evident in the *Vinz and Lou* videos that we mentioned earlier. Similar scenarios are common to all videos which seek to build and to reinforce the 'right' behavioural model and to vilify 'incorrect' behaviours.

The videos in our corpus present the main characters, including Vinz and Lou, in different situations in the classroom, the street, the park, at school or at home. A story is gradually built around the characters, linked to the themes of food and eating. In these stories, the characters are often placed in practical situations in which they have the opportunity to act independently: they shop in a store, cook at home, put away groceries, eat in the canteen, go to the restaurant or buy fruit at the outdoor market. In all of these stories, adults are almost always absent, and the children are left to fend for themselves. If some adult characters appear, they are relegated to secondary roles: Vinz and Lou's grandmother, a biology teacher, a sports teacher or a shopkeeper only appear for a few seconds. Vinz and Lou's mother never appears, and the father's role is limited to a voice heard briefly in a few episodes. Child characters are thus represented as the principal protagonists of each situation.

These characters are consistently faced with making choices: they choose their cereal in the store; they select the products they want to buy at the outdoor market; they decide what time to eat; they choose their meals at the self-service canteen; they organize their afternoon tea; they decide whether or not to go outside to play sports. Vinz and Lou are constructed as characters with full autonomy and choice, since they are never shown to be constrained by social, economic or physical determinants, or by rules, regulations or limits imposed by adults. Economic issues such as food costs or access to foods are not raised in relation to the choices they make. These protagonists exercise seemingly limitless free will in their acts and gestures.

As suggested here, the Vinz and Lou characters were designed in opposition to each other. Lou thinks about her diet, eats at regular hours, does sports, cooks, comes to the table when her father calls, washes her hands and eats fruit. Vinz does the opposite: he only eats fries in the canteen, skips meals, plays video games, prefers to have a pizza delivered, listens to music at the table and refuses to eat certain dishes at mealtimes. The characters' choices are evaluated by a moral code which results in reward or sanction. Lou's behaviour is constructed as 'good' by being rewarded. In one episode, Lou is congratulated by a delivery man for the pizza she cooked. A few seconds before the end of the video, a textual message appears: 'Eating well is also a question of balance' or 'Eating is also exchanging'. An adult voice can also be heard pronouncing these messages. The messages highlight critical lessons from the story and always praise Lou's decisions. In an episode where Lou tastes her grandmother's dish, the moral is 'Taste it, it may turn out to be good'. In an episode where Lou prefers to cook a pizza rather than order out for it, the final message explains that 'Homemade is smarter'. Lou's behaviour represents the exemplary model of what to do because she is rewarded by the moral of the story.

Morality also operates in a second, opposing dimension, by proving Vinz wrong and showing the adverse or absurd effects of his behaviour. He fractures an arm after breaking a machine calculating the nutritional value of his meal; he becomes sick after eating too many hamburgers; he has to visit the doctor after swallowing his headphones at the table; he becomes lethargic because he skipped a meal; he uses pickles instead of batteries because he did not listen during biology class. These sequences reinforce the idea that Vinz's behaviour is an example of what not to do. In the episodes entitled 'Clean Hands' and 'Eating? What For?' Lou herself judges her brother negatively: 'He is completely crazy!' She criticizes her brother's ridiculous attitude and condemns his non-adherence to 'ethical' eating behaviour. Good eating thus has a distinct moral undertone in these videos.

The *Vinz and Lou* resources seek to disseminate a model of nutritional behaviour with stories and characters who represent 'good' and 'bad' examples. From this perspective, the objective of educating children about eating is the diffusion and imposition of behavioural norms and actions to adopt on a daily basis.

Public health authorities thus approach children's nutrition education as a store of practical knowledge. In her studies of public health campaigns, Hélène Romeyer (2015) shows that eating is always defined in terms of nutritional and medical norms aimed at promoting health practices (2015: 59). These campaigns thus put forward a nutritional model (2015: 60) as a means of limiting and moderating risks: eating is seen as a guarantee of good health. In this way, public authorities legitimize their interventionist role in promoting eating behaviours deemed better for health. Geneviève Le Bihan and Corinne Delamaire have proposed that nutritional education aiming to modify behaviour emphasizes processes of individualization. For these authors, one of the limits of this education is that it does not consider the complex determinants of eating, focusing messages on the individual in isolation from his or her social, economic and cultural environment.

The educational tools developed in the context of national information campaigns on nutrition thus seek to educate children by listing 'good health' behaviours to be adopted by the individual (Berthoud 2019). As we have seen, 'good' eating practices are represented as the ability of the individual child to make choices, regardless of economic, social and cultural factors. This ability can be seen in the *Vinz and Lou* stories, in which children are rewarded or punished for choices they have made individually and independently. Simona De Iulio and Susan Kovacs have explored this tendency to emphasize individual responsibility while setting aside social factors and contexts:

> The child is depicted as being solely responsible for his actions; this explains the reluctance … to bring up the familial, psychological or hereditary causes of nutritional problems that may relate to the family, to medical issues or to cultural values. This autonomy of the child makes it possible to create an educational space free of socio-economic or genetic determinants, to draw up a portrait of the child who is master of his own destiny and thus facilitate the transmission of a message of empowerment, even of guilt. (2014: 110)

This disregard for contextual phenomena influencing behaviour can reinforce inequalities. By ignoring social, economic or medical factors which come to play in health and eating practices, these resources build a standardized model of behaviour. The risk, in the words of Caroline Ollivier-Yaniv, is 'to reinforce new forms of inequality, indexed on the differentiated social resources of actors and their re-appropriation of the injunctions of prevention policies' (2013: 109).

Our analyses of the educational resources created as part of nutritional campaigns show how public authorities have relied on prescriptive info-communication strategies in order to raise awareness and educate children about 'good' nutrition. These strategies aim to inform and sensitize children and also to 'make children act' by intervening in their behaviours, their bodies and their lives.

Our textual and discursive analysis shows that food knowledge in such resources centres on issues of health and nutrition and is in fact less concerned with learning than with teaching individual behaviours. Knowledge is presented in the form of behavioural 'prescriptions'. This discursive standardization does not address the diversity of the children for whom such prescriptions are intended. One of the objectives of our participant observations, as we now show, was to study how official discourses are appropriated in schools. Before presenting the results of our observations, the second part of this chapter discusses how these prescriptions circulate in schools, the medias and mediators by which they are disseminated and how they come to be embodied in children's learning.

The circulation of prescriptions: Institutionalization of knowledge

Food knowledge based on eating guidelines circulates in different ways in schools. Through ethnographic observations conducted over several months in five primary schools in the Lille area, we identified three modes of circulation.

The first mode comprises educational resources produced by national agencies and made available for education professionals. These tools are adapted to the school environment through their format and their discursive qualities. They allow educators to cover nutritional principles and recommendations in an entertaining way. The *Vinz and Lou* videos fit into this mode, as do educational kits entitled *Léo and Léa*. These kits were financed, produced and published as part of the PNNS nutrition campaigns. As such, they are intended to promote nutritional behaviours according to the principles of the national programme. The booklets which comprise the *Léo and Léa* kits are organized into chapters, each of them starting with a story and offering exercises, puzzles and games.

The theme of eating in these pedagogical kits is presented through a vibrant interdisciplinary approach. Food is characterized as a vital nutritional need, but is also associated with other phenomena including: sensory pleasures and discoveries (taste, cooking); particular contexts and events (lunch in the canteen, a picnic); cultural practices (soup recipes from around the world). These tools also examine the history and origins of food (the spice route); modes of production, distribution and consumption (types of crops, distribution networks); the functioning of the human body; plant life and development. Food and eating are tied to a variety of school subject matters such as biology, geography, history, reading, vocabulary or mathematics. The question of eating is also used to address more general subjects such as social interactions, good and bad habits and sharing.

In the pedagogical kit *Léo and the Earth* (a box set for children with an explanatory booklet for professionals), one of the stories takes place during the school lunch period. The 'canteen lady' is a central figure. She counsels the children and urges them to finish their meal, to taste the different foods and to favour vegetables. Described by the schoolboy character Léo as 'kind' but 'severe', she is in a way the spokesperson for the PNNS recommendations: she tells the children to eat fruit to be healthy, and to avoid salt and fat. Accompanying pedagogical materials offer ideas for activities, such as holding a debate with students on the question of eating habits. This debate, it is suggested, should centre on the issue of treats, which are 'not very good for one's health'. Exercises and activities in *Léo and the Earth* address the nutritional norms that children are expected to discover and interiorize. Activities include creating a 'balanced lunch menu' and a test entitled 'From Food to Nutrients' both designed to help children learn the benefits of eating fruits and vegetables that 'protect against diseases' and to understand the concept of 'nutritional balance'. Consumption guidelines are also included for teachers to help them 'make arguments'. The 'Seven Food Groups' table describes the main nutrients as well as their roles and benefits for the body and health. The 'PNNS Consumption Guidelines' table presents individual food groups and how much or when to consume each: 'fruits and vegetables: at least five times a day'; 'added fats: to be limited'; 'drinks: unlimited quantities of water'. In addition, posters displaying nutritional prescriptions use comic illustrations to explain 'ten ways of staying in shape' throughout the day. The poster illustrations depict a child in different real-life situations: at the table, the soccer field, the park or in the street. Below each image, a text indicates what to do or not to do during the day. These texts explain: 'I avoid snacking', 'a fatty meal is heavy and slow to digest: avoid it, if I want to be in good shape'; 'I exercise, I get into the habit of walking, and I do physical activity'; 'I take care to eat fruits and vegetables: they are good for my health.' These educational documents promote the official prescriptions of the PNNS national nutrition programmes which are themselves mentioned throughout the chapters. They are rewritten in the form of stories and exercises and thus adapted to the world of childhood and school.

A second mode of nutritional prescription circulation in schools corresponds to what sociologist Jérôme Denis has called 'guide technologies', that is to say, 'artefacts or equipment that produce guidelines to remind one of rules' (2007: 11). This mode entails using existing local structures such as the school institution to operationalize nutritional recommendations which are thus no longer only stated but directly experienced. This operationalization is visible in the school canteen, where children experience nutritional norms through the meals they eat there. An official city nutritionist prepares menus to be served at the school, strictly adhering to national health authorities' guidelines with regard to quantities, nutritional balance and daily needs. Children thus become accustomed to eating meals of a specific measured quantity, featuring vegetables and fruits and with limited amounts of fat, salt and sweets. Meals are served by kitchen staff who are trained to understand and apply nutritional guidelines. Their role is to serve children in accordance with precise regulations. Portion sizes materialize nutritional norms since all servings are calculated in grams. The catering staff receive instructions from the city nutritionist about quantities: for a child, one slice of meat, two fish fingers, an apple, one container of yoghurt or one piece of cake. Serving utensils used by staff are another means to determine portion sizes: a ladle of mash, a pincer-full of green beans, a tablespoon of sauce, a small dish of grated carrots, a glass container of applesauce or a bowl of soup. Prescriptions are therefore not only relayed by info-communication resources such as kits and videos but also by the organization of school meals.

Finally, nutritional guidelines are disseminated in schools by what Jérôme Denis defines as 'prescriptive relays', that is to say, people embodying the model and showing through their own behaviours 'how to act in compliance with the rules' (Denis 2007: 8). In schools, this function is taken on by hired lunchtime education workers, school staff or canteen staff. Through these actors the prescriptions 'crystallize in everyday situations of advice and help, while some come to show others what to do' (2007: 7). The staff who organize lunchtime breaks embody this relay structure. When they are hired, these employees undergo training organized by the city nutritionist, in order to become familiarized with the nutritional recommendations that they are expected to impart to students. During meals they take with children, these lunchtime staff members are expected to remind children of nutritional prescriptions such as eating fruits and vegetables, tasting a bit of everything and so on. Job profiles for these lunchtime staff positions explicitly state the work of relaying nutritional norms to children. Staff managers guide these employees throughout the year, and educational tools are made available to them by the local authorities or the Ministry of Education. Referring to this mission, one employee explains to us:

> At the beginning of the year, we let children discover how the canteen works, we accompany them, we explain how it works. And then, little by little, we tell them that one must taste everything, try a food at least once. They also learn to serve themselves, to carry the tray, to fetch water, to sort waste. And then we tell them about food groups, why it is good for health, we offer workshops on this.

Lunchtime school staff are thus endowed with the missions of advising, prescribing and showing. They are also expected to embody good behaviour during meals. According to the manager of support services at the Lille city hall, 'the lunchtime guide remains the main reference for the child. So, for example, he too must taste everything when he eats with the children at the table.' These mediators must 'play roles' in the sense of Erving Goffman, that is to say, they must show themselves to be good eaters who make the right choices and who favour 'healthy' foods, so as to serve as models for children.

Public health authorities have thus sought out ways to defend, promote and transmit nutritional knowledge in accessible and understandable ways. Several strategies have emerged in recent years: nutritional knowledge is rewritten in educational tools, taking the form of stories, games, school lessons. Mediators and other school professionals are called upon to take part in the dissemination of this knowledge by using educational tools and by relaying prescriptions or by embodying them in their own practice. School spaces and times such as canteen meal times are used in an effort to operationalize this knowledge. Knowledge and norms are thus institutionalized through their inscription within the context of school times, places and practices.

This hybrid circulation of nutritional prescriptions is however not a linear process. Prescriptions are continually rewritten and translated into pedagogical discourse, practical procedures or model behaviours. While various relays serve to disseminate prescriptions, they are nonetheless modified through the practices of the actors involved in this process. We address these modifications in the third part of this chapter.

The emergence of new experiential knowledge

Through the process of creative circulation we have described, nutritional knowledge is adapted, rewritten and therefore transformed by the practices of different actors. New knowledge emerges through practices of appropriation, sometimes in opposition to institutional or expert knowledge. During workshops or mealtimes in the canteen, or when info-pedagogical tools are used, professionals and children reappropriate knowledge and adapt it to particular situations. These appropriation practices can be defined as 'tactics' (De Certeau 1984) through which individuals adapt and break free from official prescriptions, inventing 'ways of doing' within the institution. By assimilating the roles and missions assigned to them (De Certeau 1984) they appropriate these roles in their own way.

The tools made available to education professionals, including posters, booklets and educational kits are rarely used in their entirety according to recommended protocols or in the given order of chapters or exercises. They are instead adapted by teachers and other staff, who use these resources to find inspiration. Educators draw ideas, images or arguments from them, creating new tools themselves for use in workshops with children through a process of 'bricolage'. During an interview, a staff member explains that these resources are unsuitable for the children with whom they work. He cites not only a lack of time available to staff to put the resources to use, but the fact that the standardized nutritional discourse is inconsistent with the diversity of the children present in schools. Official nutritional recommendations, as we have previously seen, promote one 'right' individual choice, with no consideration given to social and economic factors influencing eating practices and behaviours. During our observations, we noted for example that such standardized knowledge is ill suited to the experiences of school children from immigrant families. These children may not be familiar with the food products mentioned in some of the nutritional guidelines. Educational staff, while deeming nutritional education resources to be limited or often inappropriate, use them nonetheless as sources of inspiration for creative adaptation. One lunchtime staff member describes one such example of adaptation through his reuse of specific images:

I managed on my own, I took a world map, photos of dishes found in one of the kits, and I mixed these together.

In this specific case, the staff member worked with children of different nationalities who had recently arrived in France. A combination of elements derived from official kits, internet resources, the employee's travel photographs, children's stories about what they used to eat in their country of origin was used to produce a new tool. This new improvised tool thus relays not only nutritional knowledge but also knowledge about world cuisines, products, tastes, and cultures, and about the lived experiences of individuals. Education professionals thus adapt official discourse by different means and in so doing take into account experiential knowledge.

Mealtimes in the canteens are also do-it-yourself spaces, during which canteen staff, lunchtime mediators and children adapt guide technologies. Canteen cooks adapt or sometimes even ignore nutritional recommendations. Lunch menus, for example, prepared in strict adherence to official nutritional norms are sometimes considered ill adapted to children's tastes. Canteen cooking staff know that children often leave their vegetables and fruits on their plates, uneaten. Cooks use their imagination to decorate dishes, cutting vegetables and fruits in an aesthetic way and adding a little sauce, against official recommendations. Sometimes during the meal, canteen serving staff leave out vegetables for some children, thus ignoring one of the most often-quoted official prescriptions: 'you have to taste everything'. Food quantities are also adapted by the canteen staff to take into account children's weight and size and their appetite on a particular day. So, while nutritionists work to predefine meal portions, cooks and serving staff may add or take away a little food for a child. The cooking staff know the children personally and create ties with them.

One cook explains, for example, that she has 'her sparrows', children who tend to eat little. She explains that 'they don't even need to tell me anymore, as soon as I see them, I adapt, and I give them less'. Thus, experience as well as first-hand knowledge of individual students sometimes take precedence over official standards.

Children are also able to adapt or thwart nutritional rules. They sometimes do this individually, for example, by hiding food they do not want to eat under their napkin; or by asking the cooking staff for a little more than the official portion size; or by taking extra slices of bread that they hide under their plates. Such gestures can also be collective and reveal solidarity among children who develop common tactics. We observed one child who did not want to finish his plate of food. He was helped by his friends at the same table, each taking some of his food. The staff leader was led to believe that the child had eaten enough to be allowed to leave the table. Children are thus sometimes able to counter nutritional knowledge and official prescriptions with their own tastes and desires. Lunchtime staff also distance themselves at times from the role model they are expected to play during meals. Some employees admit that they themselves do not like certain foods. They justify their choices directly to the children, thus highlighting the importance of taste rather than nutritional norms. Other lunchtime staffers prefer not to eat with the children, thus backing away from their role as exemplary eaters by having lunch 'behind the scenes'.

School actors such as canteen staff, who find themselves caught between official dogma and real-life practice, are in effect able to appropriate, to adapt and to bypass or transgress official guidelines. Such actors respond to national protocols, normative prescriptions and generic tools with practices based on their lived experiences in schools. Far from being passive disseminators of national recommendations, school educators appropriate, oppose or even refuse and criticize the normative frameworks which they are expected to uphold. As a result, new knowledge emerges, linked to these actors' everyday experiences.

The circulation of food knowledge can thus be described as a complex process by which know-how, tools and practices are continuously adapted and recomposed. We have seen that knowledge about food in official discourse centres on nutritional knowledge and is related above all to the domains of health and medicine. As part of public authorities' ambition to modify and to model individual behaviours, this eating knowledge is translated into prescriptions dictating what to eat and what to avoid eating. Such prescriptions circulate in schools through different means. They are rewritten to appear in info-communication educational tools, they are inscribed in places such as the school canteen in order to be put into practice and they are directly embodied by professionals themselves.

Rather than knowledge as a singular body of concepts, we thus prefer to speak of forms of knowledge – in the plural – which are juxtaposed, which overlap and which sometimes present opposing views. Official nutritional knowledge is combined with pedagogical as well as experiential knowledge derived from situated practices, personal experiences, individual tastes and local contexts. In our study, knowledge about food and eating is heterogeneous, a mix of expert, institutional and lay concepts and precepts. Food knowledge in school can thus be characterized as a blend of academic discourse, practical know-how, acquired knowledge and lived experiences.

The circulation of this knowledge is a non-linear process. Knowledge relays in schools do not operate in succession but rather coexist as, for example, when pedagogical tools, actors and technology guides are present together. Knowledge circulation is thus iterative rather than sequential; different actors draw inspiration from official tools while building new forms of knowledge.

Developing a reasoned approach to food education through science teaching

Denise Orange-Ravachol and Christian Orange

The context of food education in France

Recent ministerial instructions for primary and secondary schools emphasize the importance of so-called 'educational approaches'[1] and highlight the value of interdisciplinarity. A constellation of educational concerns (educational approaches to health, sustainable development, risk, citizenship and so on) has emerged in recent years. These educational domains are included in the imposed curricula of individual school subjects, but take on as well an integrated format, via combinations or reconfigurations of several school disciplines (Audigier 2012). This context seems particularly conducive to the development, or even renewal, of food education, anchored not only in the usual scientific disciplines and topics (human nutrition, balanced diet, obesity prevention, etc.) but also within interdisciplinary sustainable development instruction (sustainable agriculture, global issues in food security, combatting food waste, etc.). In order to teach students 'good eating habits' and to 'properly socialise' them through food, schools can create the necessary conditions to engage pupils in profitable ways: teachers of various subjects (geography, life and earth sciences, physical education, modern languages, economics, etc.) can be asked to tie food and nutrition to their curricula, while other school personnel (budget officers, head chefs, school counsellors, nurses, local producers, dieticians, associations, etc.) can be encouraged to get involved as well. However, while we find that new and varied collaborative networks are indeed being formed, and that so-called islands of rationality[2] (Fourez 1997; Maingain and Dufour 2002) in relation to school subjects can indeed be built, it remains more difficult to characterize the fundamentals of food education to be taught in the school setting and beyond. It is with this concern in mind that we discuss in this chapter the problems surrounding training in critical thinking and choice making. These skills are promoted with insistence by the school institution through multiple interconnected ministerial instructions and recommendations, including core curricula guidelines for compulsory education, ministerial circulars on sustainable development education and food education, accompanying documents made available on the ministry's national pedagogical resource platform (https://edus col.education.fr/), science curricula and other resources.[3]

The 2007 Education for Sustainable Development circular (Ministry of Education 2007: 732) states for example that schools must provide explanations based on proven scientific knowledge and that 'the role of teachers is to help students develop critical thinking' because 'they must be taught "how" and not "what" to choose'. In addition, the so-called 'core curriculum' for compulsory education, outlining required aims in knowledge, skills and culture (Ministry of Education 2015) 'opens the door to knowledge and teaches judgment and critical thinking on the basis of a rational, orderly understanding of the world'.

More specifically, 'food and taste education in schools' is intended to be 'interdisciplinary, to be taught within the context of health education, citizenship education and sustainable development education'. Yet food education is faced with contradictory goals. On the one hand, the objective is to 'help students acquire healthy and responsible eating habits',[4] thus in some sense the aim is to tell students what to do. On the other hand, official texts also note that teaching these good habits requires tools and resources that can enable students to awaken their critical faculties so that they themselves can choose what and how they eat.[5]

In what ways can these guidelines, particularly those aimed at developing critical thinking skills, be translated into food education? Under what conditions can these curricular goals be reached? To address these questions, we refer to our research in sustainable development education and food education (Kovacs and Orange Ravachol 2015; Orange and Orange Ravachol 2017), and to our exploration of problematization and problem-solving activities with students of life and earth sciences (Orange Ravachol 2012), a key subject for health education. We start from the idea that acquiring critical thinking requires a break from common modes of reasoning and thereby a shift to 'extraordinary' modes of thinking (Astolfi 2008). As in all educational approaches, this rupture with conventional thinking applies to a variety of knowledge domains: biology (physiology, ecology), geography and economics (land-use planning, energy issues). We confine ourselves here to the field of nutritional physiology. We consider what this break may consist of by analysing, from an epistemological and didactic point of view, several physiological problems frequently associated with food education in schools. We first show that 'knowing about human nutrition' requires going beyond a dichotomy of 'true' and 'false' thinking. We then consider examples of student responses or textbook activities to illustrate three approaches to teaching critical thinking: systemic reasoning; avoiding explanations based on the physical properties of objects; and questioning hastily drawn correlations.

The possible and the necessary: What to know about human nutrition

The first issue we consider is human nutrition, understood as the processes by which the human body obtains matter and energy. By the end of primary school, students will have usually studied nutrition in terms of food and its transformations during the digestive process. If we accept the premises of problematized learning (Orange 2012), knowledge about nutrition cannot be reduced to descriptions of the digestive tract or of the path of food going through the digestive tract. This would be tantamount to considering food as only something that enters, moves through and exits the digestive tract; in other words, food would be seen as being of no use to the human body. Nor should students be limited to learning, even in detail, the operation of systems or organs involved in digestion. What is important is that they acquire scientific knowledge about human nutrition so that they can explain the purposes of eating (growth, maintaining organ function), the mechanisms that make the nutritional process possible and finally why a particular explanatory model is considered possible or impossible. If we focus here on the role of food, there are three necessary phenomena to be constructed by learning (Orange 2003): the necessary distribution of food-derived nutrients to the entire body; the necessary transformation of ingested foods; and finally, the necessity of a separation between what is and is not absorbed by the body. One must therefore engage students with a biological problem linking the function of nutrition ('what is the point of eating?') and the functioning that underlies it ('how does it work?'). There is nothing straightforward about this approach. Our research shows that students usually think about food by means of story-making (Bruner 2002; Orange Ravachol 2012); such stories could be replaced by other potential stories as long as no limits are imposed. As an example, the text extract that follows shows what a group of four students (ages nine and ten) in a primary school class produced when they were asked, 'How does the food I ate provide strength?'

> The hamburger and fries go down a tube called the oesophagus into the stomach. Afterwards, some food goes down the excrement tube. The rest will go down the tubes to the muscles.

The question as it is asked relates the function of nutrition ('to give strength') to the functioning of nutrition ('How the food I ate' can provide strength). The students' answer is limited to the travels of a hamburger and fries through the human body, with a distinction drawn between what goes to the muscles and what forms faeces. Nothing is said about the transformation of food into nutrients and even less about the nutritional function of food. While students mention that 'certain foods' are distributed to the muscles, they provide no indication of the reasons for this partition or what phenomena are actually at work. Students imagine only one possibility and say nothing about what might make it necessary. Yet this is precisely what 'knowing about nutrition' entails: understanding why we explain nutrition a certain way and why it cannot work any other way. Helping students go beyond story-making and towards functional argumentation is a condition for gaining critical understanding about nutrition and food. Yet it is not enough to state the functional requirements of nutrition (digestion, distribution, sorting), students must work through these questions in class. This work can be done by analysing and comparing students' proposed answers; by encouraging them to think about whether a process can work in a certain way or not;

by asking them to argue; by freeing students from the conceptual framework of true and false. Our research (Orange 2003, 2012) has shown that having students develop their explanations, individually and then in groups, by presenting and debating them, leads them to work on the possibilities and impossibilities of their proposals. Such activities considerably help students acquire reasoned knowledge that enables them to say why such a process is possible or not.

Explaining the dynamic structural stability of cells: Applying systemic reasoning

As we have just mentioned, when primary school pupils work on and rethink their own explanations, they can come to understand epistemologically relevant functional necessities in nutrition. However, this leaves us with mechanistic descriptions (the grinding, sorting and transport of food) that do not involve chemical explanations. For students at the end of secondary school, it is possible to go beyond the process of supplying all parts of the human body with nutritive substances in order to study chemical transformations which take place in the body and the dynamic structural stability of cells. In other words, teachers can help students understand that inside cells, organic molecules constantly disassemble and reassemble, while each cell, despite these renewals, remains itself over time. This problem can be grasped through compartmental modelling (nested compartments; Orange 1997) and the use of systemic reasoning (inputs and outputs for each compartment). However, this way of thinking is not immediately obvious to secondary school students, as seen in a discussion with two high school students (ages sixteen to seventeen) after their class had studied and schematized the molecular renewal of a cell in the human body. These two pupils, who were doing well at school, had difficulty with the model when revising their classwork. Hence their request for a meeting with the teacher a few days after the lesson. In the diagram studied in class, double arrows indicate that large organic molecules (LOMs) can break down to form smaller organic molecules (SOMs) and vice versa. While the content of the schema summarizes the processes (respiration and cell synthesis) that the class had successfully studied, its format had been introduced by the teacher. The aim of using such diagrams is for students to think beyond the traditional depictions of 'blood circulation/cells or organs', which favour sequential reasoning, and instead use a systemic type of modelling.

At the beginning of the meeting with the teacher one of the students said:

> Yeah, well, I didn't really understand how it actually worked … I dunno if this happened first or that, because as I understood it, SOMs are eaten, they pass through the intestine, they are absorbed and then they pass into the cell.

She tries to explain by 'telling a story' about the molecules, which means that not only is she struggling with what the diagram represents but also, and above all, she does not understand the very purpose of molecular renewal:

But then what's the point of forming them [LOMs]? ... Since they do this, then they do it again, they break apart and this forms the same SOMs ... and these SOMs, then they go away?

The didactic challenge is, therefore, to lead students to change how they explain concepts, abandoning their tendency to explain with stories. This intellectual shortcut does not allow students to think about functional necessities (each little story could potentially be different) nor does it help them to understand how a living system works. The main challenge is therefore to encourage students to adopt an 'extraordinary' way of thinking, through systemic reasoning, which can show that each type of molecule can, a priori, have a multitude of paths. This form of analysis, close to that of professional biologists, is a condition for constructing a reasoned knowledge of nutrition thus enabling students to understand that a cell or organism can have a certain lifespan although its components constantly renew themselves. This renewal is a fundamental characteristic of living systems.

In the same way, students' usual form of reasoning prevents them from understanding the value of ingesting mineral salts, which seem to enter and leave the body in the same quantity. A simple sequential vision leads one to think that mineral salts are of no use in the functioning of the body (Orange 1997).

Beyond intra-objectal reasoning: Making food choices

The third issue we wish to address concerns classifying foods and establishing guidelines for a balanced diet. The nutrition education classes in which this problem is dealt with usually use various readily accessible documents (supermarket brochures, information leaflets from the French national nutrition health programme campaigns (PNNS), textbooks, internet resources and others), which constitute shared cultural references. In this way, teachers take on a sensitive issue characterized by different and opposing scientific, cultural and societal points of view. It is also a way for them to address two significant objectives, during relatively short class periods: first, to ensure that each student in the class expresses himself freely, develops ideas, thinks about societal practices; and second, to filter and select topics raised during discussion in order to inculcate the norms expected by society. Consideration of foods, menus or eating habits thus entails focusing on the attributes or characteristics of foods – in other words, on intra-objectal explanations (Piaget and Garcia 1983). These are simplistic explanations that focus on the properties of objects rather than on their relationships. The nutritional recommendations which result from this approach are expressed in terms of statements or rules (e.g. the food pyramid). In other words, assertoric discourse (several kinds of food) is combined with normative discourse (what to eat and in what quantity) to the detriment of critical reasoning. The knowledge and authority of nutritionists prevail, but the foundations of nutritional science are neither studied nor discussed. Paradoxically, the nutritional norm is labelled 'scientific'. However, it is not scientific for the students, since the underlying foundations are not worked through in order to produce explanations. These nutritional standards are based only on appeals to authority and cannot lead to critical thinking. This 'scientifically proven' discourse in fact falls back upon cultural norms. The challenge in critical thinking and decision-making training is therefore to break away from the practice of storytelling (making up stories about food) and from explanations using the intrinsic properties of the objects studied. These explanations tend to be intra-objectal in nature, for example, foods that are good, bad, fatty, calcium-rich and so on, and are quite common in advertising and official health information campaigns. On the contrary, it is essential to think in terms of the relationships between what food can provide (including 'bad' foods), the systemic functioning of the human body (substances simultaneously entering and exiting), epidemiological studies and the like. In addition to this mode of reasoning, teachers must also change their attitude towards the discourses and documentary sources they rely on, even if these are considered authoritative: students should not base their choices on appeals to authority, but should give reasons for rules and choices and think for themselves. We shall see that the lessons in some textbooks do not help students move in this direction.

Avoiding hasty correlations in nutritional disease prevention

Science textbooks for secondary schools (middle and highschools) provide much of the material that teachers use. They are of real interest for nutrition and food education as they introduce students to different cultural practices, provide epidemiological data and give preventive advice. Exchanges, debates and in-depth discussions can follow. However, the truncated nature of the information within these textbooks as well as the types of questions addressed to students may lead to simplistic answers and faulty generalizations, which both teachers and students should be careful to avoid. As an example, we first consider two documents from the same Year 9 (pupils aged fourteen to fifteen) French life and earth sciences textbook published by Hachette (Hervé and Desormes 2008). They are statistical tables which appear on a page about the risks associated with poor nutrition and how to reduce them. One of these (Table 12.1) shows eating habits in three French cities (City 1, in the south; City 2, in the east; City 3, in the north); the other (Table 12.2) shows cardiovascular mortality in these same cities. Only the second is credited to the World Health Organization (WHO). However, our research shows that all the incorporated data come from a single study coordinated by the WHO launched in the early 1980s – 'Monitoring Trends and Determinants in Cardiovascular Disease'. This research project enabled 38 centres in 21 countries to study dietary trends around the world for over ten years. Since both documents stem from the same research project, and given their shared scientific objectives and funding source, it seems legitimate to consider them together. However, is the connection between these two tables self-evident? What could be the reasons for the differences between the cities? If we look

Table 12.1 Eating habits in three French cities
Adapted from Hervé and Desormes (2008: 219).

Diet, g/day	City 1 (South)	City 2 (East)	City 3 (North)
Bread	225	164	152
Vegetables	306	217	212
Fruits	238	149	160
Butter	13	22	20
Cheese	51	34	42
Vegetable fats	20	16	15
Wine	383	286	267

Table 12.2 Mortality rate per 100,000 people in three French cities
Adapted from Hervé and Desormes (2008: 219).

Cities	Cardiovascular mortality		Total mortality	
	Men	Women	Men	Women
City 1 (South)	140	39	575	255
City 2 (East)	216	64	887	318
City 3 (North)	224	72	1041	411

closely at the two tables, the Southern city (City 1) stands out for its relatively low mortality rate, which is almost half that of the city in the North (City 3). In terms of diet, its inhabitants consume much more bread, vegetables, fruit and wine. If the ultimate goal is to reduce cardiovascular mortality through food behaviours – this double page spread is devoted to the risks of a poor diet – what conclusions are we implicitly meant to draw? That one should consume more fruits and vegetables? Drink more wine? Why should fruits and vegetables be preferred to wine? Is it possible to isolate dietary factors in this way and draw conclusions from them alone? Who is to say that these are the only factors at play? Critical thinking requires, on the one hand, that we identify the source of these documents, information not provided by the textbook, and, on the other hand, that we resist jumping to conclusions. Is it reasonable, then, to rely on such documents without training students in the basics of epidemiology?

Graphs are another type of diagram found in textbooks that raise key issues. The graph shown in Figure 12.1, for example, compares the amount of energy which carbohydrates (glucids) and lipids provide during physical activity. The accompanying exercise asks students to 'determine the intensity of physical activity required to lose the most fat'. Given that high school students are familiar with line graphs, it can be expected that they would quickly respond that the maximum is 65 per cent VO_2 max (i.e. 65 per cent of the maximum volume of oxygen that the person can consume per unit of time). The curved line showing energy provided by

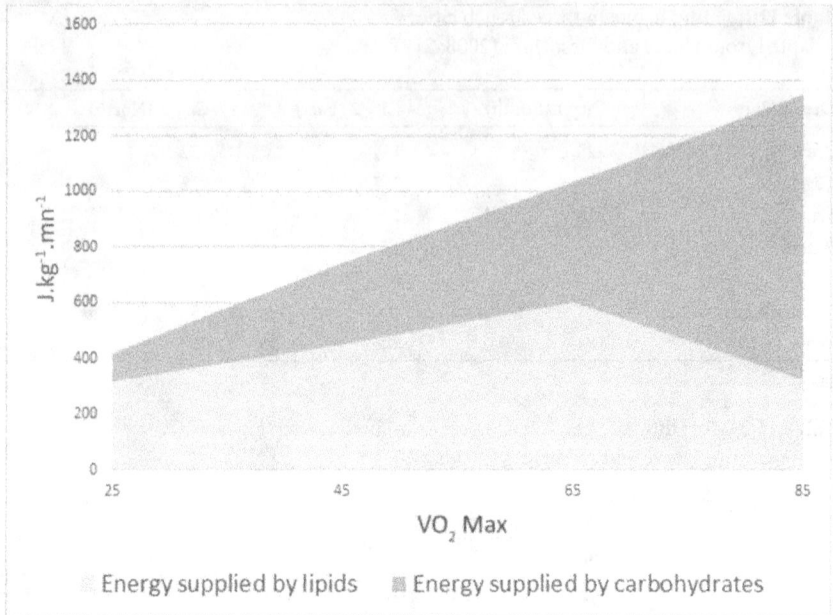

Figure 12.1 Amount of energy supplied by carbohydrates and lipids as a function of effort in five professional cyclists. Adapted from Duco (2010: 199).

fats gives the solution directly without needing to understand the deeper meaning of this graph. However, if the question is examined scientifically, several points not mentioned in the textbook need to be discussed. First, what is the source of the information featured on this graph? How can we identify energy provided by carbohydrates and energy provided by lipids? Not providing this information may lead students to think that while scientists know, because they have ways of knowing, students do not need to know such details: they are simply to trust the materials and the teacher. Of course, explaining the respiratory quotient[6] would take time, but that is the only way to fully investigate how the body uses energy. Another point for discussion is this: to burn up lipids (fats), is it better to exercise at 65 per cent VO_2 max or to exercise for twice as long at 45 per cent? Looking only at what the graph wants to show us means not considering the relationships between the various energy reserves in the body. For example, pupils might say that if 'we eat too much sugar', we store fat. So, if we do physical activity that consumes lipids instead, what makes it possible to say that the fat stores cannot be replenished from carbohydrates, for example? Can we so easily separate these variables? Here again, an investigation guided by building a global model of energy metabolism would allow us to address all these questions. However, such a model is not included in the curricula.

As we can see, while this schoolbook claims to take an investigative approach, its methods are not compatible with approaches to develop critical thinking. There is a considerable risk that the shortcuts it proposes may lead to faulty reasoning: at worst, the pupils, guided by the *contrat didactique* (didactic contract),[7] do not realize that the reasoning they are being asked to apply is fallacious or in any case based on undisclosed knowledge; at best, they conclude that the life and earth sciences are not a very rigorous discipline. In both cases, the damage is considerable. We see that it is more formative to try to understand how certain figures were produced rather than to take the graphs at face value, as raw and unquestionable truth. Moreover, what we have presented here is not exaggerated or exceptional, but corresponds to what is found in practically all life and earth science textbooks (Orange 2017). The ideal here is not to accuse textbook authors of incompetence but to point out that they are faced with a fundamental contradiction: the objective is to lead students to the desired conclusions through what looks like an investigation, but to do so quickly, with no time given for in-depth study, due in part to the ambitious scale of educational programmes.

Conclusion

While the aim of food education is not only inculcating societal norms but also employing well-thought-out education methods and training in critical thinking, such education is only possible under certain conditions. Here we have explored only a few of these conditions – those related to particular points of biological necessity. As we stated in the introduction, other fields of knowledge should be investigated and, above all, interdisciplinary problems should also be worked through in this way.

In the domain to which we confined ourselves, we sought to show the importance of helping students change the way they think about food. We summarize these points in Table 12.3. This change is not a simple matter, because discussions about food in the media, while they play an important role, are based on conventional modes of thinking, such as storytelling and object-based reasoning. In a way, schools must counter media discourses, not to dispute their claims but to enable future citizens to think about them critically.

Table 12.3 Common modes of thinking that students need to break away from in order to make rational food choices

Subjects of study	Common modes of thinking	Conditions for overcoming common modes of thinking
Food classification Menus Cultural habits	Focus on the intra-objectal (the properties of food) Little is done with the relationships between objects and simultaneous processes	Work with students on epidemiological issues; help them understand the difference between a scientific model and simple statistical correlations
The breakdown and trajectory of food and nutrients	Storytelling: short food stories	Build a systemic model of nutrition with students and use it to discuss food issues

Notes

1. We use 'educational approach' to translate the French term 'éducations à', ambitious interdisciplinary programmes at the primary and secondary school levels which aim (since the early 2000s) to develop knowledge – and especially competencies and aptitudes – with regard to domains of social interest such as food and nutrition, health, sustainability, media, civic awareness. The French 'éducations à' are similar to 'literacy' approaches yet are not strictly competency based.

2. For Fourez (1997: 218), 'an island of rationality is a theoretical construction which can be as fully elaborated as scientific concepts belonging to particular disciplines, but which falls within the domain of field sciences or technological theorisation' ('un îlot de rationalité est une construction théorique parfois aussi élaborée que des concepts scientifiques disciplinaires, mais qui relève des sciences de terrain ou de la théorisation technologique').

3. The Eduscol platform provides regularly updated pedagogical materials for teachers; thematic subsections include a 'food education' page. See http://eduscol.education.fr/cid47664/une-education-alimentation-precoce-durable.html (accessed 10 June 2018).

4. This objective of sensitizing children to the importance of responsible eating is still currently stated in the Food and Taste Education resource section of the Eduscol pedagogical resource platform, despite significant structural and discursive changes made since our analysis of the website in 2018; see: https://eduscol.education.fr/cid148288/les-enjeux-de-l-education-a-l-alimentation-et-au-gout-en-milieu-scolaire.html (accessed 10 November 2021).

5. The Eduscol platform contents have been modified and restructured since our 2018 analysis; for the current version see https://eduscol.education.fr/cid146387/eduquer-a-l-alimentation-et-au-gout-permet-d-engager-un-travail-sur-les-modalites-qui-interviennent-dans-les-choix-alimentaires.html (accessed 10 November 2021.

6. The respiratory quotient is the ratio of the volume of CO_2 released to the volume of O_2 consumed by the body over a given period. It is a function of the nutrients used by the body to obtain energy.

7. The respective expectations of the teacher and the students about knowledge and its acquisition are referred to as a *contrat didactique* (Brousseau 1998). This 'contract' is largely implicit. Here, students are confronted with documents; the teaching contract, constructed through the usual functioning of the classroom, may lead students to think that there is a relatively simple conclusion to be drawn from them.

When 'healthy' eating becomes a political issue: Parents' Association school canteens in Andalusia, Spain

Philippe Cardon and María Dolores Martín-Lagos López

Today, throughout Spain, 80 per cent of public-school canteens are run by private catering[1] companies[2] with marked differences across regions; Spain is a decentralized state that endows its autonomous communities with broad decision-making and management powers. These communities can thus legally choose the model of management they wish for public primary school canteens within their territory. Many schools choose to contract private catering companies to outsource their food preparation and delivery. In 2011, the Andalusian government revised the legal framework surrounding the operation and management of school canteens in public elementary schools to open the market to competition from catering companies. Previously, school canteens had been managed directly by the establishments with their kitchen and kitchen staff. Currently, 95 per cent of the public elementary school canteens in Andalusia are managed by private catering companies.[3]

Social movements criticizing this new management model of public-school canteens in Spain have emerged, offering alternative management solutions. In Granada, Andalusia, parent-run school canteens for pupils were created as of 2014 outside the sphere of public primary schools. The canteens welcome all children who so choose for lunch at 2 pm, as is customary in Spain (Díaz Méndez and Gutierrez Palacios 2014). On average, about seventy children attend each of the seven canteens currently operating in and around Granada.[4] These school canteens are opposed to the 2011 legislative bill regarding outsourced catering; each of the current canteens runs its own kitchen and staff. Similar organizations have existed since the nineteenth century; today's parent-run associative canteens are part of a long tradition of alternative movements promoting healthy food in what organizers consider to be a fight against the industrialization of food (Cardon, Depecker and Plessz 2019).

In Granada, these 'reform from below' organizations[5] (Cardon, Depecker and Plessz 2019) criticize both the quality of the meals prepared by outsourced catering companies and the lack of a programme to educate children on health, social and environmental issues. Indeed, in many Western countries, the school canteen (and schools in general) increasingly plays a role in educating children about these issues. Canteens espouse a 'moral project: to educate the kind of people we are, what we aspire to be and the role that food can play in the process' (Carotti et al. 2019). Schools, primarily through the school canteen, become the place of 'organized governance' (Carotti et al. 2019) aimed at educating children (and, according to a logic of delegated biopolitics, their families) on a diet deemed healthy, that is, in line with nutritional orthodoxy. Moreover, studies have shown the vital role that school canteens can play in the fight against health inequalities (Pike and Colquhoun 2014). These health, environmental and social challenges are essential, as education on these issues is not self-evident. Food practices are both levers for social standardization through the appropriation of specific standards, and areas of resistance on the part of children (Comoretto 2015). Moreover, children's social and ethnic origin plays a dominant role in the appropriation of the normative model (Bahr Bugge 2010; Nukaga 2008).

The parents who lead these organizations, as they do not consider primary schools in Spain to be fulfilling this mission, promote a double slogan: 'Do not touch my frying pan' and 'They will not poison my children'. Their objective is to offer children food that they consider to be healthy, environmentally friendly and in line with nutritional orthodoxy. To do this, these associations define themselves as spaces for the circulation of nutritional and dietetic knowledge[6] to train 'child citizens', that is, children who are aware of the health, social and environmental issues related to food. This reform movement from below aims to modify consumption practices and in so doing support the process of citizenship socialization, through activities designed to circulate knowledge about food and environmental issues.

In this chapter, we analyse these associations' educational projects with regard to food and eating. We highlight the tensions that run through such movements from below. Indeed, these organizations suffer from a twofold problem. On the one hand, the majority of the parents involved in these associations belong to the upper-middle classes; their movement does not resonate among the working classes, despite the fact of being a citizens' movement. On the other hand, although the different associations and their members are all from the upper-middle classes and are all committed to the same project of reform from below, they do not form a homogenous group. The parents belong to different strata of the upper-middle classes and carry a range of different ambitions for the future.

Methodology

This study, begun in 2017, is based on ethnographic research carried out in five parent-run school canteens currently active in Granada, Andalusia. The ethnographic study is based on repeated participant observation, primarily during children's mealtimes, in conjunction with formal interviews with association directors, children's mealtime supervisors, cooks and parents. Informal discussions also took place with the children during and after their meals and with their parents when they came to pick them up. This ethnography aims to retrace the history of parent-run canteens; the context in which they were created; how they operate and their objectives; the social and professional profiles of the parents; and more general issues related to school meals.

Using food to educate for citizenship

Whether individual structures are cooperative or entrepreneurial and regardless of the social profile of the parents who run the canteens and whose children eat there (discussed later), all of the associations share one common concern: changing children's eating habits to follow norms of dietary orthodoxy. The aim is to educate children to become *homo medicus* (Peretti-Watel 2003), that is, individuals who are conscious and rational in their food consumption behaviour. Associations also seek to educate children about environmental issues related to food, particularly with regard to production conditions (favouring organic production) and the circulation and transfer of food (proximity). Beyond health and environmental issues, members consider such learning to be a path towards citizenship, with citizenship defined as taking on the role of an actor concerned about one's health and the environment. The importance attached to citizenship can be understood through parent participants who are strong advocates of public schools and who reject private education.

To meet these goals, associations receive children daily from one or two local primary schools at 2 pm. Supervisors pick them up after school from their respective schools and bring them to the canteen where the children benefit, outside the school grounds, from a second place of education.

Education through the content of meals

This education takes place, first and foremost, through the content of the meals served in the association-run canteens. Cooks (or sometimes supervisors) explain the content of the meals to the children, emphasizing the nutritional value and environmentally friendly ethics of the meals. The associations work with local producers from Granada, purchasing directly from producers. They also promote healthy and organically produced foods. However, while organic fruits and vegetables are affordable, organic meat (or even fish) is not. Consequently, it is more difficult to buy organic meat or fish, and therefore those in charge of the canteens limit meat consumption. Through their continued promotion of local products, associations denounce meals prepared by cold line catering far from the canteens. The consumption of local organic products is also a means of criticizing catering companies' use of foods 'from far away' such as foods derived from fish farming which is considered harmful to health. In other words, as opposed to the 'long circuits' of the catering industry which they decry, parents' associations favour 'short circuits' in organic production which guarantee responsible food respectful of the environment and health. Moreover, the criticisms expressed by these associations during our study interviews were also conveyed to the press and TV. The Granada primary schools' association, Federación de las Asociaciones de Padres y Madres,[7] upholds the same convictions and deplore the same problems.

In addition to these food choices (local and organic), parents expect 'traditional' cuisine made daily from fresh produce with varied menus compliant with dietary and nutritional norms. None of the cooks currently working for these associations has had any formal culinary training. They learnt their trade on the job and through exchange of information and advice (even though the organizations have little contact with each other). They mainly rely on a cookbook published in the 2000s by the Gómez Moreno primary school's parent's association (AMPA), titled *La Cocina de Nuestro Cole* (My Schools' Kitchen). The Gómez Moreno school is located in the historic town of Albaicín de Granada (Spain) and runs a canteen, which we will discuss further in the second part of this chapter. This celebrated cookbook, featuring recipes from meals served in the Gómez Moreno school's environmentally friendly canteen won several awards and is considered the bible of canteen cooking for the associations that use it to educate children and parents. This 'traditional' cuisine, served daily, is valued as it also serves as a condemnation of the cold line meals of caterers. The parents' associations also criticize caterers for the use of plastic containers for the delivery and reheating of meals. School managers and parents cite the health risks of plastic, including risks associated with plastic molecules that penetrate food.

The canteen, or learning the rules of autonomy

The children must abide by the rules laid down by the organization before, during and after meals. This means that when they arrive at the parent-run canteen, they must take their napkin at the entrance, queue to be served and then sit at a table. While seats are not assigned, and each child is free to sit wherever they wish, children often sit in the same seats every day. After a time, while developing new friendships, they sometimes change places. In practice, children can be moved and thus cut off from their affinity group if, for example, caregivers feel that they are not focused on their meal and are 'fooling around with their friends' (to quote one caregiver). Making as little noise as possible during mealtimes is also an important social norm within the canteen; children are not allowed to talk loudly or make noise during the meal. However, they have plenty of time to be boisterous during the activities provided after the meal. According to the advocates of these associations, this system teaches children how to respect others.

The heads of these organizations, during discussions and interviews, often criticize the noisy environment that pupils are subjected to in public-school canteens, which (according to them) often causes pupils to complain. They also advocate that children should not be 'pushed' to finish a meal, but 'accompanied'. If a child has difficulty finishing a meal, a supervisor can engage with them so that they taste each dish at their own pace, but children do not necessarily have to finish the meal. As a general rule, children are encouraged to take their time to eat. Once the meal is over, the children help clear the table by taking their plate, cutlery and glass into the kitchen. Some canteens require them to rinse the cutlery and plates and put them in the dishwasher. Others ask them to place them in basins at the kitchen entrance. The canteen thus creates a favourable environment for learning hygiene habits, positive behaviour, ideas about food and fellowship. Fellowship is based on the observance of specific rules, for example, respect for others, being quiet, eating slowly, participating in food activities. Behind this learning, the aim of all these organizations is to develop children's autonomy.

In addition to healthy eating, children's education covers playtime workshops accessible after lunch. Each facility has at least one playroom adjoining the canteen with a wide range of playtime activities for children, including board games (from chess to table soccer), construction games or cardboard building blocks. In most of the facilities, there is also a library where children can browse, read and borrow books. Children's creative arts workshops, such as painting, are also an option if a parent or supervisor offers to hold one. Many of the children's artistic productions are put on display. More generally, play sessions or after-meal workshops are an opportunity for adults to pass on their values to the children, such as non-hierarchical gender roles and the fight against stereotypes. For example, girls are encouraged to play games considered to be 'masculine', such as table soccer. Also, children are encouraged to 'manage' their conflicts during arguments and even fights and to adopt 'non-violent' attitudes among themselves. During our observation sessions, it was not rare to see an adult assisting children in conflict with each other to solve the problem and maintain their friendship.

The community canteen as a social project

All games and objects used during recreation time are donated by association parent-members or by companies. These donations help support new facilities to cope with the initial costs of starting up. Donations also contribute to fostering the same community ethic that governs the organization of social relations within these structures. Indeed, all the facilities studied emphasize and value interpersonal relationships between parents and, above all, between parents and children. It is therefore not surprising that the members of these organizations consider themselves to be one big 'family'.

Association members are also opposed to the individualism of modern society. The concept of 'community' functions here in opposition to what are seen as the cold and impersonal relationships of the market economy. Their educational model is based not on traditional hierarchy, but on an adult/child relationship. This model functions through 'explicitness': rules and prohibitions are not imposed but made explicit.[8] It thus not uncommon for an adult to take the time during a meal to help a child who has difficulty eating. On the other hand, those in charge of the organizations condemn the cold and distant, even authoritarian, atmosphere that is said to characterize public canteens, which are subject to multiple constraints, particularly in terms of supervision (lack of staff, underpaid and untrained staff).

One of the main rules on which these interpersonal relationships are based is communication, which is considered to be the basis of children's education. Such communication is all the more valued since education through speech in the canteen is considered to be transferable to the family's private space, with the children carrying their learning into the domestic space and in turn educating their parents. As one facility manager put it: 'our objective is not only to educate children. What we want is for them to then go and educate their parents at home. It's like a growing circle, and that's how we're going to move forward and make things happen.' It is no coincidence therefore that some of these facilities welcome some parents for lunch at the same time as their children. The canteen is primarily reserved for children, but it also serves parents who wish to use its services. While only a few parents actually do eat lunch at the canteens, the fact that they can also take part in the meals reinforces the claimed idea of a community for sharing and educating children and their parents.

In this sense, through an educational model promoted through food and food practices, these structures encourage the figure of the consumer-citizen. The consumer-citizen is not only concerned with healthy and environmentally friendly food but is also respectful and concerned about others, feels solidarity and is committed to relationships with those around them. In this project of reform from below, education is seen as a means to transform society. This transformation is achieved by developing profound relationships between parents and children through the values transmitted in the canteen.

Defence of public and secular schools

Among the parents interviewed for this study, the importance given to responsible citizenship as well as concern for health and the environment go hand in hand with a keen appreciation for public schools. These parents defend public schools and public education which, in their view, best meet the need to train children as citizens and to combat social inequalities. Public schools embody the institution most able to compensate for social differences and inequalities by reducing differences in education in particular. According to these parents, public schools can fight social inequalities related to food. In their conversations, parents refer to the situation of children from underprivileged and poor backgrounds who do not have access to a balanced diet at home or do not eat enough to satisfy their hunger. School canteens, subsidized by the regions, should alleviate these social vulnerabilities that directly affect children by offering low prices for the poorest and most deprived families and by making the price of access to canteens dependent on household income. They explicitly denounce private schools, which, in contrast to public schools, embody and reinforce social differences through enrolment fees that make the school inaccessible to a large segment of the population.

Moreover, beyond the public dimension, the secular dimension of public schools is highly valued. The vast majority of parents in the associations claim to be non-believers or, when they are believers, hold that religion cannot be at the heart of the school organization. In a Spain that is still strongly marked by religion, especially in Andalusia, this position concerning private and religious schools marks a symbolic boundary that is widely shared by members of the parents' associations.

A culture of education through food: A double local heritage

Significantly, this movement of reform from below via parent-run school canteens has strong roots in local cultures. Other potential models available to promoters of the Grenada canteens include Gastronomic Associations such as those of the Spanish Basque Country. The vocation of such gastronomic associations is to create a collective space for the diffusion and sharing of culinary pleasure. The nuance lies in the fact that the school canteens are mainly aimed at children and their vocation is to educate (whereas Basque Country Gastronomic Associations are more general places for sharing meals). In reality, the parents in charge of the Grenada school canteens claim and perpetuate a locally rooted dual heritage, to which we now turn.

Municipal nursery schools: Food-based education

Association members recognize themselves as heirs of the Granada nursery schools and torchbearers of their philosophy. The Granada nursery schools were created at the time of the Spanish transition by the City Council of Granada. With a firm grounding in civics and citizenship, and with the goal of educating children through 'reasoned' learning of life, these nursery schools welcome children aged zero to six years. Their educational project includes developing autonomy and responsibility. The values advocated by these nursery schools since the period of their creation are achieved through a wide range of educational play activities. These nursery schools run canteens and kitchens where children learn to discover food and to cook. The schools think of food as a multidimensional learning support for addressing issues in health, environment and sociability. Although there are only three of these nursery schools today (once there were more than a dozen in the city), it is essential to note that parents of today's association-run school canteens attended these nursery schools. Even the parents who did not attend these nursery schools know them and recognize their heritage of education through food. During informal exchanges or interviews, many parents referred to these kindergartens as a model of education. The promoters and members of the parent-run canteens clearly feel that they have inherited the legacy of this model of education.

Gómez Moreno Primary School: A school canteen managed by parents

The canteens studied also consider themselves to be symbolic heirs of the Gómez Moreno Primary School, located in the Albaicín district. This school closed in 2002, due in part to insufficient enrolment. A group of parents fought against the closure by using the parents' association to set up an innovative management project: an alternative, independent educational project, based on the management of the school canteen by the parents' association itself. This educational project helped to revitalize the school, which very quickly saw its pupil enrolment numbers increase. While the aim of this essay is not to provide a detailed history of the Gómez Moreno School, we wish to emphasize three points as keys for understanding the reform movement of which associative school canteens are a part.

First, the revival of the Gómez Moreno Primary School through the food education project coincides with the gentrification process in the historically popular Albaicín neighbourhood. This gentrification began in the late 1990s (Duque Calvache 2016) with the establishment of an upper middle class from which are drawn both the parents behind the Gómez Moreno project and the parents who advocate the current community canteens. A strong social and class homogeneity can thus be found in the generations that perpetuate this educational model.

Second, parent association takeover of the Gómez Moreno school canteen has gone hand in hand with an educational project in which food plays a central role. This educational project is based on a specific concept of nutrition, of which the canteen serves as the model: nutrition that is respectful of health and the environment. This model is based on daily cooking, carried out on-site by a cook, using fresh, local organic products. Since its creation, the Gómez Moreno canteen managed by the parents' association has worked with local producers from the plains of Granada. This food model serves as a support for children's learning and training in citizenship. The parents' association school canteens claim direct inheritance from this model.

Third, the educational project of the Gómez Moreno Primary School is also materialized by the previously mentioned cookbook produced by the parents' association with the school canteen cook. Associative canteen cooks feel that they have inherited this cookbook and it is also through this resource that they are trained. From the very beginning of our ethnographic field study, this cookbook was pointed out to us as the reference work for healthy and eco-friendly cooking. This point is central because it concretely embodies the Gómez Moreno School as claimed by the majority of those in charge of associative school canteens. Beyond its role as a working tool, this culinary guide also embodies the educational model through which these organizations can be identified. It is not surprising that this book has given rise to other guides: one of the canteens, at the time of this survey, was preparing its own cookbook based on 'grandmothers' recipes' (the aim being to list all the recipes for dishes prepared by older generations in the Granada region). Another group is working with nutritionists to improve the recipes of the Gómez Moreno book.

An educational model under stress: A transitional and precarious reform movement

This local 'bottom-up' movement, with its educational model founded on the principle of learning through food, suffers from the economic model on which it is based and which places it in a precarious position. Two elements help to explain the precarity of this educational model built outside the walls of Grenada public primary schools: their economic fragility and the inequalities they seem to produce, and the social tensions that run through them.

Unequal canteens?

The first problem lies in the paradox that these associations face – they cannot benefit from regional public aid to support the price of a meal since they exist outside of the educational system. Although the cost of the meals they offer is relatively close to that of school canteens, it cannot be offset by regional subsidies. It is therefore not surprising that the socio-economic profile of the families who are members of these associations is that of the upper middle classes, or even the upper classes, that is, families with an income level adapted to this type of structure. Moreover, this economic dimension intersects with a sociological profile and lifestyle that are entirely in line with the proposed educational model, that is, a class ethos that values postmodern education and a healthy and environmentally friendly diet. The canteens are thus concretely but indirectly confronted with the problems of social inequalities in education that pervade Western countries (Martín-Lagos López 2018). The project is aimed at all children regardless of their social condition, but participants are mostly middle class with comfortable incomes. It is therefore not surprising that the detractors of these structures accuse them of practising an 'elitist' education that directly favours the already privileged social classes. In response, the associations argue that they cannot compete for management of school canteens. Thus, the children who eat in their canteens are not entitled to subsidies from the region of Andalusia.

Moreover, although this movement produces a certain level of social exclusion, it also generates a specific form of social and professional precarity: while staff members are paid, they are poorly paid. Many of the parents' associations survive economically only through members' fees and a sense of community, which can often result in underpayment of staff. Membership dues are used for the purchase of food and to pay staff (up to 5 hours a day for the cook and 3 hours for the supervisors; it should be noted that managers who are there every day work on a voluntary basis). As some of them say, they are 'half-workers, half-volunteers', a sort of in-between status which does not facilitate long-term professional advancement. If the cooks and supervisors who work at the canteens a few hours a day recognize the precariousness of their employment, they also claim pride in the structure and type of education they support. This situation is not free of identity tension, as it is linked to the precarity of work in Andalusia.

Upper-middle classes dealing with legal and economic fragility of associations

It is therefore not surprising that general assembly meetings regularly reveal significant tensions, with debates about the economic model of these structures. The associations' legal fragility is not without effects on the structuring of the movement on a broader scale. These associations share a common conception of education, claim the same legacies and put into practice the same food model. However, they find it difficult to unify and work together, if only because economic and more general management constraints do not facilitate the organizations' development. This reality is made even more difficult by the fact that association members do not necessarily all think about the future of public-school canteens and their own future in the same way. The challenge for association members is to resolve the tension between the social model they have chosen and the role they wish to play in that context.

The diversity of social profiles explains the difficulties encountered in attempts for a unified approach and in the search for a viable economic model. As previously mentioned, associative school canteens created outside the school framework share a similar sociological profile: the managers and parents of these structures belong to the upper-middle classes. There is nothing particularly unusual about this phenomenon; it has been widely demonstrated that interest in diets in line with nutritional orthodoxy increases as one moves up the social ladder. Conformity to this nutritional and environmental model is characteristic of the upper-middle classes in all Western countries (Cardon, Depecker and Plessz 2019).

However, parents who are promoters and members of associative canteens from the upper-middle classes do not constitute a homogeneous group in terms of their profession and their professional status. Behind this class homogeneity lie differences in professional profiles among members of individual organizations. While these are general trends, they constitute symbolic, even ideological, barriers between the associations studied, which account for the tensions that run through this local reform movement. We have identified three different profiles which correspond to three ways of understanding how a reform movement can be structured: the 'artists' profile referring to parents working in the arts and culture, the 'administrative executives' profile and finally the 'private sector executive' profile. Each association is dominated by one of these three profiles.

Artists: Thinking of themselves as a transitional movement to promote better investment in schools

The artist profile is characteristic of two of the five associations, the first created in 2014 and the second in 2015. This profile includes, among its leaders, parents who work in the world of culture and the arts, but also in outdoor sports activities (skiing, parachuting, paragliding, climbing). It also includes primary and secondary school teachers. This profile claims to have an ethical and philosophical commitment to healthy and responsible eating. Members feel committed to a school food reform project. They have and claim a horizontal and collective conception of power.

This conception of the organization of power has a direct impact on the management of the association, not only with regard to decision-making (majority voting in the general assembly is obligatory) but also with respect to carrying out the tasks of feeding and tending to meals. The cook and the paid supervisors who look after the children help with meal service, supervise the children and perform cleaning tasks. In addition, all the parents of the association are invited to take turns several times a month to carry out tasks related to the canteen, in particular cleaning the canteen and laundry. Most of the parents contribute, and there is a rotation in their involvement. This group of organizations exhibits the strongest commitment and adherence to the model of the community as a family. It is therefore not surprising that these associations do not define themselves as 'alternatives' but as transitional organizations. While they promote an alternative movement outside public schools, it is in a transitional way, the aim being to implement this model within public schools through a change in the law at the regional level. Thus, in the same way that they seek to expand their educational model into the heart of private familial spaces, they wish to expand this model to the public spaces of schools.

Public executives: Thinking of oneself as transitory

The 'public executives' profile refers to an association created in 2016, after the two above-mentioned canteens. Unlike these previously mentioned structures, this third associative canteen was created by two unemployed parents who took advantage of an opportunity. Having discovered the existence of parent-run school canteens and taking issue with the canteens in their children's schools, they decided to create a new association. Unlike the two 'artists' canteens, these parents are salaried employees of the association and, as such, are responsible for all food-related activities (childcare, shopping, meal preparation, canteen preparation, service and cleaning). Therefore, contrary to the first profile, the only responsibility that other parents take on is to pick up their children. Parents are also invited to participate in the organization's general assemblies. Here, the participative element is based more on the power of representation. This canteen is located on the outskirts of Granada's city centre, in a neighbourhood with many services and administrative centres. The parent members' sociological profile is very different from the first type. Parents are mainly in executive civil service positions within the public administration (especially hospital staff) and teachers (especially university faculty). Parent members can be reluctant to commit themselves beyond participation in individual meetings. The organization's discourse is characterized by demands for healthy and responsible food, as parents recognize the benefits of the food offered by their canteen. The directors' primary vocation is to lead the association 'because it provides a good service'. While the first organizational profile perfectly embodies a movement committed to food reform, this second profile is less committed to this ideal and is more opportunistic. It is perhaps here that the tension between two management models is the strongest: for the two fathers who run the association, their motivation derives from their professional situations – since both were unemployed – and their criticism of their children's school canteen. The opportunity to create a canteen outside their children's school motivated them to provide what they consider to be best for their children (healthy and environmentally friendly food) and to create work for themselves. This employment is admittedly very fragile, though the two parents acknowledge that both their wives are teachers, which made it easier to set up the project despite relatively precarious conditions. At the time of our survey, the two directors did not know what would become of their project in the future. While they strongly value the canteen project, they qualify it as transitory. They do not rule out the idea of expanding the operation or even transforming it into a business, notably because it could provide them with more stable employment.

Private sector executives: Thinking like an alternative movement

Finally, as a third profile, we identified an association where parents are recruited in advance from the private sector. Managers or independent professionals lead this recruitment. It is interesting to note that this association has chosen to become a company managed by a team of three people rather than by the general assembly so that decisions can be reached more quickly. In 2017 the founders were inspired by parents' association canteens but judged that the operating model was not sustainable. The group of parents, at the initiative of the association, decided to create a company. In this sense, the organization and management of the structure are based on a vertical power structure: decisions are made by management (composed of two couples who also founded the association). In some cases, these managers consult with parents before taking a decision.

Moreover, unlike the artist profiles, here parents are not asked to participate voluntarily in the various tasks related to the canteen. Lunches are organized by the director, the deputy director, the cook and a supervisor. While the director and deputy director also work elsewhere and are volunteers at this time, the supervisor and the cook are paid. Nevertheless, while the organizational logic of this structure differs from that of the artist profile canteens, it has an ethical and philosophical commitment to healthy and responsible eating.

While the company broadly supports the reform movement, it differs from other associations who claim transitory status. This company does consider itself to embody an alternative movement to the extent that the managers' objective is to perpetuate the structure. While the director of the structure works voluntarily, the medium-term objective is that the company should employ her. The structure also seeks to diversify its activities by setting up cultural and artistic workshops, including afternoon sessions on food and by renting its premises to professionals looking for locations to provide services such as yoga classes or painting lessons. In this sense, food would be at the heart of a broader educational and societal project marked by the diversification of activities open to a much wider public than primary school children. Moreover, it is here that the idea of educating parents is most forcefully expressed by canteen directors during the interviews we conducted as well as by the parents we met.

Conclusion

Bringing children to citizenship through food is the mantra of these primary school canteen organizations. Granada associative canteens are spaces for the circulation of nutritional and dietetic knowledge as well as for the circulation of knowledge related to health, the environment and, more generally, citizenship.

However, these associations are fragile due to their precarious social and economic situation; they do not escape the structural reproduction of social inequalities even though they operate outside the education system. Above all, this movement to reform food practices from below, as it is developing in the context of Granada via parent-run school canteens, is traversed by tensions characteristic of the identity issues apparent today among the upper-middle classes. While their levels of education and training tend to bring parent members closer together, the professions specific to each association tend to differentiate them. Their professions relate to different cultures and identities and, in the same way, to different ideas about the collective management of their facilities.

This movement as a whole represents an attempt to socialize children to citizenship through food education, but the modalities of action differ. Thus, artist parents maintain the transitional dimension of the canteen, contending that their model should be imposed in public-school canteens. In fact, by asserting the transient nature of their canteen as a non-alternative organization, artist parents can sometimes minimize the effects of their social position within the upper-middle class. On the other hand, the transitional dimension of the association is not a significant and central issue for the other parent profiles, particularly for private sector executives. For some, the structure's perpetuation offers above all a social and economic opportunity for employment.

Consequently, the mere allusion to the reform project and its forms of perpetuation causes tension. This tension runs through the political core of the movement. For artist parents, the transitional quality of the organizations embodies the political dimension of the project whose aim is to transform regional law on the management of public-school canteens. The perpetuation of structures outside schools is a hypothesis for some associations, while it is already a reality for others. The issues surrounding the meaning of reform 'from below' as addressed within the upper-middle classes constitute an exploratory field of investigation for those interested in the political dimension of food-related questions.

Notes

1. In the discourses of both Andalusian institutions and these different actors (organizations, parents), the English term 'catering' is used to refer to these companies.
2. Since the Ministry of Education and Culture's 1992 decree, there are three possible forms of management of public canteens in primary education: outsourcing by invitation to tender; direct management by the administration, i.e. autonomous communities, municipal councils, departmental councils; management by parents' associations through direct management or an enterprise contract.
3. On 17 June 2019, the Governing Council of the Andalusian government amended the specifications of the school canteen service to introduce new requirements to facilitate the participation of companies from the municipality and smaller entities. Greater use of local products in the preparation of menus is also encouraged (Noticias de la Junta 2019). It is too early to know the real impact of this change, especially since what is taken into account in tenders is the turnover of the companies.
4. In Spain, school hours are from 9 am to 2 pm, Monday to Friday. The majority of schools have a canteen which opens at 2.15 pm. Spain is the only European country where lunch is served at around 3 pm on average (Díaz Méndez and Gutierrez Palacios 2014).
5. By 'reform movement', we mean social actions that aim to bring about a lasting change in practices and even representations. The 'reform movement from below' refers to all organizations and groups that try to transform eating habits. It differs from reform

movements driven by states and public policies, which are characterized by the verticality of their actions. Christian Topalov (1999) proposed this concept, which has the advantage of being used to study movements at different historical periods.

6. The associations use the scientific distinction between nutrition (the science of metabolic food processing) and dietetics (concerned with the practice of a balanced diet).

7. Federación de las Asociaciones de Padres y Madres (FAMPA) is a federation of all parents' associations.

8. Roles and prohibitions are 'imposed' when they are stated as overriding principles that are non-negotiable, non-justified; they are 'explicit' when they are formulated as principles that are justified and subject to negotiation.

References

Introduction

Biltekoff, C. (2013), *Eating Right in America: The Cultural Politics of Food and Health* (Durham, NC: Duke University Press).

Cramer, J. M., C. P. Greene and L. M. Waters, eds (2011), *Food as Communication, Communication as Food* (New York: Peter Lang).

Felt, U., R. Fouché, C. A. Miller and L. Smith-Doerr, eds (2017), *The Handbook of Science and Technology Studies* (Cambridge, MA: MIT Press).

Flowers, R., and E. Swan, eds (2015), *Food Pedagogies* (Farnham: Ashgate).

Gentilcore, D., and M. Smith, eds (2019), *Proteins, Pathologies and Politics: Dietary Innovation and Disease from the Nineteenth Century* (London: Bloomsbury Academic).

Jeanneret, Y. (2008), *Penser la trivialité: La vie triviale des êtres culturels* (Paris: Hermès Lavoisier).

Latour, B. (1987), *Science in Action: How to Follow Scientists and Engineers through Society* (Cambridge, MA: Harvard University Press).

Neswald, E., D. F. Smith and U. Thoms, eds (2017), *Setting Nutritional Standards: Theory, Policies, Practices* (Woodbridge: University of Rochester Press).

Östling, E. Sandmo, D. Larsson Heidenblad, A. Nilsson Hammar, K. H. Nordberg eds (2018), *Circulation of Knowledge: Exploration in the History of Knowledge* (Lund: Nordic Academic Press).

Penders, B. (2010), *The Diversification of Health: Politics of Large-Scale Cooperation in Nutrition Science* (Bielefeld: Transcript Verlag).

Pike, J., and P. Kelly, eds (2014), *The Moral Geographies of Children, Young People and Food* (Basingstoke: Palgrave Macmillan).

Pike, J., and P. Kelly, eds (2017), *Neo-Liberalism and Austerity: The Moral Economies of Young People's Health and Well-Being* (London: Palgrave Macmillan).

Sarasin, P., and A. Kilcher (2011), 'Editorial', *Nach Feierabend: Züricher Jahrbuch für Wissensgeschichte*, 7.

WHO (2001), *Information, Education, Communication: Lessons from the Past; Perspectives for the Future*, 3.

Chapter 1

Boccardi, V., R. Calvani, F. Limongi, A. Marseglia, A. Mason, M. Noale, D. Rogoli, N. Veronese, G. Crepaldi and S. Maggi (2018), 'Consensus Paper on the "Executive Summary of the International Conference on Mediterranean Diet and Health: A Lifelong Approach", an Italian Initiative Supported by the Mediterranean Diet Foundation and the Menarini Foundation', *Nutrition*, 51–2: 38–45.

Borgmeier, I., and J. Westenhoefer (2009), 'Impact of Different Food Label Formats on Healthiness Evaluation and Food Choice of Consumers: A Randomized-Controlled Study', *BMC Public Health*, 9: 1–12.

Brosse, J. (1994), *Mitologia degli alberi* (Milan: Rizzoli).

Brown, R. D. (2011), 'The Traffic Light Diet Can Lower Risk for Obesity and Diabetes', *NASN School Nurse*, 26(3): 152–4.

Cappellini, M. (2018), 'ONU, agroalimentare italiano sotto accusa: "Olio e Grana come il fumo" ', *Il Sole 24 Ore*, 17 July.

Carandini, A. (2016), *Roma. Il primo giorno* (Rome: Laterza).

Cattabiani, A. (2017), Florario. *Miti leggende e simboli di fiori e piante* (Milan: Mondadori).

Epstein, L., and S. Squires (1988), *Diet for Children: An Eight-Week Program for Parents and Children* (New York: Little, Brown).

Garcia-Martinez, O., C. Ruiz, A. Gutierrez-Ibanez, R. Illescas-Montes and L. Melguizo-Rodriguez (2018), 'Benefits of Olive Oil Phenolic Compounds in Disease Prevention', *Endocrine, Metabolic & Immune Disorders – Drug Targets*, 18(4): 333–40.

Geertz, C. (1973), *The Interpretation of Cultures* (New York: Basic Books).

Giardina, A., ed. (2011), *Roma antica* (Rome: Laterza).

Gramsci, A. (1973), *Lettere dal carcere* (Turin: Einaudi).

Granet, M., and M. Mauss (1975), *Il linguaggio dei sentimenti* (Milan: Adelphi).

Graves, R., and R. Patai (1980), *I Miti Ebraici* (Milan: Longanesi).

Hagen, K. (2010), 'Nutritional Information: Traffic Light Labelling Is the Best Way to Reach Consumers', *DIW Weekly Report*, 19(6), 141–51.

Johnson, T., J. Vergara, C. Doll, M. Kramer, G. Sundararaman, H. Rajendran, A. Efrat and M. Hingle (2014), *A Mobile Food Recommendation System Based on The Traffic Light Diet*, Cornell University preprint archive, arXiv:1409.0296 [cs.CY].

Julia, C., E. Kesse-Guyot, M. Touvier, C. Méjean, L. Fezeu and S. Hercberg (2014), 'Application of the British Food Standards Agency Nutrient Profiling System in a French Food Composition Database', *British Journal of Nutrition*, 112(10): 1699–705.

Keys, A. (1987), 'Olive Oil and Coronary Heart Disease', *The Lancet*, 329(8539): 983–4.

Keys, A., and M. Keys (1959), *Eat Well and Stay Well* (Garden City, NY: Doubleday).

Kovacs, S., and D. Orange-Ravachol (2015), 'La pyramide alimentaire: permanence et mutations d'un objet polymorphe controversé', *Questions de communication*, 27: 129–49.

Lévi-Strauss, C. (1962), *Le totémisme aujourd'hui* (Paris: Presses Universitaires de France).

Lévi-Strauss, C. (1967), *Razza e storia e altri studi di antropologia* (Turin: Einaudi).

Moro, E. (2014), *La dieta mediterranea: Mito e storia di uno stile di vita* (Bologna: Il Mulino).

Moro, E. (2018), 'Nascita di un nome. Esercizi di memoria sul patrimonio immateriale della dieta mediterranea', *Archivio antropologico mediterraneo*, 20(1). Available online: http://journals.openedition.org/aam/298 (accessed 5 April 2021).

Moro, E., and M. Niola (2017), *Andare per i luoghi della dieta mediterranea* (Bologna: Il Mulino).

Niola, M. (2012), *Non tutto fa brodo* (Bologna: Il Mulino).

Niola, M. (2015), *Homo dieteticus: Viaggio nelle tribù alimentari* (Bologna: Il Mulino).

Pini, V. (2018), 'Lotta ONU a grassi e sale: nel mirino il parmigiano', *La Repubblica*, 18 July.

Pintó, X., M. Fanlo-Maresma, E. Corbella, X. Corbella et al. (2019), 'A Mediterranean Diet Rich in Extra-Virgin Olive Oil Is Associated with a Reduced Prevalence of

Nonalcoholic Fatty Liver Disease in Older Individuals at High Cardiovascular Risk', *Journal of Nutrition*, 149(11): 1920–9.

Scarpi, P. (1989), 'La rivoluzione dei cereali e del vino: Demeter, Dionysos, Athena', in O. Longo and P. Scarpi, eds, *Homo Edens. Regimi, Miti e Pratiche dell'alimentazione nella civiltà del Mediterrane* (Verona: Diapress/Documenti).

Scarpi, P. (2005), *Il senso del cibo: Mondo antico e riflessi contemporanei* (Palermo: Sellerio).

Serra-Majem, L., B. Román-Viñas, A. Sanchez-Villegas, M. Guasch-Ferré, D. Corella and C. La Vecchia (2019), 'Benefits of the Mediterranean Diet: Epidemiological and Molecular Aspects', *Molecular Aspects of Medicine*, 67: 1–55.

Seward, M. W., J. P. Block and A. Chatterjee (2016), 'A Traffic Light Label Intervention and Dietary Choices in College Cafeterias', *American Journal of Public Health*, 106(10): 1808–14.

Westermarck, E. (1926), *Ritual and Beliefs in Morocco*, 2 vols (London: Macmillan).

Willet, C. W., F. Sacks, A. Trichopoulou, G. Drescher, A. Ferro-Luzzi, E. Helsing and D. Trichopoulos (1995), 'Mediterranean Diet Pyramid: A Cultural Model for Healthy Eating', *American Journal of Clinical Nutrition*, 61: 1402S–1406S.

Wills, J. (2004), *The Traffic Light Diet* (London: Orion Books).

Yubero-Serrano, E. M., J. Lopez-Moreno, F. Gomez-Delgado, J. Lopez-Miranda et al. (2019), 'Extra Virgin Olive Oil: More Than a Healthy Fat', *European Journal of Clinical Nutrition*, 72: 8–17.

Chapter 2

Albala, K. (2002), *Eating Right in the Renaissance* (Berkeley: University of California Press).

Argaud, É. (2009), 'Les enjeux des représentations des langues savantes et vulgaires en France et en Europe aux XVIᵉ et XVIIᵉ siècles. Affirmer des prééminences et construire une hiérarchisation', *Documents pour l'histoire du français langue étrangère ou seconde*, 43. Available online: https://doi.org/10.4000/dhfles.815 (accessed 22 October 2021).

Brockliss, L. W. B., and C. Jones (1997), *The Medical World of Early Modern France* (Oxford: Clarendon Press).

Bruno, C. (2009), 'La langue claire de Descartes', *Rue Descartes*, 65: 20–34.

Céard, J. (1982), 'La diététique dans la médecine de la Renaissance', in *Pratiques et discours alimentaires à la Renaissance* (Paris: Maisonneuve et Larose).

Charbonneau, F. (2002), 'Melon pervers. Attraits et périls de la bonne chère au siècle de Vatel', *Dix-septième siècle*, 217: 583–94.

Defaux, G., ed. (2003), *Lyon et l'illustration de la langue française à la Renaissance* (Paris: ENS Éditions).

Du Chesne, J. (1606), *Le Pourtraict de la santé, où est au vif représentée la reigle universelle & particuliere de bien sainement & longuement vivre* (Paris: Claude Morel).

Fouquet, F. ([1678] 1712), *Recueil des remedes faciles et domestiques choisis, experimentez & trés-approuvez pour toutes sortes de Maladies internes & externes, & difficiles à guerir* (Paris: Jean Musier).

La Framboisière, N.-A. de (1600), *Le Gouvernement nécessaire à chacun pour vivre longuement en santé* (Paris: Sonnius).

La Framboisière, N.-A. de (1613), *Les Œuvres de Nicolas Abraham de La Framboisière* (Paris: Veuve Marc Orry).

Galen (2017), *Galen. Selected Works*, trans. P. N. Singer (Oxford: Oxford University Press).

Gentilcore, D. (2016), *Food and Health in Early Modern Europe: Diet, Medicine and Society, 1450–1800* (London: Bloomsbury Academic).

Giacomotto-Charra, V., and J. Vons, eds (2017), *Formes du savoir médical à la Renaissance* (Paris: Maison des sciences de l'homme d'Aquitaine).

Grmek, M. D., ed. (1995), *Histoire de la pensée médicale en Occident, 1. Antiquité et Moyen Age* (Paris: Seuil).

Grmek, M. D. (1997), *Le chaudron de Médée: l'expérimentation sur le vivant dans l'Antiquité* (Paris: Le Plessis-Robinson, Synthélabo).

Hill Curth, L. (2003), 'Lessons from the Past: Preventive Medicine in Early Modern England', *Medical Humanities*, 29(1): 16–20.

Jacquelot, P. ([1630] 1633), *L'Art de vivre longuement, sous le nom de Medee, laquelle enseigne les facultez des choses qui sont continuellement en nostre usage, et d'où naissent les Maladies, ensemble la méthode de se comporter en icelles & le moyen de pourvoir à leurs offences* (Paris: J. Jost).

Kahn, D. (2007), *Alchimie et paracelsisme en France à la fin de la Renaissance* (Genève: Droz).

Koźluk, M. (2012), *L'Esculape et son art à la Renaissance: le discours préfaciel dans les ouvrages français de médecine, 1528–1628* (Paris: Classiques Garnier).

Koźluk, M. (2016), 'Le régime de Guy Patin: de l'enseignement à la polémique', *Histoire des sciences médicales*, L(4): 467–76.

Koźluk, M. and J.-P. Pittion (2009), 'La *Médée* de Pierre Jacquelot: médecine, culture humaniste et thérapeutique des passions', in J. Vons, ed., *Pratique et pensée médicales à la Renaissance. Actes du 50ᵉ colloque international d'Études Humanistes* (Paris: Boccard Edition-Diffusion), 187–200.

Lafont, O. (2010), *Des Médicaments pour les pauvres: ouvrages charitables et santé publique aux XVIIᵉ et XVIIIᵉ siècles* (Paris: Pharmathèmes).

Le Long, M. (1637), *Le Régime de santé de l'Eschole de Salerne* (Paris: Nicolas & Jean de la Coste).

Lunel, A. (2008), *La Maison médicale du roi: XVIᵉ-XVIIIᵉ siècles* (Seyssel: Champ Vallon).

Martin, H.-J. ([1969] 1999), *Livre, pouvoirs et société à Paris au XVIIᵉ siècle (1598–1701)* (Genève: Droz).

Mikkeli, H. (2000), *Hygiene: In the Early Modern Medical Tradition* (Helsinki: Finnish Academy of Science & Letters).

Mimoso-Ruiz, D. ([1978] 1982), *Médée antique et moderne: aspects rituels et socio-politiques d'un mythe* (Paris: Éditions Ophrys), 81–9.

Nicoud, M. (2012), 'La rhétorique des régimes de santé', in J. Coste, J. Danielle and J. Pigeaud, eds, *La rhétorique médicale à travers les siècles* (Genève: Droz), 171–207.

Patin, G. (1632), *Traité de la conservation de santé, par un bon régime et légitime usage des choses requises pour bien & sainement vivre* (Paris: Jean Jost).

Patin, G. ([1633] 1667), 'Traité de la conversation de santé', in P. Guybert, ed., *Le Médecin charitable* (Lyon: Antoine Beaujollin).

Pigray, P. ([1609] 1619), *Épitomé des preceptes de medecine & chirurgie, avec ample declaration des remedes propres aux maladies* (Lyon: Pierre Rigaud).

Renaudot, T. ([1632–42] 2004), *De la petite fille velue et autres conférences du Bureau d'adresse* (Paris: Klincksieck).

Sorel, C. ([1664] 2015), *La Bibliothèque française* (Paris: H. Champion).

Chapter 3

Amalvi, C. (2002), *Répertoire des auteurs de manuels scolaires de 1660 à 1960* (Paris: La Boutique de l'Histoire).

Baumert, H. (2013), *Plaidoyer pour l'enseignement des pratiques culinaires* (Paris: L'Harmattan).

Berlivet, L. (2010), *De l'hygiénisme à l'éducation à la santé* (Paris: Éditions Sciences Humaines).

Borde, R., and C. Perrin (1992), *Les offices du cinéma éducateur et la survivance du muet 1925–1940* (Lyon: PUL).

Brison, M. (1982), 'L'école et l'enfant à Lyon: le problème de l'alimentation dans les cantines scolaires', *Revue d'histoire de la seconde Guerre mondiale*, 125 (January): 37–71.

Carré, S., and J. Watin-Augouard (1995), 'Saga La Pie qui Chante', *Revue des marques*, 11 (July). Available online: https://la-revue-des-marques.fr/sagas_marques/la_pie_qui_chante/la_pie_qui_chante.php (accessed 30 December 2021).

Chachignon, M. (1993), *Bon appétit les enfants!* (Paris: Éditions de l'Union des personnels de la restauration scolaire).

De Iulio, S. (2009), 'Notes pour une histoire de la publicité destinée aux enfants: théories, méthodes et pratiques en France (1900–1970)', in *Managerial Thought and Practice in France, 19th–21st Centuries: Assessment and Future Prospects* (Oxford: Royaume-Uni). Available online: https://hal.archives-ouvertes.fr/hal-02013424/document (accessed 10 July 2020).

De Pastre-Robert, B., M. Dubost and F. Massit-Follea, eds (2004), *Cinéma pédagogique et scientifique. A la découverte des archives* (Lyon: ENS Éditions).

Everaere, M., and H. Braillon (1954), Leçons de choses: Cours moyen (Paris: Hachette).

Faye, S. (1932), Morale pour l'enseignement primaire supérieur, programme de 1920 (Paris: Hachette).

Freyssinet-Domingeon, J., and D. Nourrisson (2009), *L'Ecole face à l'alcool* (Saint-Etienne: PUSE).

Frioux, S., and D. Nourrisson (2015), *Propre et sain: Un siècle d'hygiène à l'école en images* (Paris: Armand Colin).

Gosselin, C. F. J. (1908), *Les cantines scolaires* (Paris: Ollier Henri).

Guiot, F. (2018), 'Cantines et colonies pour "enfants débiles": Les secours alimentaires apportés aux enfants de faible constitution lors de la Première Guerre mondiale en Belgique', in D. Nourrisson, ed., *Boire et manger: Une histoire culturelle* (La Diana: Montbrison), 91–109.

Jeunet, P., and D. Nourrisson, eds (2001), *Cinéma-Ecole: aller-retour* (Saint-Etienne: PUSE).

Juranville, C. (1879), *Le savoir-faire et le savoir-vivre dans les diverses circonstances de la vie. Guide pratique de la vie usuelle à l'usage des jeunes filles* (Paris: Larousse).

Moll-Weiss, A. (1906), 'Les cantines scolaires', *La Revue*, 15 May 4(62): 151–61.

Moll-Weiss, A. (1931), *L'alimentation de la jeunesse française* (Paris: Léon Eyrolles).

Nourrisson, D., ed. (2002a), *A votre santé! Education et santé sous la IVᵉ République* (Saint-Etienne: PUSE).

Nourrisson, D., ed. (2002b), *Education à la santé XIXᵉ-XXᵉ siècle* (Rennes: ENSP).

Nourrisson, D. (2008), *La saga Coca-Cola* (Paris: Larousse).

Nourrisson, D. (2013), *Crus et cuites: Histoire du buveur* (Paris: Perrin).

Nourrisson, D. (2014), 'L'alliance de l'éducation et de la santé à l'école: une histoire ancienne et tourmentée (XVIIIe–XXe siècles)', in S. Parayre and A. Klein, eds, *Education et santé: des pratiques aux savoirs* (Paris: L'Harmattan), 59–70.

Nourrisson, D. (2017a), *Une histoire du vin* (Paris: Perrin).

Nourrisson, D. (2017b), 'Dire et voir le vin en gastronomie: l'école du goût dans les années 1950', in J. Pérard and O. Jacquet, eds, *Vin et gastronomie: Regards croisés* (Dijon: EUD), 117–25.

Nourrisson, D. (2019), 'Pédagogie de l'eau', in D. Nourrisson, ed., *L'eau, source de vie* (Montbrison: La Diana).

Orieux, M., M. Everaere and H. Braillon (1959), *Sciences appliquées: Classe de fin d'études (écoles rurales de garçons)* (Paris: Hachette).

Rosset, P. (2017), *La cantine, ventre de l'école?* (Paris: L'Harmattan).

Stengel, K. (2012), *Une cantine peut-elle être pédagogique? La place de la transmission dans la restauration scolaire* (Paris: L'Harmattan).

Thénard-Duvivier, F. (2012), *Hygiène, santé et protection sociale de la fin du XVIIIe siècle à nos jours* (Paris: Ellipses).

Wagnon, S., and H. André, eds (2014), 'Le film fixe, objet d'étude et de recherche de l'histoire matérielle de l'éducation', *Trema, Revue internationale des sciences de l'éducation et didactique*, 41(June).

Chapter 4

ARS [Agence régionale de santé] Ile-de-France (2011), *Prévention de la dénutrition et Qualité de la nutrition en Etablissements d'Hébergement pour Personnes Agées Dépendantes* (Paris: Agence Régionale de Santé). Available online: http://www.bioelys.fr/wp-content/uploads/2016/08/Pr%C3%A9vention-de-la-d%C3%A9nutrition-et-Qualit%C3%A9-de-la-nutrition-rn-EHPAD.pdf (accessed 2 November 2021).

Berlivet, L. (2004), 'Une biologie de l'éducation pour la santé: La fabrique des campagnes de prévention', in D. Fassin and D. Memmi, eds, *Le gouvernement des corps* (Paris: Éditions de l'École des Hautes Etudes en Sciences Sociales), 38–75.

Borsa, S. (1985), *La vie quotidienne des hôpitaux en France au XIXe siècle* (Paris: Hachette).

Bribing, A. (1939), 'Sur l'alimentation du vieillard', PhD thesis, University of Paris.

Chauffard, A. (1902), *De la réforme du régime alimentaire des hôpitaux* (Paris: Annales d'hygiène publique de médecine légale).

Cribier, F., and É. Feller (2013), 'Parcours de fin de vie et recours aux hébergements. Évolution des trajectoires, dispositifs et attitudes au cours du XXe siècle', in Y. Marec and D. Réguer, eds, *De l'hospice au domicile collectif: La vieillesse et ses prises en charge de la fin du XVIIIe siècle à nos jours* (Rouen: Presses universitaires de Rouen et du Havre), 479–93.

Cros-Mayrevieille, G. (1912), *Traité de l'assistance hospitalière* (Paris: Éditeurs Berger-Levrault).

Dechambre, A. (1885), *Dictionnaire usuel des sciences médicales* (Paris: Masson Éditeur).

De Groot, L., W. A. Van Staveren and J. Hautvast (1991), 'EURONUT-SENECA: Nutrition in the Elderly in Europe', *European Journal of Clinical Nutrition*, 3(43): 105–9.

Depecker, T., A. Lhuissier and A. Maurice, eds (2013), *La juste mesure: Une sociologie historique des normes alimentaires* (Rennes: Presses universitaires de Rennes).

Durand-Fardel, M. (1854), *Traité clinique et pratique des maladies des vieillards* (Paris: G. Baillière).

Ennuyer, B. (2002), *Les malentendus de la dépendance: De l'incapacité au lien social* (Paris: Dunod).

François, J. (1958), 'Les bases physiologiques d'une alimentation rationnelle du vieillard normal', PhD thesis, University of Paris.

Gemmerle, M. (1987), *Cent ans de la vie d'un hospice, 1888–1988, Les établissements hospitaliers départementaux* (Bischwiller: Eds Bischwiller).

Guérin, L. (2016), 'Manger ensemble. mourir ensemble. Ethnographie du repas collectif en Ehpad', PhD dissertation, Ecole des Hautes Etudes en Sciences Sociales.

Guérin, L. (2018), 'L'essentiel est qu'il(s) mange(nt): Participation sollicitée ou empêchée des résidents en EHPAD', *Participations*, 3(22): 159–83.

Guillemard, A.-M. (1981), *À la découverte d'une politique de la vieillesse* (Paris: Comité d'Histoire de la Sécurité Sociale & Association pour l'étude de l'Histoire de la Sécurité Sociale).

Hamburger, J. (1950), *Petite Encyclopédie Médicale: Guide de pratique médicale*, Neuvième édition (Paris: Editions Médicales Flammarion).

HAS [Haute autorité de santé] (2007), Stratégie de prise en charge en cas de dénutrition protéino-énergétique chez la personne âgée. Recommandations de bonnes pratiques professionnelles (Paris: Haute Autorité de santé). Available online: https://www.has-sante.fr/jcms/c_546549/fr/strategie-de-prise-en-charge-en-cas-de-denutrition-proteino-energetique-chez-la-personne-agee (accessed 2 November 2021).

Hémon, D., and E. Jougla (2004), 'La canicule du mois d'août 2003 en France', *Revue d' Épidémiologie et de Santé Publique*, 52(1): 3–5.

Hutet, O. (2013), 'Finir ses jours à l'hôpital (1840–1940): L'exemple des hôpitaux du Havre et de Fécamp', in Y. Marec and D. Réguer, eds, *De l'hospice au domicile collectif: La vieillesse et ses prises en charge de la fin du XVIIIe siècle à nos jours* (Rouen: Presses Universitaires de Rouen et du Havre), 349–56.

Jean, A., and F. Bloch (2005), *Dénutrition du sujet âgé. La rechercher, la diagnostiquer, la prendre en charge* (Paris: Éditions scientifiques L & C).

Landouzy, T., and L. Joseph (1907), *La loi de 1905 sur l'Assistance obligatoire aux Septuagénaires et l'Alimentation rationnelle du Vieillard assisté* (Paris: La Presse Médicale).

Lassablière, P. (1941), *Manger pour vivre en bonne santé: Petite encyclopédie de l'alimentation hygiénique et gastronomique* (Paris: Maloine).

Loux, F. (1997), 'Place et fonction de l'alimentation dans les représentations populaires: Le vin est le lait des vieillards', in A. Nardin, ed., *L'appétit vient en mangeant: Histoire de l'alimentation à l'hôpital XVe–XXe siècles* (Paris: Exhibition Catalogue, Musée de l'Assistance Publique des Hôpitaux de Paris).

Marquier, R. (2013), *Vivre en établissement d'hébergement pour personnes âgées à la fin des années 2000* (Paris: DREES).

Nardin, A. (2007), 'Les établissements hospitaliers au cœur des premières politiques de la vieillesse: Regards sur le secteur de la gériatrie', in F. Démier and C. Barillé, eds, *Les maux & les soins: Médecins et malades dans les hôpitaux parisiens au XIXe siècle* (Paris: Éditions Action artistique de la ville de Paris), 225–37.

Ngatcha-Ribert, L. (2012), *Alzheimer. La construction sociale d'une maladie* (Paris: Dunod).

Pouyet, V. (2015), 'Attractivité et mémoire des aliments chez les personnes âgées atteintes de la maladie d'Alzheimer', PhD thesis, AgroParisTech.

PNNS (2006), *Le guide nutrition pour les aidants des personnes âgées. Guide de l'Agence française de sécurité sanitaire des aliments, Programme National Nutrition Santé.* Available online: https://www.sraenutrition.fr/wp-content/uploads/2019/04/Livret-daccompagnement-destin%C3%A9-aux-aidants-familiaux-Guide-nutrition-pour-les-aidants.pdf (accessed 2 November 2021).

Randoin, L., P. Le Gallic, J. Causeret and G. Duchêne (1951), *Les rations alimentaires équilibrées* (Paris: Société scientifique d'hygiène alimentaire).

Robin, M. P. (1975), 'Le médecin praticien face à la dénutrition des sujets âgés', PhD thesis, University of Bobigny.

Rossigneux-Méheust, M. (2013), 'Boire à l'hospice. Morales, tensions et contestations autour de la consommation de vin chez les vieillards parisiens dans la deuxième moitié du XIXe siècle', *Histoire, économie & société*, 32(3): 46–60.

Séré, G.-J. (1936), 'L'alimentation du malade à l'hôpital: De l'alimentation traditionnelle à la diététique scientifique', PhD thesis, University of Bordeaux.

Tourtel, R., J. Favard and H. C. R. Napias (1900), *L'Assistance publique en 1900* (Montévrain: Impression de l'école d'Alembert).

UFC-Que Choisir (2015), *Alimentation en Ehpad: Une politique de prévention s'impose!*

Vinit, F. (1974), *L'Alimentation des personnes âgées en collectivité* (Paris: Éditions E.S.F.).

Zazzo, J.-F., S. Antoun and A. Basdevant (2010), *Dénutrition: Une pathologie méconnue en société d'abondance* (Paris: Programme National Nutrition Santé).

Chapter 5

Albert, A. (2013), 'Les midinettes parisiennes à la Belle Époque. Bon goût ou mauvais genre?', *Histoire, économie & société*, 3: 61–74.

Bouchet, T., S. Gacon, F. Jarrige, F. X. Nérard and X. Vigna, eds (2016), 'Introduction', in *La gamelle et l'outil: Manger au travail en France et en Europe de la fin du XVIIIe siècle à nos jours* (Nancy: Arbre Bleu).

Bruegel, M. (2004), 'Le repas à l'usine. Industrialisation, nutrition et alimentation populaire', *Revue d'histoire moderne & contemporaine*, 51–3(3): 183–98.

Distrifruits (2017), 'Project Framework Document', 43.

Gacon, S. (2014), 'Cantines et alimentation au travail: Une approche comparée, du milieu du XIXe siècle à nos jours', *Le Mouvement Social*, 247(2): 3–25.

Geoffroy, F. (2019), 'Existe-t-il un effet Hawthorne?' *Gérer et comprendre*, 135: 42–52.

Hatzfeld, N. (2002), 'La pause casse-croûte. Quand les chaînes s'arrêtent à Peugeot-Sochaux', *Terrain*, 39: 33–48.

Lécuyer, B.-P. (1994), 'Deux relectures des expériences de Hawthorne, problème d'histoire et d'épistémologie', in J.-P. Bouilloud and B.-P. Lécuyer, eds, *L'invention de la gestion: Histoire et pratiques* (Paris: L'Harmattan), 93–118.

Lhuissier, A. (2007), *Alimentation populaire et réforme sociale: Les consommations ouvrières dans le second XIXe siècle* (Paris: Éditions de la Maison des sciences de l'homme).

Marey, E.-J. (1868), *Du mouvement dans les fonctions de la vie* (Paris: Germer Baillière).

Oswald, A. J., E. Proto and D. Sgroi (2015), 'Happiness and Productivity', *Journal of Labor Economics*, 33(4): 789–822.

Pagès, R. (1961), 'Sociologie du travail et sciences de l'homme', in G. Friedmann and P. Naville, eds, *Traité de sociologie du travail* (Paris: Armand Colin).

Rabinbach, A. (1990), *The Human Motor. Energy, Fatigue, and the Origins of Modernity* (London: Basic Books).

Rabinbach, A. (2004), *Le moteur humain: L'énergie, la fatigue et les origines de la modernité*, trans. M. Luxembourg (Paris: La Fabrique).

Rosa, H. (2013), *Accélération. Une critique sociale du temps* (Paris: Éditions La Découverte).

Scholliers, P. (1994), 'Le temps consacré à l'alimentation par les familles ouvrières en Europe aux XIXe et XXe siècles', in M. Aymard, C. Grignon and F. Sabban, eds, *Le temps de manger: Alimentation, emploi du temps et rythmes sociaux* (Paris: Éditions de la Maison des sciences de l'homme/INRA), 111–37.

Scholliers, P. (2020), 'La controverse culinaire: La réception de la calorie en Belgique, 1890–1913', *Les enjeux de l'information et de la communication*, 19(1): 6–20. Available online: https://enjeux-univ-grenoble-alpes.fr (accessed 27 June 2021).

Siegfried, K. (1998), *The Salaried Masses: Duty and Distraction in Weimar Germany*, trans. Q. Hoare (London: Verso).

Thompson, E. P. (1967), 'Time, Work-Discipline, and Industrial Capitalism', *Past & Present*, 38: 56–97.

Thompson, E. P. (2004), *Temps, discipline du travail et capitalisme industriel*, trans. I. Taudière (Paris: La Fabrique).

Toner, J. (2015), *L'art de gouverner ses esclaves* (Paris: Presses Universitaires de France).

Chapter 6

Aaron Allen & Associates (2018), 'European Fast Food: Where to Grow and Where to Be Cautious'. Available online: https://aaronallen.com/blog/european-fast-food (accessed 6 February 2020).

Allard-Huver, F. (2016), 'Émergence de nouvelles pratiques alimentaires et controverses', in G. Fumey, ed., *L'alimentation demain* (Paris: Les Essentiels d'Hermès), 27–46.

Allard-Huver, F. (2019), 'Discours et pratiques militants au cœur des controverses environnementales: une tension entre stratégie et tactique', in V. Carlino and M. Muller-Stein, eds, *Les paroles militantes dans les controverses environnementales* (Metz: Éditions universitaires de Lorraine), 291–306.

Allard-Huver, F., and N. Gilewicz (2013), 'Digital Parrhesia as a Counterweight to Astroturfing', in M. Folk and S. Apostel, eds, *Online Credibility and Digital Ethos: Evaluating Computer-Mediated Communication* (Hershey: IGI Global), 215–27.

Allard-Huver, F., and N. Gilewicz (2015), 'Digital Parrhesia 2.0: Moving beyond Deceptive Communications Strategies in the Digital World', in D. Harrisson, ed., *Handbook of Research on Digital Media and Creative Technologies* (Hershey: IGI Global), 404–16.

ANIA (2017), *Fraude sur les œufs au fipronil priorité à l'action et à la concertation. Lettre ouverte de Jean-Philippe Girard, président de l'ANIA, en réponse aux propos de Michel Édouard Leclerc.* Available online: https://www.ania.net/vie-de-lagro/oeufs-lettre-ouverte (accessed 6 February 2020).

ANIA-TNS-Sofres (2013), 'Les Français et l'alimentation: baromètre TNS Sofres – ANIA'. Available online: https://www.tns-sofres.com/publications/les-francais-et-lalimentation-juin-2013 (accessed 6 February 2020).

ANSES (2017), 'Note d'appui scientifique et technique de l'Agence nationale de sécurité sanitaire de l'alimentation, de l'environnement et du travail relatif à "la concentration *maximale en fipronil à ne pas dépasser dans les ovoproduits et autres produits transformés à base d'œufs, pour que l'exposition du consommateur reste inférieure à la valeur toxicologique de référence aiguë*"'. Available online: https://www.anses.fr/fr/sys tem/files/ERCA2017SA0183.pdf (accessed 6 February 2020).

Bateson, G. (1972), *Steps to an Ecology of Mind: Collected Essays in Anthropology, Psychiatry, Evolution, and Epistemology* (Chicago: University of Chicago Press).

BBC (2013), 'Findus Beef Lasagne Contained Up to 100% Horsemeat, FSA Says', *BBC*, 7 February. Available online: https://www.bbc.com/news/uk-21375594 (accessed 6 February 2020).

Beck, U. (1986), *Risikogesellschaft: auf dem Weg in eine andere Moderne* (Frankfurt a.M.: Suhrkamp).

Bran, M., and L. Girard (2013), 'L' "affaire Findus" effraie les consommateurs', *Le Monde*, 11 Februray. Available online: https://www.lemonde.fr/economie/article/2013/02/11/l-affa ire-findus-effraie-les-consommateurs_1830010_3234.html (accessed 6 February 2020).

Bray, F., and C. Faquet (2014), 'Mai 2011, la bactérie E. coli déstabilise la filière des légumes', *LSA*. Available online: https://www.lsa-conso.fr/15-ans-de-lsa-fr-mai-2011-la-bacterie-e-coli-destabilise-la-filiere-des-legumes,175861 (accessed 6 February 2020).

ChassotVi (2011), 'Alerte à la bactérie tueuse', *Le Matin*, 25 May.

Collins, D. (2013), 'Ring of Steel, High Chimneys and Few Windows: Horse Meat Lasagne Factory Revealed', *The Mirror*, 19 February. Available online: https://www.mirror. co.uk/news/uk-news/horse-meat-lasagne-factory-revealed-1595234 (accessed 6 February 2020).

Daumin, D. (2017), 'Le scandale des poules pondeuses tué dans l'œuf', *La Nouvelle République Dimanche*, 6 August.

Déniel, P. (2013), 'Agroalimentaire: l'étrange supply chain de Findus', *L'Usine Nouvelle*, 14 February. Available online: https://www.usinenouvelle.com/article/agroalimentaire-l-etrange-supply-chain-de-findus.N191453 (accessed 6 February 2020).

Department of Agriculture, Food and the Marine (2013), *Equine DNA & Mislabelling of Processed Beef Investigation Report March 2013*, 14 March. Available online: https:// www.agriculture.gov.ie/media/migration/publications/2013/EquineDNAreportMarc h2013190313.pdf (accessed 6 February 2020).

Department of Health and Social Care (2012), 'Businesses Pledge for More Fruit and Veg'. Available online: https://www.gov.uk/government/news/businesses-ple dge-for-more-fruit-and-veg (accessed 6 February 2020).

DGAL (2017a), 'Fipronil dans les œufs: la France renforce ses contrôles'. Available online: https://agriculture.gouv.fr/fipronil-dans-les-oeufs-la-france-renforce-ses-controles (accessed 6 February 2020).

DGAL (2017b), 'Fipronil dans les œufs: l'Anses confirme l'absence de risque pour la santé humaine'. Available online: https://agriculture.gouv.fr/fipronil-dans-les-oeufs-lanses-confirme-labsence-de-risque-pour-la-sante-humaine (accessed 6 February 2020).

DGAL (2017c), 'Fipronil dans les œufs: toute l'actualité'. Available online: https://agricult ure.gouv.fr/fipronil-dans-les-oeufs-toute-lactualite (accessed 6 February 2020).

DGAL (2017d), 'Œufs contaminés: point sur la situation sanitaire en France'. Available online: https://agriculture.gouv.fr/oeufs-contamines-point-sur-la-situation-sanita ire-en-france (accessed 6 February 2020).

DGAL (2018), *Rapport d'activité DGAL 2017 – Les faits marquants*. Available online: https://agriculture.gouv.fr/telecharger/89125?token=c75095fffc600df294100 9f95a5022fb (accessed 6 February 2020).

Die Zeit (2011), 'EU stoppt Import ägyptischer Sprossensamen', *Die Zeit*, 5 July. Available online: https://www.zeit.de/wissen/gesundheit/2011-07/aegyptische-samen-einfuhrst opp (accessed 6 February 2020).

Echkenazi, A. (2011), 'Alerte au concombre venu d'Espagne', *Aujourd'hui en France*, 27 May.

Elliot, C. (2014), *Elliott Review into the Integrity and Assurance of Food Supply Networks – Final Report: A National Food Crime Prevention Framework, July 2014*. Available online: https://assets.publishing.service.gov.uk/government/uploads/system/uploads/attachment_data/file/350726/elliot-review-final-report-july2014.pdf (accessed 6 February 2020).

Euractiv (2013), 'EU Debates Tighter Food Labelling Rules after Horsemeat Scandal', *Euractiv*. Available online: https://www.euractiv.com/section/health-consumers/news/eu-debates-tighter-food-labelling-rules-after-horsemeat-scandal/ (accessed 6 February 2020).

European Commission (2012), 'Europeans' Attitudes towards Food Security, Food Quality and the Countryside'. Available online: https://ec.europa.eu/commfrontoffice/publicopinion/archives/ebs/ebs_389_en.pdf (accessed 6 February 2020).

European Commission (2013a), 'Commission Publishes European Test Results on Horse DNA and Phenylbutazone: No Food Safety Issues but Tougher Penalties to Apply in the Future to Fraudulent Labelling'. Available online: https://ec.europa.eu/commission/presscorner/detail/en/IP_13_331 (accessed 6 February 2020).

European Commission (2013b), 'Horse Meat – Questions and Answers'. Available online: https://ec.europa.eu/food/safety/official_controls/food_fraud/horse_meat/qanda_en (accessed 6 February 2020).

European Commission (2014), 'Food Safety'. Available online: https://www.youtube.com/watch?v=MYt_FRwNu7w&feature=youtu.be (accessed 6 February 2020).

European Food Safety Authority (2012), 'E. coli: Rapid Response in a Crisis'. Available online: https://web.archive.org/web/20181120064044/http:/www.efsa.europa.eu/en/press/news/120711 (accessed 6 February 2020).

Foodwatch (2017), *Œufs contaminés au fipronil en France aussi? Les autorités 'ne l'excluent pas'*, Available online: https://www.foodwatch.org/fr/presse/communiques-de-pre sse/page-detail-communiques-de-presse/oeufs-contamines-au-fipronil-en-fra nce-aussi-les-autorites-ne/ (accessed 12 December 2019).

Foodwatch (2020), *About Us*. Available online: https://www.foodwatch.org/en/about-us/ (accessed 6 February 2020).

Frank, C., D. Werber, J. P. Cramer et al. (2011), 'Epidemic Profile of Shiga-Toxin-Producing Escherichia coli O104:H4 Outbreak in Germany', *New England Journal of Medicine*, 365: 1771–80.

Freud, S. (2012), *Totem and Taboo* (London: Routledge Classics).

Fumey, G. (2016), *L'Alimentation demain. Cultures et médiations* (Paris: Les Essentiels d'Hermès).

Geisler, B. (2011), 'Spanische Salatgurken aus Malaga sind EHEC-Quelle', *Hamburger Abendblatt*, 26 May. Available online: https://www.abendblatt.de/ratgeber/gesundh eit/article106539332/Spanische-Salatgurken-aus-Malaga-sind-EHEC-Quelle.html (accessed 6 February 2020).

Govan, F. (2011a), ' "Killer Cucumbers" Row between Spain and Germany', *Daily Telegraph*, 30 May.

Govan, F. (2011b), 'Spanish Cucumbers Banned after E. coli Outbreak', *Daily Telegraph*, 31 May.

Govan, F. and H. Wallop (2011), 'Our Cucumbers Clear of E.coli, Say Supermarkets after 16 Die in Europe', *Daily Telegraph*, 1 June.

Greimas, A. J. (1966), 'Éléments pour une théorie de l'interprétation du récit mythique', *Communications*, 8: 28–59.

Hamburg, H. (2011), 'Labortest zeigt: Zwei in Hamburg untersuchte Gurken nicht Quelle der EHEC-Epidemie'. Available online: https://www.hamburg.de/bgv/pressemitte ilungen/nofl/2917528/2011-05-31-bgv-hus-ehec-erkrankungen.html (accessed 6 February 2020).

Hickman, M. (2013), 'Findus Leak Reveals Horse in "Beef" for Six Months', *The Independent*, 9 February.

Hickman, M., and T. Paterson (2011), 'Cucumbers Blamed for 10 Deaths in Germany "Not on Sale in UK"', *The Independent*, 30 May. Available online: https://www.inde pendent.co.uk/life-style/food-and-drink/news/cucumbers-blamed-for-10-deaths-in-germany-not-on-sale-in-uk-2290796.html (accessed 6 February 2020).

Interfel (2015), 'Nouvelle campagne collective de promotion et d'information pour les fruits et légumes frais et la pomme de terre fraîche', *Les fruits et légumes frais – Interfel*. Avalaible online: https://www.lesfruitsetlegumesfrais.com/_upload/ressources/ presse/2015/535/2015-02-23_cp_lancement_campagne_collective_fruits_et_legumes_ frais_et_pommes_de_terre.pdf (accessed 6 February 2020).

IRSN (2018), '2018 Baromètre IRSN: La perception des risques et de la sécurité par les Français'. Available online: http://barometre.irsn.fr/wp-content/uploads/2018/10/201810 04_IRSN%20BAROMETRE-Les_essentiels.pdf (accessed 6 February 2020).

IRSN (2019), *2019 Baromètre IRSN: La perception des risques et de la sécurité par les Français*. Available online: http://barometre.irsn.fr/barometre2019/#p=17 (accessed 6 February 2020).

Jasanoff, S. (1986), *Risk Management and Political Culture* (New York: Russell Sage Foundation).

Jullien, B. (2013), 'Comment Findus a géré la crise', *La revue des marques*, 84 (October): 33–5. Available online: http://www.prodimarques.com/documents/ gratuit/84/comment-findus-a-gere-la-crise.php.

La Croix (2011), 'ALLEMAGNE Une bactérie dangereuse et d'origine inconnue inquiète', *La Croix*, no. 38981, 26 May.

Lang, T. (2013), 'Horsemeat Scandal Was a Damning Indictment of the State of Our Food', *The Conversation*, 13 December. Available online: https://theconversation.com/horsem eat-scandal-was-a-damning-indictment-of-the-state-of-our-food-21490 (accessed 6 February 2020).

Latour, B. (1999), *Politiques de la nature. Comment faire entrer les sciences en démocratie* (Paris: La Découverte).

Lawrence, F. (2013), 'Horsemeat Scandal: The Essential Guide', *The Guardian*, 15 February. Available online: https://www.theguardian.com/uk/2013/feb/15/horsemeat-scan dal-the-essential-guide#101 (accessed 6 February 2020).

Leclerc, M. (2017), 'La transparence vaut mieux que toute polémique!' *De quoi je me MEL*, 25 August. Available online: https://www.michel-edouard-leclerc.com/categorie/ economie/actus-debats/la-transparence-vaut-mieux-que-toute-polemique (accessed 6 February 2020).

Le Figaro (2017), 'Oeufs contaminés: des lots livrés en France', *Le Figaro*, 8 July. Available online: http://www.lefigaro.fr/flash-eco/2017/08/07/97002-20170807FILWWW00 198-oeufs-contamines-des-lots-livres-en-france-en-provenance-des-pays-bas.php (accessed 6 February 2020).

Lemaître, F. (2011), 'Alerte aux légumes tueurs dans le nord de l'Allemagne', *Le Monde*, 26 May. Available online: https://www.lemonde.fr/a-la-une/article/2011/05/26/alerte-aux-legumes-tueurs-dans-le-nord-de-l-allemagne_1527653_3208.html (accessed 6 February 2020).

Le Matin (2011), 'La bactérie tueuse vient des concombres', *Le Matin*, 27 May.

Lentschner, K. (2013), 'Viande de cheval: comment Findus a démasqué la fraude', *Le Figaro*, 20 February. Available online: https://www.lefigaro.fr/societes/2013/02/20/20005-20130220ARTFIG00711-viande-de-cheval-comment-findus-a-demasque-la-fraude.php (accessed 6 February 2020).

Lévêque, T. (2011), 'La France demande la "transparence" sur la bactérie Escherichia', *BFMTV*, 31 May, Available online: https://www.bfmtv.com/societe/france-demande-transparence-bacterie-escherichia-164087.html (accessed 6 February 2020).

Levi-Strauss, C. (1970), *The Raw and the Cooked* (London: Jonathan Cape).

L'Obs (2019), 'C'est quoi "l'agribashing", contre lequel manifestent les agriculteurs?' *L'Obs*. Available online: https://www.nouvelobs.com/societe/20191022.OBS20150/c-est-quoi-l-agribashing-contre-lequel-manifestent-les-agriculteurs.html (accessed 6 February 2020).

Luhmann, N. (2003), *Soziologie des Risikos* (Berlin: Walter de Gruyter).

McPartland, B. (2013), 'Horsemeat Scandal: "Just a Labelling Problem"', *The Local*, 11 February. Available: https://www.thelocal.fr/20130211/horsemeat-scandal--authorities-raid-french-firms (accessed 6 February 2020).

Ministry for Food, Rural Affairs, and Consumer Protection Baden Württemberg (2011), 'EHEC-Infektionen: Bislang keine Hinweise auf belastete Gurken in Baden-Württemberg'. Available online: http://www.mlr.baden-wuerttemberg.de/EHEC_Infektionen_Bislang_keine_Hinweise_auf_belastete_Gurken_in_Baden_Wuerttemberg/97331.html (accessed 6 February 2020).

Neville, S. (2013), 'Horsemeat Lasagne Scandal Leaves Findus Reputation in Tatters', *The Guardian*, 8 February. Available online: https://www.theguardian.com/business/2013/feb/08/horsemeat-lasagne-scandal-findus-reputation (accessed 6 February 2020).

NewsPress (2011), 'Une mystérieuse épidémie liée à la consommation de légumes crus', *NewsPress*, 25 May.

Observatoire des aliments (2013), 'Viande hachée, minerai: le grand flou pour le consommateur', *Observatoire des aliments*, 24 February. Available online: https://observatoire-des-aliments.fr/qualite/minerai-et-viande-hachee-le-grand-flou-pour-le-consommateur (accessed 6 February 2020).

Quet, M. (2015), 'L'art narratif dans les controverses globales', *Hermès, La Revue*, 73(3): 39–44.

Richard, D. (2017), 'Les oeufs au fipronil symboles du mal européen', *Sud Ouest*, 20 August.

RKI (2011), 'Gemeinsame Stellungnahme von BfR und RKI'. Available online: https://www.rki.de/DE/Content/InfAZ/E/EHEC/EHEC_O104/Gemeinsame_Stellungnahme_RKI_BfR.html (accessed 6 February 2020).

Rosenweg, D. (2017), 'Oeufs contaminés: opacité et omerta chez les industriels', *Aujourd'hui en France*, 17 August.

Sentker, A. (2011), 'Die Angst sprießt', *Die Zeit*, 9 June. Available online: https://www.zeit.de/2011/24/01-Ehec (accessed 6 February 2020).

Sheil, S. (2013), 'Horsemeat Fraud in the Food Chain', *Library of the European Parliament*. Available online: https://www.europarl.europa.eu/RegData/bibliotheque/briefing/2013/130493/LDM_BRI(2013)130493_REV1_EN.pdf (accessed 6 February 2020).

Spiegel (2011), 'Two-Year-Old Boy Dies in German E. Coli Outbreak', *Spiegel International*, 14 June. Available online: https://www.spiegel.de/international/germany/death-toll-reaches-37-two-year-old-boy-dies-in-german-e-coli-outbreak-a-768278.html (accessed 6 February 2020).

Tageschau (2013), 'Pferdefleisch-Skandal in Deutschland Welche Produkte und Händler sind betroffen?' *Tageschau*, 22 February. Available online: https://www.tagesschau.de/inland/pferdefleisch-deutsche-supermaerkte102.html (accessed 6 February 2020).

Torre, M. (2013a), 'Affaire Findus: sur la piste de la viande de cheval suspecte', *La Tribune*, 14 February. Available online: https://www.latribune.fr/actualites/economie/fra nce/20130214trib000748805/affaire-findus-sur-la-piste-de-la-viande-de-cheval-suspe cte.html (accessed 6 February 2020).

Torre, M. (2013b), 'Comment Findus tente de se dépêtrer de "l'affaire" en soignant sa réputation sur le web', *La Tribune*, 18 February. Available online: https://www.latrib une.fr/entreprises-finance/20130218trib000749453/comment-findus-tente-de-se-depet rer-de-l-affaire-en-soignant-sa-reputation-sur-le-web.html (accessed 6 February 2020).

Vattimo, G. (1992), *The Transparent Society* (London: Polity).

Watters, S. (2015), 'The Spectacular Origins of the EU Horse Meat Scandal', *Graduate Journal of Food Studies*, 2(2): 6–17.

Chapter 7

Assal, J.-P., M. Berger and J. Canivet (1982), 'History and Aims of the Diabetes Education Study Group', *Excerpta Medica, International Congress Series*, 624: 3–7.

Berger, M., and I. Mülhausser (1995), 'Implementation of Intensified Insulin Therapy: A European Perspective', *Diabetic Medicine*, 12(3): 201–8.

Bliss, M. (1982), *The Discovery of Insulin* (Chicago: University of Chicago Press).

Boltanski, L. (1971), 'Les Usages Sociaux du Corps', *Annales Économies, Sociétés, Civilisations*, 26(1): 205–33.

Bouchardat, A. (1875), *De la Glycosurie ou diabète sucré, son traitement hygiénique* (Paris: Librairie Germer Bailliere).

Bourdieu, P. (1979), *La distinction* (Paris: Les Éditions de Minuit).

Bourdieu, P. (1980), *Le sens pratique* (Paris: Les Éditions de Minuit).

Chabanier, H. and C. Lobo-Onell (1938), *Le diabète* (Paris: Grasset).

Chantelau, E., G. E. Sonnenberg, I. Stanitzek-Schmidt, F. Best, H. Altenär and M. Berger (1982), 'Diet Liberalization and Metabolic Control in Type I Diabetic Outpatients Treated by Continuous Subcutaneous Insulin Infusion', *Diabetes Care*, 5(6): 612–16.

Chevandier, C. (2009), *L'hôpital dans la France du XXe siècle* (Paris: Perrin).

Coussaert, A. (1991), 'La Santé et Son Sujet Dans Les Écoles de Diabétologie', in Arlette Lafay, ed., *Le Statut Du Malade. XVIe –XXe Siècle*(Paris: L'Harmattan), 65–110.

Darmon, M. (2012), 'A People Thinning Institution: Changing Bodies and Souls in a Commercial Weight-Loss Group', *Ethnography*, 13(3): 375–98.

Darmon, M. (2020), 'The School Form of the Hospital: How Does Social Class Affect Post-Stroke Patients in Rehabilitation Units?' *Qualitative Sociology*, 43: 235–54.

Depecker, T. (2010), 'Les Cultures Somatiques: Usages Du Corps et Diététique', *Revue d'Etudes en Agriculture et Environnement*, 91(2): 153–84.

D'Ivernois, J.-F., and R. Gagnayre (1995), *Apprendre à éduquer le patient* (Paris: Payot).

Elias, N. (1973), *La civilisation des mœurs* (Paris: Calmann-Lévy).

Elias, N. (1976), *La Dynamique de l'Occident* (Paris: Calmann-Lévy).

Feudtner, C. (2003), *Bittersweet: Diabetes, Insulin, and the Transformation of Illness* (Chapel Hill: University of North Carolina Press).

Guelpa, G. (1911), 'La guérison du diabète', *Communication à la société de médecine*.

HAS and INPES (2007), 'Structuration d'un programme d'éducation thérapeutique du patient dans le champ des maladies chroniques', *Guide méthodologique*.

Job, D., E. Eschwege, C. Guyot-Argenton, J.-P. Aubry and G. Tchoubroutsky (1976), 'Effect of Multiple Daily Injections on the Course of Diabetic Retinopathy', *Diabetes*, 25(5): 463–9.

Labbé, M. (1933), *Le traitement du diabète*, 4th edn (Paris: Masson).

Lecorché, E. (1893), *Traité du diabète sucré* (Paris: Rueff).

Lestradet, H., J. Besse and P. Grenet (1968), *Le diabète de l'enfant et de l'adolescent dans l'exercice journalier de la médecine praticienne* (Paris: Maloine).

Lhuissier, A. (2006), 'Éducation alimentaire en milieu populaire: des normes en concurrence', *Journal des anthropologues*, 106–107: 61–76.

Longchamp, P. (2014), 'Goûts de Liberté, Goûts de Nécessité: Quand La Diététique s'en Mêle', *Sociologie et Sociétés*, 46(2): 59–82.

Marchand, C. (2014), 'Le Médecin et l'alimentation: Principes de Nutrition et Recommandations Alimentaires En France (1887–1940)', PhD diss., University François-Rabelais, Tours.

Mauck, A. (2010), 'Managing Care: The History of Diabetes Management in Twentieth-Century America', PhD diss., Harvard University, Cambridge.

Mauriac, P. (1941), *Le traitement du diabète en pratique médicale* (Paris: Masson).

Monin, E. (1896), *Hygiène et traitement du diabète*, 3rd edn (Paris: Société d'éditions scientifiques).

Moore, M. D. (2018), 'Food as Medicine: Diet, Diabetes Management, and the Patient in Twentieth-Century Britain', *Journal of the History of Medicine and Allied Sciences*, 73(2): 150–67.

Mülhausser, I., U. Bott, H. Overmann, W. Wagner, R. Bender, V. Jörgens and M. Berger (1995), 'Liberalised Diet in Patients with Type 1 Diabetes', *Journal of Internal Medicine*, 237(6): 591–7.

O'Donnell, S. (2015), 'Changing Social and Scientific Discourses on Type 2 Diabetes between 1800 and 1950: A Socio-Historical Analysis', *Sociology of Health & Illness*, 37(7): 1102–21.

Pinell, P. (1996), 'Modern Medicine and the Civilising Process', *Social Science & Medicine*, 18(1): 1–16.

Presley, J. W. (1991), 'A History of Diabetes Mellitus in the United-States, 1880–1990', PhD diss., University of Texas, Austin.

Régnier, F., and A. Masullo (2009), 'Obésité, Goûts et Consommation', *Revue Française de Sociologie*, 50(4): 747–73.

Rollo, J. (1798), *Cases of the Diabetes Melittus with the Results of the Trials of Certain Acids, and Other Substances, in the Cure of the Lues Venerea* (London: C. Dilly).

Royer, P. and H. Lestradet (1958), *Le traitement du diabète infantile en régime libre* (Paris: Flammarion).

Sanabria, E. (2015), 'Sensorial Pedagogies, Hungry Fat Cells and the Limits of Nutritional Health Education', *BioSocieties*, 10(2): 125–42.

Sinding, C. (2000), 'Une molécule espion pour les diabétologues, l'innovation en médecine entre science et morale', *Sciences sociales et santé*, 18(2): 95–120.

Sinding, C. (2002), 'Making the Unit of Insulin: Standards, Clinical Work, and Industry, 1920–1925', *Bulletin of the History of Medicine*, 76(2): 231–70.

Sinding, C. (2004), 'The Specificity of Medical Facts: The Case of Diabetology', *Studies in History and Philosophy of Science Part C: Studies in History and Philosophy of Biological and Biomedical Sciences*, 35(3): 545–59.

Sinding, C. (2005), 'Les Multiples Usages de La Quantification En Médecine: Le Cas Du Diabète Sucré', in G. Jorland, A. Opinel and G. Weisz, eds, *Body Counts. Medical Quantification in Historical & Sociological Perspective* (Montréal: McGill-Queen's University Press), 127–44.

Sinding, C. (2006), 'Flexible Norms? From Patients' Values to Physicians' Standards', in E. Waltraud, ed., *Histories of the Normal and the Abnormal: Social and Cultural Histories of Norms and Normativity* (New York: Routledge), 225–44.

Tchobroutsky, G. (1978), 'Relation of Diabetic Control to Development of Microvascular Complications', *Diabetologia*, 15(3): 143–52.

Uhry, P. (1951), *Traitement du diabète* (Paris: Masson).

Vincent, G. (1980), *L'école primaire française: étude sociologique* (Lyon: PUL).

Chapter 8

AFDN and HAS (2006), Association des Diététiciens de Langue Française and Haute Autorité de santé, *La consultation diététique réalisée par un diététicien. Recommandations pour la pratique clinique*. Available online: https://www.hassante.fr/upload/docs/application/pdf/consultation_dietetique_recos.pdf (accessed 20 May 2020).

Berthoud, M. (2018), 'Info-educational Dispositives to Educate Children about Nutrition', in V. Clavier and J.-P. De Oliveria, eds, *Food and Health: Actor Strategies in Information and Communication*, Vol. 2 (London: ISTE-Wiley), 129–50.

Bourret, C. J. (2011), 'Évolution du rôle des patients et nouvelles organisations d'interface en santé. Éléments pour une approche comparée: France, Royaume-Uni, Catalogne (Espagne)', *Recherches en Communication*, 32: 71–85.

Calenge, B. (2015), *Les bibliothèques et la médiation des connaissances* (Paris: Éditions du Cercle de la Librairie).

Cardon, P. and S. De Iulio, eds (2021), *Cantine et friandises: l'école et l'alimentation des enfants* (Tours: Presses universitaires Francois Rabelais).

Cecchi, C. (2008), 'La place de l'information dans la décision en santé publique', *Santé Publique*, 20(4): 387–94.

Clavier, V. (2018), 'Information Resources and Information Practices in the Context of the Medicalization of Food', in V. Clavier and J.-P. De Oliveria, eds, *Food and Health: Actor Strategies in Information and Communication*, Vol. 2 (London: ISTE-Wiley), 163–87.

Clavier, V. (2019), 'La place de l'information dans les pratiques professionnelles des diététicien.nes: au croisement des missions d'éducation, de prévention et de soin', *I2D – Information, données & documents*, 11: 114–33.

Clavier, V., and C. Paganelli (2015), 'Activités informationnelles et organisation des connaissances: résultats et perspectives pour l'information spécialisée', *Les cahiers de la Société Française des Sciences de la Communication*, 11: 170–5.

Couzinet, V. (2018), 'Métamorphoses du document: enjeux d'un objet médiateur fondamental', *Études de communication*, 50(1): 75–90.

De Iulio, S., S. Kovacs, C. Orange, D. Orange-Ravachol and D. Borrelli (2018), 'Food at School: Between Science and Norm', in *Food and Health: Actor Strategies in Information and Communication*, Vol. 2 (London: ISTE-Wiley), 99–127.

Fainzang, S. (2009), 'La communication d'informations dans la relation médecins-malades. Une approche anthropologique', *Questions de communication*, 15(1): 279–95.

Fournier, C., and S. Kerzanet (2007), 'Communication médecin-malade et éducation du patient, des notions à rapprocher: apports croisés de la littérature', *Santé Publique*, 19(5): 413–25.

Gardiès, C., and I. Fabre (2015), 'Médiation des savoirs: de la diffusion d'informations numériques à la construction de connaissances, le cas d'une 'classe inversée', *Distances et médiations des savoirs*, 12: 1–19.

Hercberg, S. (2014), 'Pour une politique nutritionnelle à la hauteur des enjeux de Santé Publique!', *Santé Publique*, 26(3): 281–2.

Hjørland, B. (2018), 'Library and Information Science (LIS)', Part 1, *Knowledge Organization*, 45(3): 232–54.

Hugol-Gential C., S. Bastien, H. Burzala-Ory and A. Noacco (2018), 'From Health Responsibility to Ethical Responsibility: The Legitimization of New Vegetable Experts in France', in V. Clavier and J.-P. De Oliveria, eds, *Food and Health: Actor Strategies in Information and Communication*, Vol. 2 (London: ISTE-Wiley), 53–74.

Jeanneret, Y. (2008), *Penser la trivialité. Vol. 1: La vie triviale des êtres culturels* (Paris: Hermès-Lavoisier).

Krempf, M. (2003), Rapport sur l' évolution du métier de diététicien. Programme National Nutrition Santé (PNNS). Available online: http://www.afdn.org/fileadmin/pdf/rapport _krempf.pdf (accessed 20 May 2020).

Le Barzic, M. (2001), 'Le syndrome de restriction cognitive: de la norme au désordre du comportement alimentaire', *Diabetes & Metabolism*, 27(4): 512–16.

Liquète, V. (2011), 'Des pratiques d'information à la construction de connaissances en contexte: de l'analyse à la modélisation SEPICRI (Systèmes, Environnement, Pratiques Individuelles, Collectives et Représentations de l'Information)', Mémoire d'habilitation à diriger des recherches (Université de Rouen). Available online: https://tel.archives-ouvertes.fr/tel-00670700/document (accessed 20 May 2020).

Livre Blanc (2017), Le livre blanc des diététiciens. Des besoins reconnus, des actes toujours attendus. #onpassealacte, Publication issue de la contribution de l'AFDN à la Grande conférence de santé organisée par le ministère des Affaires sociales et de la Santé (novembre 2015). Available online: http://www.afdn.org/fileadmin/ pdf/1704-livre-blanc.pdf (accessed 20 May 2020).

McKenzie, P. J. (2003), 'Communication Barriers and Information-Seeking Counterstrategies in Accounts of Practitioner–Patient Encounters', *Library & Information Science Research*, 24: 31–47.

Martin, A. (2009), La formation à la nutrition des professionnels. Rapport public au Ministre de la Santé. Available online: http://www.ladocumentationfrancaise.fr/ rapports-publics/094000169-la-formation-a-la-nutrition-des-professionnels (accessed 20 May 2020).

Meyriat, J. (1978), 'De l'écrit à l'information: la notion de document et la méthodologie de l'analyse du document', *Inforcom 78*, 1: 23–32.

Meyriat, J. (1993), 'Information', in R. Estivals, ed., *Les sciences de l'écrit: encyclopédie internationale de bibliologie* (Paris: Retz), 326–38.

Miège, B. (1997), *La société conquise par la communication: La communication entre industrie et espace public* (Grenoble: Presses universitaires de Grenoble).

Pinell, P. (2005), 'Champ médical et processus de spécialisation', *Actes de la recherche en sciences sociales*, 156–7(1): 4–36.

Poulain, J.-P. (2009), *Sociologie de l'obésité* (Paris: Presses Universitaires de France).

Romeyer, H. (2015), 'Le bien-être en normes: les programmes nationaux nutrition santé', *Questions de communication*, 27(1): 41–61.

Savolainen, R. (1995), 'Everyday Life Information Seeking: Approaching Information Seeking in the Context of "Way of Life"', *Library & Information Science Research*, 17(3): 259–94.

Savolainen, R. (2011), 'Asking and Sharing Information in the Blogosphere: The Case of Slimming Blogs', *Library & Information Science Research*, 33: 73–9.

Staii, A., L. Balicco, M. Bertin, V. Clavier, E. Mounier and C. Paganelli (2006), 'Information Practices of the Medical Staff in University Hospital Centers: Crossroad of the Scientific Logic and the Professional Culture', *Canadian Journal of Information and Library Science*, 30(1/2): 69–90.

Wilson, T. D. (2000), 'Human Information Behavior', *Informing Science*, 3: 49–55.

Chapter 9

Akrich, M., and C. Méadel (2009), 'Les échanges entre patients sur l'internet', *La Presse Médicale*, 38(10): 1484–90.

Åsbring, P., and A. L. Närvänen (2004), 'Patient Power and Control: A Study of Women with Uncertain Illness Trajectories', *Qualitative Health Research*, 14(2): 226–40.

Attfield, S. J., A. Adams and A. Blandford (2006), 'Patient Information Needs: Pre- and Post-Consultation', *Health Informatics Journal*, 12(2): 165–77.

Ayers, S. L., and J. J. Kronenfeld (2007), 'Chronic Illness and Health-Seeking Information on the Internet', *Health*, 11(3): 327–47.

Bai, J. C., and C. Ciacci (2017), 'World Gastroenterology Organisation Global Guidelines: Celiac Disease', *Journal of Clinical Gastroenterology*, 51(9): 755–68.

Barbot, J., and N. Dodier (2000), 'L'émergence d'un tiers public dans le rapport malade-médecin. L'exemple de l'épidémie à VIH', *Sciences Sociales et Santé*, 18(1): 75–117.

Baszanger, I. (1986), 'Les maladies chroniques et leur ordre négocié', *Revue Française de Sociologie*, 27(1): 3–27.

Beardsworth, A., A. Bryman, T. Keil, J. Goode, C. Haslam and E. Lancashire (2002), 'Women, Men and Food: The Significance of Gender for Nutritional Attitudes and Choices', *British Food Journal*, 104(7): 470–91.

Beverly, E. A., C. K. Miller and L. A. Wray (2008), 'Spousal Support and Food-Related Behavior Change in Middle-Aged and Older Adults Living with Type 2 Diabetes', *Health Education & Behavior*, 35(5): 707–20.

Blandford, A., and A. Adams (2005), 'Digital Libraries' Support for the User's Information Journey', in Proceedings of the 5th ACM/IEEE-CS Joint Conference on Digital Libraries, IEEE, 160–9.

Caiata-Zufferey, M., A. Abraham, K. Sommerhalder and P. J. Schulz (2010), 'Online Health Information Seeking in the Context of the Medical Consultation in Switzerland', *Qualitative Health Research*, 20(8): 1050–61.

Chamak, B. (2008), 'Autism and Social Movements: French Parents' Associations and International Autistic Individuals' Organisations', *Sociology of Health and Illness*, 30(1): 76–96.

Cohen, P., and E. Legrand (2011), 'Alimentation et cancers. Personnes atteintes et autorités alternatives', *Anthropologie & Santé*, 2. Available online: https://journals.openedition.org/anthropologiesante/629 (accessed 8 February 2020).

Counihan, C. M., and S. L. Kaplan (1998), *Food and Gender: Identity and Power* (London: Routledge).

Cresson, G. (1998), *Le travail domestique de santé* (Paris: L'Harmattan).

Fournier, T. (2012), 'Suivre ou s'écarter de la prescription diététique. Les effets du "manger ensemble" et du "vivre ensemble" chez des personnes hypercholestérolémiques en France', *Sciences sociales et santé*, 30(2): 35–60.

Fournier, T., J. Jarty, N. Lapeyre and P. Touraille (2015), 'L'alimentation, arme du genre', *Journal des anthropologues*, 140–1. Available online: https://journals.openedition.org/jda/6022 (accessed 8 February 2020).

Fox, S., and D. Fallows (2003), 'Internet Health Resources', 16 July, TPRC. Available online: https://ssrn.com/abstract=2054071 (accessed 8 February 2020).

Gagnon, É. (1999), 'La communication, l'autre, l'indicible. De l'entraide des malades', *Anthropologie et sociétés*, 23(2): 61–78.

Haicault, M. (1984), 'La gestion ordinaire de la vie en deux', *Sociologie du Travail*, 26(3), 268–77.

Herzlich, C. (1995), 'Les difficultés de constitution d'une cause', *Sciences sociales et santé*, 13(4): 39–44.

Huyard, C. (2011), 'Pourquoi s'associer? Quatre motifs d'entrée dans un collectif dans les associations de maladies rares', *Revue française de sociologie*, 52(4): 719–45.

Johnson, J. D. (2003), 'On Contexts of Information Seeking', *Information Processing & Management*, 39(5): 735–60.

Kirchgässler, K., E. Matt and F. Laroche (1987), 'La fragilité du quotidien: les processus de normalisation dans les maladies chroniques', *Sciences sociales et santé*, 5(1): 93–114.

Knivsberg, A. M., K. L. Reichelt, T. HØien and M. NØdland (2002), 'A Randomised, Controlled Study of Dietary Intervention in Autistic Syndromes', *Nutritional Neuroscience*, 5(4): 251–61.

Knobé, S. (2009), 'Logiques d'engagement des malades dans les associations de lutte contre le cancer', *Socio-logos*. Available online: http://journals.openedition.org/socio-logos/2346 (accessed 8 February 2020).

Lecimbre, E., R. Gagnayre, A. Deccache and J. d'Ivernois (2002), 'Le rôle des associations de patients dans le développement de l'éducation thérapeutique en France', *Santé Publique*, 14(4): 389–401.

Lee, C. J., S. W. Gray and N. Lewis (2010), 'Internet Use Leads Cancer Patients to Be Active Health Care Consumers', *Patient Education and Counseling*, 81: 63–9.

Leis, Á., M. Á. Mayer, J. Torres Niño, A. Rodríguez-González, J. M. Suelves and M. Armayones (2013), 'Grupos sobre alimentación saludable en Facebook: características y contenidos', *Gaceta sanitaria*, 27(4): 355–7.

Lemire, M. (2008), 'Application du concept de responsabilisation personnelle aux usages sociaux des technologies d'information et de communication en santé', *tic&société*, 2(1). Available online: http://ticetsociete.revues.org/351 (accessed 8 February 2020).

Lupton, D. (1995), *The Imperative of Health: Public Health and the Regulated Body* (London: Sage).

McMullan, M. (2006), 'Patients Using the Internet to Obtain Health Information: How This Affects the Patient–Health Professional Relationship', *Patient Education and Counseling*, 63(1–2): 24–8.

Maher, J., S. Fraser and J. Wright (2010), 'Framing the Mother: Childhood Obesity, Maternal Responsibility and Care', *Journal of Gender Studies*, 19(3): 233–47.

Nabli, F., and L. Ricroch (2012), 'Enquête Emploi du temps 2009–2010', *Insee Résultats*, 130.

Naulin, S. (2014), 'La blogosphère culinaire. Cartographie d'un espace d'évaluation amateur', *Réseaux*, 183(1): 31–62.

Naulin, S. (2015), 'Pourquoi partager sa passion de la cuisine sur internet?' *Revue de la BNF*, 49(1): 38–43.

Naulin, S. (2017), *Des mots à la bouche. Le journalisme gastronomique en France* (Rennes/Tours: Presses Universitaires de Rennes/Presses Universitaires François Rabelais).

Nutbeam, D. (2008), 'The Evolving Concept of Health Literacy', *Social Science & Medicine*, 67(12): 2072–8.

OCHA, CREDOC (2018), 'Etudes Evictions' (n.p.).

Rabeharisoa, V. and M. Callon (2000), 'Les associations de malades et la recherche. I. Des self-help groups aux associations de malades', *Médecine/sciences*, 16(8–9): 945–9.

Renahy, E., and P. Chauvin (2006), 'Internet Uses for Health Information Seeking: A Literature Review', *Revue Epidémiologique de Santé Publique*, 54(3): 263–75.

Rochedy, A. (2019), 'La bonne parentalité dans l'assiette. Autismes et régimes "sans"', *Revue des sciences sociales*, 61: 56–65.

Romeyer, H. (2008), 'TIC et santé: entre information médicale et information de santé', *tic&société*, 2(1). Available online: http://journals.openedition.org/ticetsociete/365 (accessed 8 February 2020).

Romeyer, H. (2012), 'La santé en ligne', *Communication*, 30(1). Available online: http://journals.openedition.org/communication/2915 (accessed 8 February 2020).

Sapone, A., et al. (2012), 'Spectrum of Gluten-Related Disorders: Consensus on New Nomenclature and Classification', *BMC Medicine* 10(13).

Tijou-Traoré, A. (2010), 'L'expérience dans la production de savoirs profanes sur le diabète chez des patients diabétiques à Bamako (Mali)', *Sciences sociales et santé*, 28(4): 41–76.

Warde, A., S. L. Cheng, W. Olsen and D. Southerton (2007), 'Changes in the Practice of Eating. A Comparative Analysis of Time-Use', *Acta Sociologica*, 50(4): 363–85.

Werner, M., and B. Zimmermann (2003), 'Penser l'histoire croisée: entre empirie et réflexivité', *Annales. Histoire, Sciences Sociales*, 58(1): 7–36.

Wolff, V. (2019), 'Sensibilités alimentaires et séditions corporelles: de la vulnérabilité à un idéal moral?' *Ethnologie francaise*, 176(4): 735–50.

Wolff, V. (2020), 'Le partage de savoirs et savoir-faire "sans gluten" sur Internet', *Les Enjeux de l'information et de la communication*, 21(3): 43–57.

Chapter 10

Appadurai, A. (1986), 'Commodities and the Politics of Value', in A. Appadurai, ed., *The Social Life of Things* (Cambridge: Cambridge University Press), 3–63.

Apple, R. D. (1988), ' "They Need It Now": Science, Advertising and Vitamins, 1925–1940', *Journal of Popular Culture*, 22(3): 65–83.

Apple, R. D. (1996), *Vitamania. Vitamins in American Culture* (New Brunswick, NJ: Rutgers University Press).

Apple, M., and L. Christian-Smith (1991), 'The Politics of the Textbook', in M. Apple and L. Christian-Smith, eds, *The Politics of the Textbook* (Abingdon: Routledge), 1–21.

Babou, I., and J. Le Marec, eds (2005), Sciences, médias et société, Actes de colloque (Lyon: École normale supérieure Lettres et Sciences humaines).

Bal, A., G. Fugiglando, C. Tortora et al. (2003), *Sciences de la vie et de la terre, 3e: programme 1999, modifié en 2000* (Paris: Nathan).

Barthes, R. (1961), 'Pour une psycho-sociologie de l'alimentation contemporaines', *Annales. Economies, sociétés, civilisations*, 16(5), 977–86.

Bergeron, J., G. Gohau, J.-C. Hervé et al. (1980), *Biologie humaine: Géologie. 3e* (Paris: Hatier).

Biltekoff, C. (2013), *Eating Right in America: The Cultural Politics of Food and Health* (Durham, NC: Duke University Press).

Bonnemain, B. (2007), 'La publicité pharmaceutique et parapharmaceutique des Annales vertes en 1927', *Revue d'histoire de la pharmacie*, 355: 307–28.

Brun-Cottan, F., M.-P. Debrune and M. Debrune (1980), *Sciences naturelles. Cours Debrune. Biologie humaine. Géologie 3e* (Paris: Belin).

Clément, P. (2004), 'Science et idéologie: exemples en didactique et en épistémologie de la biologie', in J. Le Marec and I. Babou, eds, *Sciences, médias et société, Actes du colloque à l'Ecole normale supérieure lettres et sciences humaines* (Paris: Ecole normale supérieure), 53–69.

Cooter, R., and S. Pumfrey (1994), 'Separate Spheres and Public Places: Reflections on the History of Science Popularization and Science in Popular Culture', *History of Science*, 32(3): 237–67.

Dodds, R. E., E. Tseëlon and E. L. Weitkamp (2008), 'Making Sense of Scientific Claims in Advertising: A Study of Scientifically Aware Consumers', *Public Understanding of Science*, 17(2): 211–30.

Floch, J.-M. (1990), *Sémiotique, marketing et communication* (Paris: PUF).

Grossman, M. (2008), 'On the Concept of Health Capital and the Demand for Health', *Journal of Political Economy*, 80(2): 223–55.

Heinich, N. (2017), 'Dix propositions sur les valeurs', *Questions de communication*, 31(1): 291–313.

Horrocks, S. M. (1995), 'The Business of Vitamins: Nutrition Science and the Food Industry in Inter-war Britain', in H. Kamminga and A. Cunningham, eds, *The Science and Culture of Nutrition, 1840–1940* (Leiden, The Netherlands: Brill), 235–58).

Jeanneret, Y. (2008), *Penser la trivialité: La vie triviale des êtres culturels* (Paris: Hermès Lavoisier).

Kamminga, H. (2000), ' "Axes to Grind": Popularising the Science of Vitamins, 1920s and 1930s', in D. F. Smith and J. Phillips, eds, *Food, Science, Policy and Regulation in the Twentieth Century* (London: Routledge), 83–100.

Kovacs, S. and D. Orange-Ravachol (2019), 'Knowledge and Values Youngsters Can Trust: Nutrition and Food Practices in French Life Science Teaching since 1945', *Food & Foodways*, 27(1–2): 123–43.

Larue, R., J. Hatem, J. Gelé et al. (1980), *Sciences naturelles. Biologie, géologie: Classe de troisième, collèges* (Paris: Hachette Classiques).

Levenstein, H. A. (1988), *Revolution at the Table: The Transformation of the American Diet* (New York: Oxford University Press).

Levenstein, H. A. (2013), *Fear of Food. A History of Why We Worry about What We Eat* (Chicago: University of Chicago Press).

Lutz, R. (2016), 'Still Life with Vitamins: Art and Science at the 1939 New York World's Fair', *Environmental History*, 21: 365–78.

Nestle, M. (2003), *Food Politics: How the Food Industry Influences Nutrition and Health* (Berkeley: University of California Press).

Oria, M., and J. Raffin (1966), *Sciences naturelles. 3e. Anatomie, physiologie, microbiologie, hygiène* (Paris: Hatier).

Orieux, M., and M. Everaere (1972), *Sciences naturelles 3e* (Paris: Hachette).

Paniel, J. (1959), *Hygiène. 3ème.* (Paris: Hachette Classiques, Collection Sciences naturelles Cours Obré).

Périlleux, E., A. Delettré, J.-P. Desloges et al. (1989), *Biologie 3e* (Paris: Nathan).

Perrier, M.-F. (2002), 'Lire la santé dans les manuels scolaires', in D. Nourrisson, ed., *A votre santé! Éducation et santé sous la IVe république* (Saint-Étienne: Publications de l'université de Saint-Étienne), 97–124.

Pitrelli, N., F. Manzoli and B. Montolli (2006), 'Science in Advertising: Uses and Consumptions in the Italian Press', *Public Understanding of Science*, 15(2): 207–20.

Rojat, D., J.-M. Pérol and B. Salviat, eds (2008), *SVT Programme 2008. Sciences de la Vie et de la Terre 3e* (Paris: Nathan).

Séguy, L. (2014), 'De la nutrition à l'étiquetage nutritionnel: une histoire de la domestication marchande et politique des nutriments', Doctoral thesis, Université Toulouse Le Mirail, Toulouse.

Wigelsworth, J. R. (2010), *Selling Science in the Age of Newton: Advertising and the Commoditization of Knowledge* (Farnham: Ashgate).

Chapter 11

Berthoud, M. (2019), 'Des dispositifs info-pédagogiques pour éduquer les enfants à la nutrition', in V. Clavier and J.-P. De Oliveira, eds, *Alimentation et santé: logiques d'acteurs en information-communication* (Paris: ISTE Édition), 125–45.

Boubal, C. (2019), 'L'art de ne pas gouverner les conduites. Étude de la conception des campagnes de prévention en nutrition', *Revue française de sociologie*, 60: 457–81.

Darbellay, F., ed. (2012), *La circulation des savoirs. Interdisciplinarité, concepts nomades, analogies, métaphores* (Berne: P. Lang).

De Certeau, M. (1984), *The Practice of Everyday Life*, trans. Steven F. Rendail (Berkeley: University of California Press).

De Certeau, M., L. Giard and P. Mayon (1994), *L'invention du quotidien. 2, Habiter, cuisiner* (Paris: Gallimard).

De Iulio, S., and S. Kovacs (2014), 'Communiquer, prévenir, éduquer', *Communication & Organisation*, 45: 99–114.

Delamotte, É., ed. (2004), *Du partage au marché: Regards croisés sur la circulation des savoirs* (Villeneuve d'Ascq: Presses Universitaires du Septentrion).

Denis, J. (2007), 'La prescription ordinaire: Circulation et énonciation des règles au travail', *Sociologie du Travail*, 49(4): 496–513.

Jeanneret, Y. (2008), *Penser la trivialité: Volume 1, La vie triviale des êtres culturels* (Paris: Hermès Lavoisier).

Jeanneret, Y. (2014), *Critique de la trivialité: les médiations de la communication, enjeu de pouvoir* (Paris: Éditions Non Standard).

Kovacs, S., and D. Orange-Ravachol (2015), 'La pyramide alimentaire: permanence et mutations d'un objet polymorphe controversé', *Questions de communication*, 27: 129–49.

Le Bihan, G., and C. Delamaire (2012), 'Education nutritionnelle', in J.-P. Poulain, ed., *Dictionnaire des cultures alimentaires* (Paris: Presses universitaires de France), 430–2.

Odin, R. (2011), *Les espaces de communication: introduction à la sémio-pragmatique* (Grenoble: Presses Universitaires de Grenoble).

Ollivier-Yaniv, C. (2013), 'Communication, prévention et action publique: proposition d'un modèle intégratif et configurationnel. Le cas de la prévention du tabagisme passif', *Communication & langages*, 176(2): 93–111.

PNNS (2011), Ministère du travail, de l'emploi et de la santé, *Programme National Nutrition Santé 2011–2015*, Paris. Available online: https://solidarites-sante.gouv.fr/IMG/pdf/pnns_2011-2015-2.pdf (accessed 15 July 2021).

Quet, M. (2014), 'La circulation des savoirs: Interdisciplinarité, concepts nomades, analogies, métaphores', *Revue d'anthropologie des connaissances*, 8(1): 221–4.

Rayou, P. (2002), 'La circulation des savoirs entre sociologie de l'éducation et société: Présentation', *Éducation et sociétés*, 9(1): 5–11.

Romeyer, H. (2015), 'Le bien-être en normes: les programmes nationaux nutrition santé', *Questions de communication*, 27: 41–61.

Tichit, C. (2015), 'Du repas familial au snack entre copains: le point de vue des enfants sur leur alimentation quotidienne (enquête en milieu scolaire à Paris, France)', *Anthropology of Food*. Available online: http://journals.openedition.org/aof/7883 (accessed 2 November 2021).

Chapter 12

Audigier, F. (2012), 'Les éducations à. Quels significations et enjeux théoriques et pratiques? Esquisse d'une analyse', *Recherches en didactiques*, 13: 25–38. Available online: https://www.cairn.info/revue-recherches-en-didactiques-2012-1-page-25.htm# (accessed 29 June 2021).

Astolfi, J.-P. (2008), *La saveur des savoirs* (Paris: E.S.F.).

Brousseau, G. (1998), *Théorie des situations didactiques* (Grenoble: La Pensée Sauvage).

Bruner, J. (2002), *Pourquoi nous racontons des histoires?* (Paris: Retz).

Duco, A., ed. (2010), *SVT 2e* (Paris: Belin).

Fourez, G., A. Maingain and B. Dufour, eds (2002), *Approches didactiques de l'interdisciplinarité* (Brussels: De Boeck).

Fourez, G. (1997), 'Qu'entendre par "îlot de rationalité" et par "îlot interdisciplinaire de rationalité"?' *ASTER*, 25: 217–25. Available online: http://ife.ens-lyon.fr/publications/edition-electronique/aster/RA025-10.pdf. (accessed 29 June 2021).

Hervé, M.-C. and H. Desormes, ed. (2008), *Sciences de la vie et de la Terre 3e* (Paris: Hachette).

Kovacs, S., and D. Orange-Ravachol (2015), 'La pyramide alimentaire: permanence et mutations d'un objet polymorphe controversé', *Questions de communication*, 27: 129–49.

Ministry of Education (France) (2007), Circular 2007-077, 29 March 2007, Second Phase of Sustainable Development Education, *Bulletin officiel (BO)*, 14, 5 April. Available online: https://www.education.gouv.fr/bo/2007/14/MENE0700821C.htm (accessed 15 October 2021).

Ministry of Education (France) (2015), Decree 2015-372, 31 March 2015: Socle commun de connaissances, de compétences et de culture, *Bulletin officiel*, 17, 25 April 2015. Available online: https://www.education.gouv.fr/bo/15/Hebdo17/MENE1506516D.htm (accessed 15 October 2021).

Orange, C. (1997), *Problèmes et modélisation en biologie* (Paris: PUF).

Orange, C. (2003), 'Débat scientifique dans la classe, problématisation et argumentation: le cas d'un débat sur la nutrition au cours moyen', *ASTER*, 37: 83–107.

Orange, C. (2012), *Enseigner les sciences: problèmes, débats et savoirs scientifiques en classe* (Brussels: De Boeck).

Orange, C. (2017), 'Les régimes de vérité dans les manuels français de Sciences de la vie et de la Terre', *Carrefours de l'éducation*, 44: 14–30.

Orange-Ravachol, D. (2012), *Didactique des SVT, Entre phénomènes et événements* (Rennes: PUR, Païdeia collection).

Orange, C., and D. Orange-Ravachol (2017), 'Problématisations scientifiques fonctionnalistes et historiques en éducation relative à l'environnement et au développement durable: le cas de l'évolution climatique', *Formation et pratiques d'enseignement en questions*, 22: 21–38.

Piaget, J., and R. Garcia (1983), *Psychogenèse et histoire des sciences* (Paris: Flammarion).

Chapter 13

Bahr Bugge, A. (2010), 'Young People's School Food Styles: Naughty or Nice?' *Young*, 18(2): 223–43.

Cardon, P., T. Depecker and M. Plessz (2019), *Sociologie de l'alimentation* (Paris: Armand Colin, Collection U).

Carotti, S., M.-A. Richard, M. Dupuis and P. Sultant (2019), 'Education alimentaire de la jeunesse', Interministerial report: Ministry of Education (France), Ministry of Agriculture and Food (France). Available online: https://www.vie-publique.fr/sites/default/files/rapport/pdf/194000247.pdf (accessed 30 December 2021).

Comoretto, G. (2015), 'Manger entre pairs à l'école. Synchronisme et complémentarité des processus de socialisation', PhD thesis, Université de Versailles SaintQuentin-en-Yvelines, Guyancourt.

Díaz Méndez, C., and R. Gutierrez Palacios, ed. (2014), 'Comida y alimentación: hábitos, derechos y salud', *Panorama Social*, 19: 186–209.

Duque Calvache, R. (2016), *Procesos de gentrificación en cascos antiguos: el Albaicín de Granada* (Madrid: CIS Editorial).

Martín-Lagos López, M. D. (2018), 'Educación y desigualdad: una metasintesis tras el 50 aniversario del Informe Colman', *Revista de Educación*, vol.138.

Nukaga, M. (2008), 'The Underlife of Kids' School Lunchtime: Negotiating Ethnic Boundaries and Identity in Food Exchange', *Journal of Contemporary Ethnography*, 37(3), 342–80.

Noticias de la Junta (2019), 'El gobierno andaluz modifica la contratación de comedores escolares para facilitar el acceso a los pymes locales', 17 June.

Peretti-Watel, P. (2003), *Sociologie du risque* (Paris: Armand Colin Collection U).

Pike, J., and D. Colquhoun (2014), 'The Relationship between Policy and Place: The Role of School Meals in Addressing Health Inequalities', *Health Sociology Review*, 18(1): 50–60.

Topalov, C., ed. (1999), *Laboratoires du nouveau siècle. La nébuleuse réformatrice et ses réseaux en France (1880–1914)* (Paris: Edition de l'EHESS).

Index

www.ingramcontent.com/pod-product-compliance
Lightning Source LLC
Chambersburg PA
CBHW050423280326
41932CB00013BA/1975